THE CHEROKEE NATION

THE

Cherokee Nation

By MARION L. STARKEY

"To find if any country still
Might do obeisance to an honest word."

JG PRESS

Published in the USA 1995 by JG Press
Distributed by World Publications, Inc.

The JG Press imprint is a trademark of JG Press, Inc.,
455 Somerset Avenue, North Dighton, Mass. 02764.

This edition published by special arrangement with
W.S. Konecky Associates.

ISBN: 1-57215-122-6

Printed and bound in the USA

TO THE SCHLEISSNERS,

KAREL, VJERA, FRANTICEK, *and* HANNI;

and to all my friends in Hluboka nad Vltavou

who died on the European Trail of Tears

Preface

Research for this volume, which began in 1938, has taken me far afield, from Massachusetts to Oklahoma, with frequent stopovers in the Great Smokies, Chattanooga, and Georgia, and by a stroke of great good luck to the unbombed wing of the Newspaper Annex of the British Museum. Historical research is a grimy business; old manuscripts are dusty and a strain on the eyes, and you spend long, frustrating hours exploring blind alleys. But also, continued long enough, it is a very wonderful thing. It is with the historian rather as it was with the prophet Ezekiel: as one digs through the dry bones of the recorded past, bone joins to bone and takes on flesh and sinew, until presently here are the living men. As I worked, the Cherokees came forward from the past and repossessed their story—one of the great stories of American history.

Any piece of historical research is inevitably in part a co-operative experiment. I am indebted to a great number of generous people, some of whom, alas, have not lived long enough for me to thank them officially. Among these is the late Dr. Enoch Bell, onetime secretary to the American Board of Foreign Missions in the great tradition of Jeremiah Evarts. Dr. Bell gave me not only access to the most human source of Cherokee history, the Mission Papers, but also, through the warmth of his personality and the breadth of his understanding, insight into the character of the missionaries to the Indians. Other members of the Mission Board, particularly Mrs. Maurice P. Dunlap, librarian, have also earned my gratitude for their kind assistance.

Robert Sparks Walker, of Chattanooga, Tennessee, historian, naturalist, and poet, has never failed to respond to my frequent calls for help with cheerful promptitude. He has helped me run down elusive information and find some of my most valuable pictures, and it is thanks to him and the Georgian historian George G. Ward, of Columbus, that I have been able to trace the approximate sites of the missions for my map.

In Oklahoma I received many courtesies and sound practical advice from Mr. and Mrs. Grant Foreman of Muskogee. Mrs. Leon Ross (granddaughter-in-law of Chief John Ross) gave me access to such documents and mementos as were in her possession in her home in Tahlequah. I was received most hospitably in other homes in Tahlequah by Oklahomans of Cherokee ancestry, and, thanks to their frank discussion of matters of mutual interest, learned something of the extraordinary vitality of the historic Ross-Ridge controversy.

I enjoyed similar hospitality in my four visits to the Qualla Reservation in Cherokee, North Carolina, where descendants of my characters live to this day. They are the best of good company, the Cherokees; you sit on a casual stump to admire the view and they invite you up the mountain a piece to visit their homes. To name every Cherokee who showed me his garden and spring place and sat on the front porch to discuss the family version of the Tsali legend would be impossible. I must, however, mention the Reverend and Mrs. William Fitzgerald, local authorities in Cherokee history, who gave me many suggestions.

My thanks to Miss Emily Marsh, of Cornwall, Connecticut, for valuable information on the brief but dramatic sojourn of Boudinot and young Ridge in her leafy town, and to Mrs. William L. Tisdel for the visit to Cornwall itself.

Libraries and museums to whose staffs I am indebted

include the British Museum in London, the library of the University of Oklahoma in Norman, the American Antiquarian Society in Worcester, Massachusetts, the Chattanooga Public Library, the Harvard-Andover, Widener, and Houghton Libraries, and the Fogg and Peabody Museums at Harvard. John M. Carroll of the Boston Public Library has been especially helpful.

The motto on the titlepage is reprinted, with permission, from *Huntsman, What Quarry?* published by Harper & Brothers. Copyright, 1933, 1934, 1936, 1937, 1938, 1939, by Edna St. Vincent Millay.

Assistance of a more intangible nature has been given me by Dr. Robert E. Moody of Boston University, Laurence L. Winship and Donald B. Willard of the *Boston Globe*, and the late Edwin Francis Edgett, long literary editor of the *Boston Transcript*.

And without my father, Arthur E. Starkey, I should never have got through the grim job of getting this manuscript ready for the printer.

M. L. S.

April 1946

Contents

THE CHEROKEE NATION

CHAPTER I

The Cherokees

In the heart of the Great Smokies, close to the Tennessee line, lives a scattered community of Cherokee Indians. They have a neat tribal council house near the government Indian Agency of the Qualla Reservation at Cherokee, North Carolina. Other settlements are scattered through that lovely upland country and in the Carolina hamlets of Birdtown, Soco, Big Cove.

It is not a conspicuous community. Cherokee itself, to be sure, achieves some effect of studied quaintness. It has tourist shops and camps where genuine Cherokee baskets sway in the wind, and some of these places are attended by equally genuine Cherokees in buckskin breeches and war bonnets of more dubious authenticity. Indeed, the bonnets are in derivation Sioux rather than Cherokee, but American tourists like to see their Indians properly feathered, and the Cherokees are an obliging folk.

Actually the tourist shops have little to do with the Cherokees; Council has leased them to the whites as a concession. The Cherokees profit, of course. Matrons weave baskets, mold pottery, work beaded belts, and some men whittle wood to be sold in the shops; but such employment is rarely full-time occupation. Most Cherokees are farmers.

Some of them who live along the highways have mod-

ern electrified homes, neatly painted and carefully kept
up. Others live on more primitive terms in little un-
painted cabins scattered on the mountainsides; but even
the grayest of cabins is characteristically placed under
a smother of mountain laurel, which grows to the stature
of small trees in the pleasant latitudes of the Cherokees.
Even if a cabin is dingy within, it doesn't matter too
much, for the Cherokees are a front-porch race by nature,
and in their hours of leisure and sociability like to sit on
the porch or under the hemlocks by the inevitable spring
place.

There are today approximately 3,000 Eastern Cherokees, and many of these are of mixed blood. They are the
sole legatees in the East of one of the most numerous of
Indian nations, and their legacy is a very small remnant
of what was once in extent an empire.

2.

Four centuries ago, when De Soto first ran across them,
the Cherokees are estimated to have numbered as many
as 25,000. There was no more potentially powerful nation
in the East, and none possessed of a vaster hunting range.
The latter covered not only the Appalachian Highlands
in the western extremities of both Carolinas and the northwest portion of Georgia, but also northern Alabama, the
Cumberland Plateau in Tennessee west to Muscle Shoals
and north to the Ohio, and even the interlocking borders
of both Virginias and Kentucky. There were, however, no
formal boundaries to this range, and possession of it was
frequently contested by other Indian tribes.

To the east the Tuscarora and Catawba nations kept
the Cherokees from expanding into the Atlantic coastal
plains. The Creeks and Chickasaws held them in check
on the south; the Shawanos disputed with them the
Cumberland Plateau; in the north they were threatened

by their kinsmen, the mighty Iroquois. Once in 1654 a band of Cherokees (known at the moment as Rickahockens) made a sensation in the precarious Virginia Colony by annihilating a force of the Paumunkeys, settling at the James River Falls, and forcing—briefly—an ignominious peace on the Old Dominion.

Their strength, however, was not commensurate with their numbers. Indeed, in very early days their numbers were against them, for under the loose early tribal system of government they were far too numerous, too diversified as to dialect, and too scattered to have any concept of national unity. "There was no king in Israel." There were local chiefs and local councils, but no principal chief or general council, and though the Cherokees were later to be known as a peaceable folk, capable of magnificent self-control under provocation, in their early semi-nomadic days they fought not only their neighbors but sometimes each other.

3.

They lived by hunting and fishing, and their preserves, being wide, contained not only deer, rabbit, 'possum, bear, and turkey, but even buffalo. They dressed themselves when at all—De Soto called them "naked"—in skins, and sometimes their women wove a kind of cloth of turkey feathers sewn to strips of soft bark.

But husbandry was not altogether unknown. As they became more settled in their range (which they seem to have entered in prehistoric times by way of the Ohio), they built up a form of community dignified by the name of "town," and there cultivated communal corn and bean patches. One of their most solemn tribal ceremonies, the Green Corn Dance, grew out of this custom; only after this rite in July or August did the women begin to pound the corn into meal in stone metates or in stumps hollowed out by fire. The meal was for cakes cooked in hot ashes;

but some corn was always saved to parch in the ear. Every proper household had earthen jars or reed baskets for the storage of these things.

The Cherokees also gathered herbs in the hills and greens by the water, wild grapes in the mountains. It was the custom late in fall to set carefully tended fires to clear away the underbrush in the chestnut groves to make the nuts easier to gather. It was to become a proverb in the Smokies that Indian summer with its soft smoky haze, its gentle warmth, was created by these autumn fires.

Cherokee society was originally divided into a series of clans, once considered more binding than blood relation-ship—Wolf, Blind Savannah, Paint, Long Hair, Bird, Deer, Holly. This tradition survives in modern Cherokee. "She was a Bird until she married a Wolf," people still say, explaining a relationship.

Early society took the form of a polygamous matri-archy. Though polygamy was not universal, it was not uncommon for a man to take a family of sisters in one ceremony, an act of benevolence that insured against a woman's going childless and manless even in time of war. If the marriage did not work out well, the man merely said good-by and went away, leaving his cabin, his corn patch, and his livestock to his children and his wives. There was seldom, according to observers, any acrimony on such occasions. Ill-adjusted Cherokee spouses did not quarrel; they simply parted.

The position of the women seems to have been rela-tively high. Their activities, to be sure, were circumscribed by a series of taboos imposed by the usual primitive mas-culine horror of such biological functions as pregnancy and menstruation. But early folklore contains some tradi-tion of women warriors, and in their later days a place was specially reserved for women in the Council House, and though they could not vote or participate directly in the deliberations of the chiefs, they did express their views on occasion. A document survives in which a delegation of women directed "our beloved children, the head men and warriors, to hold out to the last in support of our common rights."

4.

The basis of the aboriginal Cherokee moral code was the so-called "blood law," a Cherokee version of the Old Testament doctrine of an eye for an eye. Under this rule any violent death, even accidental, was punishable by death; and execution was vested not in judge or jury but in the family of the deceased.

Such a custom was productive of feud and other complications. Payne records the story of a killer who was too great a warrior to be allowed to atone personally for his crime. By family agreement his blood guilt was shifted to a puny nephew as scapegoat, and the lad spent two years hiding from vengeance. One day the youth rebelled against his fate, confronted his uncle at a townhouse dance, and shot him dead. The Cherokees appreciated the justice of this act, and the youth became a hero.

That among the primitive Cherokees there was a tendency to question the equity of such a law was indicated by their appointing "cities of peace" where fugitives from vengeance might have sanctuary. Eventually they were to renounce this law, pronounce a general act of oblivion for all outstanding crimes, and set up a kind of police force (the "Lighthorse Guard") and system of courts to administer justice. This act, which came in 1810, was one of their most significant steps in the direction of an orderly national government. However, as will be seen in their subsequent history, the spirit of the old blood law was not completely exorcized. It was later to be deliberately invoked in a special context, and many bloody pages in Cherokee history were to result.

5.

The true nature of primitive Cherokee religion can probably never be accurately known. By the time experts from the Smithsonian got to the Smoky Mountain Cherokees it was already late in their national decline, and while forms remained, inner spiritual significances were often lost. An investigator who knew them intimately in their days of glory, the missionary Daniel S. Butrick, was fascinated by their folklore but was rather unfortunately obsessed by a determination to prove that American Indians in general and the Cherokees in particular were one of the lost tribes of Israel. What he therefore collected and recorded with greatest zeal were often only garbled forms of Biblical tales learned from the very early missionaries and assimilated into Cherokee lore.

Reference to the "Great Spirit" occurs in early Cherokee documents; their land, for instance, was given them by this authority. The concept may have itself had an unconscious derivation in early Christian preaching. But, significantly, recent study of Cherokee rites of conjure has established that prayer in its true sense may properly be addressed only to the Ancient Red, the spirits of Sun and Fire. Also with the Cherokees the east is the source of light and life, the west the home of the dreaded Black Man, whose domain is death.

Though some myths assume that the Cherokees were created in and of their hills (and indeed their tawny soil and they are strikingly of a match), and that it was from a cave in Black Mountain, near Asheville, that Wild Boy released all the ills upon the earth, there are also vague traditions of primeval wanderings. For an inland people whose experience of water is limited to what riffles by in their mountain streams, their myth is strangely preoccupied with vast quantities of it. The earth, some say, is only an island held up in a vast sea by cords attached to the flinty firmament, and one day those cords will break. It is as though the Cherokees had a faint ancestral impression of the Pacific over which anthropologists say their fathers came, just as white folk came from beyond the Atlantic, America being only a stepmother to humankind.

Cherokee legend discloses a very animistic and pluralistic universe. Thunder is incarnate in the Thunder Man and Thunder Boys, who rove the hills in summer, flashing and grumbling, but who never strike a Cherokee. It was Thunder who befriended the Cherokees by lighting their first fire in the sycamore tree. The stars are also people, with downy, feathery bodies, heads like turtles, and blinking owlish eyes; this the Cherokees know because occasionally star people, drooping low over a ridge, have been entangled in the treetops and caught and examined by hunters.

Long Man the River is very important. The waters of the mountain streams must not be defiled, and pious Cherokee families insure their good health by "going to the river" or bathing with appropriate rites at the time of the new moon, or during illness, pregnancy, or on other vital occasions. The rivers are the path to the underworld, and spring places the gates thereof.

Little People rove the hills, befriending hunters who respect them, and the mountains harbor Lost Tribes, whose people obtained immunity from white persecution by fasting and prayer, and Bear People who have townhouses and hold council and talk quite as fluently as human beings, though they find it convenient to conceal this accomplishment. All animals are people too, and the early Cherokee hunting economy is reflected in a wealth of old tales about deer and bear and wolf and rabbit. Uncle Remus himself came directly from Cherokee country in upstate Georgia.

The Cherokees also had and still preserve in their remoter communities the complex lore of the medicine or conjure man and his *materia medica* of herb and root. All the medicine man's rites are closely interwoven with religion, for the spirits of animals or fire or sun may be appealed to in banishing an ailment, and illness has all sorts of mystic causes, such as the pathetic reluctance of the dead to leave the living, or the malice of a witch-wise enemy.

A childlike, deadly logic pervades the system. All epidemic illness followed the white man into the country; ergo, the white man is the cause of epidemic. A "strong" disease such as smallpox can be treated only by a "strong" remedy, that is, "going to the river." Such logic the medicine men applied in the earliest smallpox epidemic, and the results were tragic.

6.

The Cherokees first learned that white men infested an otherwise agreeable planet in 1540, when De Soto found them. His reputation probably preceded him, for though the Cherokees offered his party such hospitality as their code required them to show any wayfarer who came in peace, they did not outdo themselves. Indeed, De Soto's historian got the impression that the Cherokees were a very poor folk with insufficient supplies of corn to provide their horses adequately, and though quite possibly Cherokee agriculture was then in a very low state of development, it is also possible that the Cherokees deliberately avoided encouraging a prolonged stay on the part of the strangers. However, they were generous with their turkeys: the hills were full of them.

De Soto did not stay long, but he brought away with him some evidence that the hills contained both gold and copper, and other Spaniards presently returned to prospect farther. In deference to the territorial claims of the British, they worked secretly; evidence of their activity is archæological, vestiges of mining shafts and camps found in upper Georgia. As late as 1690 an explorer from South Carolina was told by the Cherokees of a Spanish mining camp twenty miles from theirs. The Cherokees have no tradition of the occupation at all, but it can hardly have pleased them. An absence of gullibility in their later relationship with English colonists suggests that they had early taken the measure of the whites and had developed a disinclination for closer acquaintance.

However, the Indians derived some profit in a material sense from these early encounters. Quite likely they had their first ponies from the Spaniards; they were to become impassioned horsemen and connoisseurs of horseflesh. They may have had their first firearms at this time. According to old people living in Revolutionary times, these were introduced about 1700; in any case, by 1715 Cherokee warriors were fairly well armed and were having difficulty in getting a sufficient supply of ammunition.

7.

Aside from the surprise attack on the Virginia Colony already noted, early Cherokee experience of English-speaking colonists came via those of South Carolina, with whom they are supposed to have made a treaty as early as 1684. At first the South Carolinians made fewer difficulties for the Cherokees than they made for the Catawbas and the Tuscaroras, and since these were traditional enemies, the Cherokees regarded their misfortunes with complacence. But in 1691 some Carolinians made an unprovoked attack on Cherokee settlements, plundering and killing, and by 1705 the Cherokees had so considerable a list of grievances against the Colonists that they lodged a formal complaint with Governor Moore. First on their list of indignities was the fact that white traders had been seizing Cherokees to sell them as slaves to the

West Indies, and that the governor, far from disapproving, rewarded such enterprise.

In this connection it is to be noted that the Cherokees did not denounce such slavery on high humanitarian grounds. For the sake of getting ammunition for their new rifles, their own warriors were quite willing to take captives among the Creeks and Catawbas to sell to the whites. As of that date they had no concept of the preservation of the integrity of the red men; their exclusive interest was the preservation of the Cherokees, and less the Cherokees at large than the tribe to which they belonged. Their sentiments were pronouncedly isolationist.

However, the impact of white aggression was drawing the Cherokees together. Effective protests to Charleston could not be arranged without a consultation between tribal chiefs. A common danger was welding the Cherokees into a common front; the concept of nationality was being born, and in 1721 they elected, for the first time in their recorded history, a principal chief to represent them all.

This crucial step was not taken entirely on their own initiative. It had been preceded by more trouble with South Carolina. In 1715 the Cherokees had to some extent joined the federation of Indian nations against the whites that had resulted in the Yamassee massacre of a white settlement. In the following winter they had been invaded by several hundred white and Negro troops. In 1721 Governor Nicholson, desiring to prevent further disorders by fixing a boundary between white settlements and red, invited a delegation to Charleston and persuaded them to elect one general chief with whom he could deal.

The Cherokees, a reasonable people, willing to learn even from their enemies, found this innovation of practical value and did not discard it. Out of the casual conference in Charleston eventually developed the custom of sending local representatives or chiefs periodically to one general council to elect a principal chief and discuss other matters of general concern; thus began the national government of the Cherokees.

This tendency was reinforced in 1736 when the Cherokees received their first missionary, the Jesuit Christian Priber, who was acting as French agent. The French had been infiltrating from the west for some time and had made a favorable impression on the Indians, for their ways seemed fairer and friendlier than those of most British settlers. In 1730 the Crown had diverted the Cherokees from a formal alliance with the French by sending seven Cherokee chiefs on a most interesting educational trip to England, where they concluded a treaty, impressively, at Whitehall. But the French continued to penetrate and the Cherokees to like them. Priber himself was a remarkable character. He applied himself to the study of Cherokee dialects, compiled a scholarly grammatical analysis thereof, which he intended for publication in Paris, and, besides giving the Cherokees their first acquaintance with Christianity, worked with them to centralize and strengthen their newborn national government.

His work ended in 1741 when he was seized by the British and left to die in prison; but though his philological treatise was lost, his religion forgotten by the Cherokees (except as certain parables, especially those of Moses or "Waši" the lawgiver, became blended with their own lore), the impetus he had given them to consolidate an independent national government remained. The truly enlightened self-government that the Cherokees were to evolve in the next decades was to some extent an unconscious tribute to the forgotten Priber.

8.

By their vigilance the British had maintained their ascendancy over the Cherokees. In 1740 the latter permitted the opening of a path for saddle horses to be run from Augusta into the headwaters of the Savannah, to facilitate the trade in furs in which the Indians had been long engaged. At the outbreak of the French and Indian wars fifteen years later, the Cherokees consented to a reluctant alliance with the British and even permitted the latter to build a stronghold, Fort Loudon, not far from the Tennessee and near their new capital, Echota. But so outrageously were Cherokee warriors mistreated by white settlers on their way home from the campaign that they rose against their late allies and seized Fort Loudon. For this insurgence they were invaded, their "Middle-town" settlements on the Tennessee devastated, and in 1761 they were forced to conclude a treaty that sheared off much of their range to the east and shrank them closer to their hills.

The outbreak of the Revolution forced a similar pattern of indignity on the Cherokees, but on a more disastrous scale. Again they allied themselves with the British, this time without reluctance. In the interim between wars they had made the discovery that it was the frontier settler, the "American," who regarded the Indians as vermin and ignored the very concept of treaty rights; representatives of the Crown on the other hand, the licensed British traders, were more like the French. They respected agreements made with the Indians, and some of them, like the French, intermarried and settled down as respected members of the Cherokee community.

But destiny was against this alliance with the British. The latter had small attention to spare their red allies; not so the rebelling colonists. In 1776 strong forces from North Carolina and Virginia invaded Cherokee country, systematically looting and burning their towns and massacring such Indians as they could catch. Even worse was the smallpox, which had first come to the Cherokees from South Carolina in 1738 and, besides inflicting a terrible mortality, had so disfigured survivors that many warriors, seeing their faces in the streams, are said to have committed suicide. The epidemics of Revolutionary times also took a great toll. But even so, decimated and starving, the Indians held out longer than their great ally. It was not until 1785, three years after Cornwallis, that they made their peace with the Americans in the Treaty of Hopewell. On that date the Cherokees as a nation forever forswore the warpath against the whites. They accepted their destiny.

9.

During all the humiliation and disaster of the eighteenth century the Cherokees had been gradually "progressing," according to the white man's use of that debatable term. The Cherokees were in their own right a people of genius. This genius had found little recognizable expression in the old, semi-nomadic hunting economy, their neolithic civilization, which had only one medium, thoroughly undependable, for preserving wisdom and glory, that of oral tradition. But under the ruthless impact of white man's civilization they were disclosing an adaptability that was in time to develop them into one of the most remarkable communities in America.

They were a people capable of learning from and profiting by their misfortunes. From 1730 on, the pressure of the white men had been driving them out of their early range into their hills, always a refuge in times of trouble. Every treaty with white men had demanded yet more territorial concessions; they had, for instance, been treatied right out of South Carolina. Even Hopewell in 1785 was not the end, for the close of the Revolution gave a fresh impetus to westward expansion, and white men, in defiance of all treaties and of the generous, outspoken wrath of George Washington, crowded into Cherokee land to the west of the Smokies. In 1794 the new state of

Tennessee was established there, nearly half of it, including Nashville, on what was Cherokee property until new treaties legalized white settlements and land speculations.

By the turn of the century their land was so shrunken that even though in the course of war and pestilence the population was shrunken also, probably to about 17,000, Cherokees at large could no longer hope to live by the hunt or by trapping for the fur trade. Their only hope for survival as a nation lay in making the transition to an agricultural economy.

Fortunately this transition had already begun. The Cherokees had always cultivated corn and beans after a fashion; in their two centuries of exposure to the ways of white men they had received other gifts besides firearms, firewater, and smallpox. Horses they probably had from the Spaniards, and by Revolutionary times some of them had poultry, sheep, cattle, and milch cows and had learned how to preserve the milk in their spring houses and to make butter and cheese. They had hogs, and some of these ran wild in the hills and grew very fat on nuts and acorns. Some Cherokees had learned the art of beekeeping.

The farmers had made the acquaintance of new crops: potatoes, grain, and later flax and cotton, which Cherokee women were learning to spin and weave. Cherokees began to take an interest in white men's agricultural implements as an improvement on the sharp stone lashed to a crotched stick that had been their primeval hoe. This advance became accelerated after the Revolution, when under the humane and far-seeing government policy on Indian affairs an agency was set up on the Hiwassee at Rattlesnake Springs and was assigned as one of its functions the responsibility of teaching the Cherokees the use of plow and loom and the care of livestock, and of facilitating their acquisition of such improvements. George Washington himself sent the Cherokees a personal message advising them to apply themselves to agriculture, and this message the Cherokees solemnly debated in their local forums, the townhouses, and in General Council.

Now they began to abandon their aboriginal custom of communal cultivation of corn patches and to spread out their settlements away from the center of their "towns," the heart of which remained the log townhouse on the banks of the river, and to operate their farms on an individual basis. Thus individual differences developed according to the fertility of the soil or the enterprise of the farmer. In upper Georgia, on the rich bottom lands along the headwaters of the Coosa and the Savannah, large-scale cultivation of cotton was possible; here real Southern plantations, cultivated in part by Negro slaves, began to appear by the end of the century, and some fine homes were built, for instance the old Ross homestead in Rossville, and the Vann home at Spring Place, both of which have survived the years. But whether the individual farm was such an establishment or the meagerest little cabin and corn patch, the land itself always remained communal property, not to be disposed of without tribal sanction. This point was to become of great importance in subsequent Cherokee history.

The Cherokees, of course, did not achieve the progress described *en masse* and in a straight line of development. There were at almost every phase of their history some Cherokees who bitterly objected to renunciation of the old male freedom of the hunt in favor of a system that rooted them to the soil like one of their own vegetables. Observers were to note quite late in the day that once the crop was in, many of the men considered their responsibilities at an end and spent the rest of the year in "frolic." It was the women who, applying themselves to such year-round pursuits as spinning and weaving, showed the stabler progress.

Thoughtful Cherokees began to observe that women

and children profited under the new arrangement. Babies were more apt to live and grow fat in a home place of their own than in the hunting camps of the old semi-nomadic days. Indeed the Cherokee communities were now perceptibly growing, just like white settlements, and, seeing this, the chiefs exerted themselves to persuade more and more of their people to apply themselves to husbandry.

10.

An interesting—but obscure—phase of Cherokee development was the effect of the infiltration of Negroes among them. That the first were runaway slaves from the Colonies is indicated by a provision in the treaty of 1730 whereby the Cherokees agreed to surrender such fugitives. Although they were later to become scrupulous in the fulfillment of such treaty obligations, their government was then so rudimentary that it is unlikely that this contract was very strictly adhered to. Negro runaways meantime were also taking refuge with neighboring Indian tribes, and when the Cherokees took the warpath against these they sometimes took Negroes with their other captives. The aboriginal Cherokee had no moral bias against slavery, though it was with him of a very different nature from the "peculiar institution" of the South of later days. Indian slaves at least, especially if young, were eventually absorbed into Cherokee family life.

In early days there was probably no prejudice against intermarriage. Later, when the Cherokees had assimilated more of the American folkways and were anxious to prove themselves "civilized," some such prejudice did develop. The famous warrior Shoe Boots, being deserted by his white wife and their two children, took to wife his Negro slave Lucy, and presently petitioned Council to give their children the status of free men. Council acceded, but cautioned Shoe Boots against begetting any more such legal problems. Later the old warrior was induced by a white man to set his mark to a paper as a gesture of friendship, and after his death this paper proved to be a will bequeathing his children to the white man. Again an appeal was made to Council, but in such dark days of Cherokee history that the white man probably eventually had his way.

Slavery grew with the expansion of the Cherokee plantations in upper Georgia. A census of 1825 disclosed the presence of 1,227 Negro slaves in the country, and some of these must have been bought on the slave market. But the institution still remained even more peculiar than it was in the white South. When schools were founded, Cherokee masters often encouraged small slaves to attend with their own children. There was one pious and literate Negro couple who taught their Cherokee mistress to read her Bible. Thus the Negro, too, played his silent, subtle part in Cherokee history.

11.

So the Cherokees advanced, some against their will, up the steep road to what white men called civilization. The shrinkage of their lands that had turned them perforce to agriculture had also unified them and consolidated their government. From Revolutionary times on, their chiefs were strong enough to execute their treaties with the whites with an incongruous fidelity; incongruous because their white neighbors seldom felt under any such obligation. But the Cherokees had the right to send delegates to Washington City to discuss their difficulties with Congress; this right they exercised, and the delegations themselves became a factor in their education.

Also there were friendly, honorable white men who took Cherokee wives, and whose children grew up in the tribe—the prosperous traders of the Ross family, near modern Chattanooga, for instance. There were—more rarely—some white women who settled down contentedly with Cherokee husbands. Thus Cherokee blood became early blended with white, and being a Cherokee was at the turn of the century less a matter of genetics than a state of mind. This interbreeding meant a further assimilation of white men's ways.

Finally, thanks to the kindly interest of George Washington and to the shrewd observation of the Cherokee delegates in Washington, a remarkable thing happened. Cherokee leaders, looking with attentive eyes on the young republic next door, discovered in it something new, something hopeful, a positive force to admire and emulate in their own country.

12.

In the early 1800's the American Republic was still the youngest of nations; many of its founding fathers were still alive, and its prevailing faith retained a glow of idealism.

This faith was embodied in the Declaration of Independence and the Bill of Rights. In practice there were discrepancies, slavery for instance, and sharp practice on the frontiers, where early settlers did not think, as has been observed, that the phrase "certain inalienable rights" had been coined with the red men in mind. But such inconsistencies, disturbing though they were to the practicing idealist, could then be regarded hopefully as purely transitory survivals of a less idealistic past; to the idealist, the beginning was the word; facts would in time be shaped to fit the wonderful words of Mr. Thomas Jefferson.

The Indian nations on the periphery of the Atlantic settlements were not alone in regarding this aspect of America with new hope. Although the capacity of the young republic to survive either the encroachments of outside powers or the contentiousness of its own several states was still untested, it had in friendly foreign eyes a prestige beyond its years. There were young Frenchmen, for instance, who watched the development of America with ardor. Here in their believing eyes was that liberty, equality, fraternity which in their own country had been submerged under the imperialistic ambitions of Napoleon. Even among the English, whose blood relationship naturally inclined them to skepticism, there were young zealots who dreamed happy insubstantial dreams of founding pantocracies on these guiltless shores.

English people who came to see for themselves were less impressed. Mrs. Trollope, for instance, was revolted by the very proclamation of idealism because of the cynicism with which, or so it seemed to her, it was disregarded in practice. But even the hard-bitten Englishwoman was aware that by her side stood infatuate French idealists, and that when she said, "How revolting," they were saying with equal sincerity, "But how magnificent." Young America was a highly controversial national experiment.

But if there was any validity in its ideals, it was also a highly hopeful experiment. Slowly, in the course of many delegations to Washington City, in consultation with Washington and Jefferson, in their discussions in Council of such documents as the Declaration, Cherokee leaders grew not only to respect the American ideal but presently to embrace it with enthusiasm and to dream of reorganizing their now compact government into a red man's republic dedicated to Mr. Jefferson's ideals.

Nor was this an impulse towards blind imitation. The Cherokees did more than ape; they grasped inner significances. They had observed the stabilizing effect of the adoption of the constitution; until it replaced the uneasy confederation it had been impossible to make a lasting peace with white men. Thoughtful Cherokees saw more clearly than most white men that the basis of the great sister republic was moral—a respect for the inviolability of compact, the giving and honoring of an honest word. In such a concept there was no conflict with aboriginal virtues, and besides, the Cherokees' long and hopeless resistance against the whites had awakened in them, as it awakens eventually in most oppressed people of intelligence, a conviction that their only hope of survival against superior strength lay in the recognition of moral purpose by both sides. The Americans had founded their commonwealth on such a purpose; thenceforth the Cherokees would accept the moral leadership of the Americans.

13.

The Cherokees, of course, did not achieve this point of view in any one act of decision and never entertained it unanimously. Whites continued to press upon their borders, and many Cherokees were dissatisfied with their lot. When Jefferson, disturbed by the presence of enclaves of Indian country in the Eastern states, offered to exchange their land for territory in the newly acquired Louisiana Purchase, some Cherokees responded in 1805 and 1806, and set up a Cherokee Nation West in the so-called Arkansas country. In 1808, Council seriously considered a proposal for national migration, a measure that according to tradition was balked by the passionate denunciation of a comparatively young chief, The Ridge.

Not long after, in 1811, the Cherokees gave some heed to a proposition to resist the whites again by force. The suggestion came from Tecumseh, who, having federated the tribes in the Northwest Territory in an alliance against white aggression, and having reached a tentative understanding with the British in Canada, came to win the southern Indians to his plan and to include the Choctaws, Chickasaws, Creeks, and Cherokees in his grand strategy.

His visit to the Cherokees coincided with a movement fostered by some of the medicine men and old chiefs in reaction to the Cherokee aping of white man's ways. These were preaching that the Cherokees were offending the spirits of their fathers and risking their birthright by accepting such corrupt gifts as looms, plows, tables, books, and cats; that they had angered the spirit of the Great White Deer, who was causing the game to leave the hills. Salvation lay in destroying the white man's gifts, painting their faces, and becoming Indians again.

One of the prophets put his preaching to a test. He called on the faithful to abandon everything they had from the white men and assemble on a mountaintop while he raised a storm to destroy the apostates remaining in the valley below. The faithful obeyed; they climbed the mountain, and in a day or so climbed down again, for nothing had come of this medicine.

Nothing, that is, except that Tecumseh's message became associated with the ridicule that followed and was rejected by the Cherokees.

14.

Tecumseh's only success in the East was with the Creeks, and that was an imperfect success. Only one faction responded, the Red Sticks, and they with fanaticism rather than wisdom. Instead of waiting on grand strategy and prearranged signals, they brought the whites down on them at once by massacring Fort Mims, Alabama.

Also they committed depredation on their neighbors, including the Cherokees, whose old chief, the gentle Pathkiller, was greatly disturbed by their threats. When one Andrew Jackson took the field against them as general of the Tennessee militia, he had with him Indian allies—some loyal Creeks, and a whole army of Cherokees.

The Creek campaign brought together a significant group of characters. Besides Jackson himself, the white men included his old friend General John Coffee, Sam Houston, and a young Indian scout, the Tennesseean

David Crockett. George Gilmer of Georgia was also involved, though not with Jackson or the Cherokees; he
served on the Georgian front, where the campaign did not
develop to anyone's glory.

The Cherokees were led by Pathkiller, "the old king,"
as white men liked to call him. With him came The Ridge,
the patriot whose oratory was said to have dissuaded
Council from consenting to mass migration to the West.
The Ridge, a prosperous trader and planter at the Head
of Coosa, was credited with recruiting 800 Cherokees to
fight the Creeks, and had been rewarded by Jackson with
the title of major. A Cherokee-minded, mixed-blood scion
of a Scottish trading family that had settled in pre-
Revolutionary times at the foot of Lookout Mountain,
young John Ross, was also present, and also won a majority. And there was Shoe Boots, who made the Alabama
swamps ring with his cock's crow, his private war cry.
"The old cock," Jackson called him.

With these others marched one of the world's immortals, Sequoia. But the Cherokees had not taken the
measure of Sequoia in those days. He served inconspicu-
ously and had no honors from Jackson.

15.

The opening of the campaign was not very satisfactory
for either Jackson or the Cherokees; the former had a
way of detailing the latter to the more inglorious tasks,
such as guarding supplies, and this was a frustrating experience. But Jackson could not always depend on his own
Tennesseans, an unstable lot given to striking out for
home in mid-campaign regardless of military consequences
whenever their terms ran out. There were wintry moments
when Jackson had very little to rely on but his insuffi-
ciently appreciated Indian allies. There was one surprise
attack in January 1814, when Coffee was wounded and

Jackson, forced back, might have suffered disaster but for the timely intervention of the Indians from the rear.

The climax of the campaign came on March 27, 1814, when the Red Sticks made a fanatic last stand in an all-day battle at Horse Shoe Bend on the Tallapoosa. The Cherokees, as usual, had been relegated to the rear, across the river from the enemy encampment, where they were supposed to cut off the retreat of the Red Sticks. But the latter, true suicide fighters, had no intention of retreating, nor the Cherokees of missing the fight. When Jackson's artillery began and war cries rang out and the woods exhaled the heady smell of gunpowder, Coffee could not hold back his Indians. Some of them, Ross for one, swam the river and came back with the Red Sticks' canoes; in these the Cherokees swarmed across the river to take on the Red Sticks in hand-to-hand combat without cover.

This was a very glorious feat and very bloody. The Cherokee losses were all out of proportion to their numbers—eighteen dead and thirty-six wounded. The Red Sticks had refused Jackson's offer of surrender in mid-afternoon and kept on until of their thousand there was hardly one alive.

Shoe Boots was a casualty. He could not be found when the fighting stopped and the dead were counted.

"Poor old cock," said Jackson. "He's crowed his last."

But Shoe Boots, though wounded, was alive and within earshot. His crow, quavering at first, then lusty, replied to Jackson out of a thicket, and the Cherokees whooped, took up his crow until the whole forest rang with it, and went crowing back to the Nation. For it had been a very great victory.

16.

It was also a very Pyrrhic victory. Some unpleasant surprises awaited the Cherokees on their return. During their absence, white men had been plundering their homes.

The treaty that Jackson concluded with the Creeks during the summer at Fort Jackson dismayed them. By way of indemnity he exacted half the Creek country, terms that punished the loyal Creeks who had helped him as severely as the Red Sticks themselves. Worse, when the Cherokees looked into the transaction they discovered that no less than four million acres of the land appropriated by Jackson was not Creek at all, but their own.

The loss was permanent. To be sure, Secretary of War Crawford returned their land when they pointed out the inequity, but Jackson, outraged by such officiousness, went back and managed to talk it out of them for very meager compensation. His persuasion, according to the Cherokees, was unpleasantly reinforced by a threat to deal with a minority if Council refused his demands. The Cherokees, who had admired his handling of the campaign, were now haunted by memories of the terrible valor of the Red Sticks. Had it been altogether well done that they had helped the man they now called Sharp Knife to annihilate their own blood brothers? For now that the Creeks had been crushed, there could be no possibility again of resisting white men by force. The Cherokees stood alone.

Yet a victory is a great thing. Although the Cherokees had now forever renounced the possibility of taking the warpath against the white men, they had proved themselves warriors still. Besides, Cherokee confidence in the integrity of white man's government had been restored by the promptness with which Secretary Crawford had honored their protest. In the last analysis white man's strength was based not on musketry but on the law, and his law was with the Cherokees. In the flush of victory the Cherokees set to work to improve their land and their government; for the first time they addressed themselves seriously to the problem of educating their children to a point where they could hold their own against the whites.

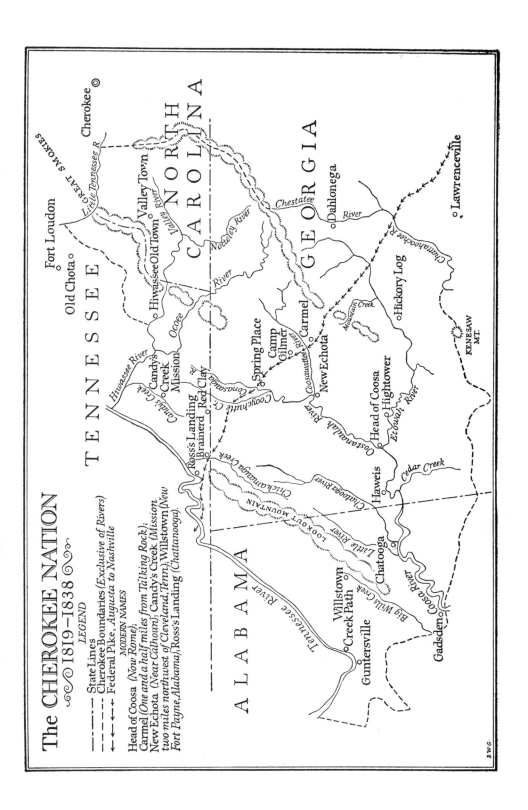

The CHEROKEE NATION
1819–1838

LEGEND

— · — · — State Lines
— — — — Cherokee Boundaries (Exclusive of Rivers)
←———→ Federal Pike, Augusta to Nashville

MODERN NAMES

Head of Coosa (Now Rome);
Carmel (One and a half miles from Talking Rock);
New Echota (Near Calhoun); Candy's Creek (Mission
two miles northwest of Cleveland, Tenn); Willstown (New
Fort Payne, Alabama); Ross's Landing (Chattanooga).

17.

Now that the Cherokees had set themselves firmly against any further cessions of their territory, and were protected in their resolve by the fact that the formerly troublesome state of Tennessee had no further territorial demands to make, it is time to appraise what remained to them—to indicate the boundaries of the Cherokee Nation in the days of its approaching prime.

"The last little," old Chief Pathkiller plaintively called what was left to them. But their territory was insignificant only by contrast with the vastness of their old and precariously held range. The acreage that they now subjected to an increasingly orderly and efficient government was roughly equal to that of the state of Massachusetts, and it was as lovely and various a piece of country as existed anywhere in the East.

The land of greatest fertility lay in northwest Georgia along the headwaters of the tobacco-colored Coosa and the Savanah, and in northeastern Alabama along the Tennessee to modern Guntersville and down the Coosa approximately to Gadsden; in old-time Cherokee parlance these were the Lower and Middle Settlements respectively; the latter also crossed into southeastern Tennessee.

At least half the Cherokee population was centered in the rolling upland country of upstate Georgia, which was crossed by the Federal Pike, opened between Augusta and Nashville in 1815, and along which Cherokees operated inns and public houses. The new capital, New Echota, was being set up in this section of the country, near present-day Calhoun, and all the more substantial chiefs lived on the rich river lands within a range of about forty miles from the capital.

Georgia is walled in to the north by the blue range of the Great Smokies, highest and most magnificent of eastern mountains. Within their valleys and along the Tennessee–North Carolina borders, where the mountains are at their most rugged, one entered into the wildest part of the Nation, the Valley Town region, a part of which was presently to become known as the Aquohee District. Here there were no plantations or great houses; tribal customs were most tenacious and least diluted here; yet these people too had been debating the Declaration in their town-houses and had grasped the moral basis of white man's civilization.

This remains a lyrical country of high clean sweet airs, and haunted by the hurried, musical voices of Long Man the River and his hundreds of chattering children. In June some hills blossom like great wild rose gardens with the mountain laurel; other hills carry the stately masses of the rhododendrons; flame azaleas bloom in craggier places; on the grim talus slopes that drop down into Tennessee are white splashes of bloom in the star magnolia.

In June also, climbing a Cherokee mountain you pass from deep-leaf summer in the valleys to all degrees of spring in the heights, the leaves delicately folding back into the bud as you climb, the little pale violet bluets reappearing on the summit. It is a country that summer is reluctant to leave, where autumn smolders interminably, and winter, in proper seasons at least, is an intermittent, mild-mannered visitor.

It is an amiable country, designed to harbor an amiable people. Also a very stubborn people, as their story will demonstrate.

The Cherokees came out of the Creek campaign firm in the conviction that, having helped America in its need, they had forever established in American eyes their right to perfect their government and improve their land in peace. How right they were, and how wrong, is the substance of this story.

CHAPTER II

The Mission Schools

The Cherokees were devoted to their children, "passionately" so, said the missionaries. A Cherokee woman preferred to die in the attempt to give birth rather than live to old age without a child. Cherokee men took time from more serious occupations to construct minute bows and arrows or blowguns wherewith small hunters could shoot crickets, and whatever their age and dignity they liked to sit by the chimney or on their porches cuddling the warm bodies of babies.

When the mother of John Arch died in his babyhood, the father thought it no shame to sling the baby on his back in a woman's carrying-cloth and take him down the trails while he attended to his hunting and trapping. Presently he initiated the child into these pursuits; young John could shoot before he could walk or talk. The life of such a one as The Ridge, warrior, trader, planter, a "king" in Council and national ambassador to the Creeks, was bound up in that of his son John.

There was nothing that the Cherokees would not do for their children. It was for their sakes that soon after the Creek campaign the chiefs admitted missionaries to the country on a large scale.

Except for the Jesuit Priber, the early Cherokees had shown little response to such missionaries as occasionally

[29]

strayed their way; their experience with white man's practice had made them skeptical of his preaching. In 1801, however, they had given the Moravian Brethren a trial on the express stipulation that in return for the privilege of expounding their religion they open a school for Cherokee children; the chiefs had held the Moravians very strictly to this bargain, once threatening to expel them when they procrastinated about setting up the school.

In the course of the years the Moravians, whose school at Spring Place became one of the finest the Cherokees were ever to have, acquired real influence among the Indians, an influence to which the Cherokee renunciation in 1810 of their old code of vengeance bore witness. The Moravians had served as a kind of ambassador of the more idealistic aspects of white man's civilization. In 1816 the Cherokees were ready to experiment further; in quick succession Council admitted the Baptists, the Methodists, and both Congregational and Presbyterian representatives of the American Board of Foreign Missions. All of these were admitted on the same conditions as the Moravians in 1801: they might preach what they would, but they must center their attention on educating the children.

Independent efforts of the Cherokees to educate their children had met with little success. Here and there a community such as The Ridge's had tried setting up a schoolhouse for a schoolmaster from one of the white settlements; but too often these turned out to be shams, loafers of vicious habits bent on sponging on Cherokee credulity. Dependent in any case on white men for book learning, the Cherokees after such experiments turned the more gratefully to the overtures of the mission societies; if all of these could be judged by the gentle Moravians, their motives, at least, would be disinterested. So the missionaries came and remained to play a vital part in the further development of the Cherokees.

2.

Each of the four mission groups had its special appeal. The Moravians were perhaps the most loved and venerated by those who knew them. They had been there longest, had attained wisdom in dealing with the Indian character, were never known to bicker either among themselves or with rival denominations. Far from resenting the incursion of the American Board in 1816–17, the Moravians went out of their way to make the newcomers welcome. But the influence of the Moravians did not extend very far beyond the delightful herb garden at Spring Place. The majority of the Cherokees hardly knew they were there.

The Baptists had the advantage of a ritual somewhat reminiscent of the Cherokee rite of "going to the river." Once during a proper baptism a hitherto unregenerate Cherokee woman surprised the preacher by wading in after the others and asking to be immersed. The preacher complied and thereby gave offense to more enlightened members of his flock who knew that the sudden convert was confusing Christianity with conjure.

The Baptists were active in the Valley Towns, where they set up a mission and school so well conducted as to win the admiration of Jeremiah Evarts, who visited the Nation in 1822.

The Methodists also set up schools in the Valley Towns, preached widely, and won many converts at camp meetings, which more conservative missionaries deplored for the very reason that Cherokees liked them: because they were lively and dramatic, almost as exciting as ball plays. At prayer meeting the whole congregation was encouraged to give voice simultaneously to independent supplications; the voices were piercing and the din was terrific. Members of the scholarly American Board, who were on cordial terms with all other missionaries, were very dubious of the spiritual benefits of such exercises, and were the more dismayed when the well-educated and intelligent John Ross became a "seeker" in this faith though his wife Quatie remained with the conservative Moravians.

Whatever the appeal of the various missions to the private consciences of the Cherokees, there is no doubt which made the most conspicuous contribution to Cherokee history. This was the American Board; a powerful organization, created in 1810 with the intention of converting the whole world to Christianity in the space of a generation, it sent missionaries not only to the Cherokees, but also to their neighbors the Creeks, Chickasaws, and Choctaws, and far afield to the Sandwich Islands and India. In answer to appeals published in the Board's *Mission Herald* the ladies not only of New England but also of the Middle Atlantic States set to sewing on garments for sketchily clad Indian children, and kind gentlemen raised money to keep them in school. Very distinguished men, the courageous Jeremiah Evarts for instance, served on the Prudential Committee in Boston; the philologist William Pickering put his learning at their disposal and interested European scholars in the achievements of the Cherokees.

Their missionaries were to serve the Cherokees far above and beyond the call of educational and pastoral duty. For one thing, they bore constant witness to Cherokee history in every homely detail of its development in their voluminous letters and diaries, all meticulously preserved in the mission rooms at Boston. For another, they were destined to become not merely spectators but actors in that drama. Two, indeed, were for a time to play leads and provide the means whereby the Cherokee drama was brought upon the national stage.

Important to this story among the earliest of the mission group are William Chamberlin, Daniel S. Butrick, and Elizur Butler. Chamberlin, first Presbyterian schoolmaster to the Cherokees, had an ear for language that enabled him to get into intimate communication with his flock.

Butrick, young, a sworn celibate, came fresh from his ordination in Boston. He was, at this remove at least, one of the most endearing of the missionaries, and though himself a very serious apostle, made no small contribution to the gaiety of the Nation. His unbounded and versatile capacity for enthusiasm, his love of riding out among his flock, made him a valuable reporter. These same qualities also got him into quandaries; it was he who was caught in a storm after dark on the wrong side of a river and had to be protected from wolves by the building of bonfires on the opposite bank, and he who tumbled off the ridgepole at a log-raising, and he who because of his manifold crotchets and his tenderhearted partisanship of Cherokee sensibilities was most frequently at odds with his fellows. "Butrick, dear man," Chamberlin used to call him, writing with raised eyebrows yet another explanation to Boston, rendered virtually omniscient by all the confidential reports the missionaries wrote about each other. Even the Cherokees smiled at Butrick, but they liked him. He was to play a minor but continuous role in their history, and to be permitted to share their cup of sorrow to its dregs, a privilege denied the more realistic and better-balanced Chamberlin.

The third of these early arrivals, Elizur Butler, less a scholar than most of his colleagues, having never been to college, had had some medical training and at first practiced among the Cherokees. He was capable and unpretentious and was eventually to prove himself very brave. It was he who, with Worcester, a later arrival, was to take the spotlight in the Cherokee drama.

Other early arrivals included Cyrus Kingsbury, who, to the disappointment of the Cherokees, almost immediately transferred to the Choctaws, and Ard Hoyt and his numerous family. Hoyt was put in charge of the first mission, and was later relieved when it became plain that his abilities were unequal to the responsibility. However, he remained with the Cherokees and died among them in 1828.

3.

For its first station the American Board chose Chickamauga, later named Brainerd, on the eastern outskirts of present-day Chattanooga, where the little overgrown cemetery still remains. It was not far from the Tennessee River, was near Mount Lookout, which became a favorite excursion for the daring, was within neighborly reach of the Ross homestead, and was not near much else. Indeed, set as it was in Tennessee in the northwest extremity of the Nation, the site was a disappointment to the Cherokees; their own center of gravity lay to the south and east, approximately at New Echota, where they were setting up a new capital. Even before the missionaries had reached Brainerd on their way up from Savannah they were stopped by local chiefs and importuned to settle where they were.

"Sir," read an invitation from the people of Hightower, "We have agreed for you to teach school for us natives here in this settlement. We want you to commence as quick as possible. We want our children to Larn. We want you to pick out the place to set up your schoolhouse."

But the missionaries were committed to Brainerd, and for the first two years, 1817–1819, had all they could do to get it properly under way. In its out-of-the-way situation it must of necessity be a boarding school, and it must also be self-sustaining as far as possible. Houses must be built for the mission families; there must be a meetinghouse, one schoolhouse for boys and another for "females," multiple little cabins, granaries; and added to all this was the labor of clearing the fields for corn and pasture. Cherokee labor at this remote spot was neither abundant nor dependable, and good "Father" Hoyt was no efficiency expert. Early days at Brainerd were marked by a series of small domestic disasters.

The mission roof leaked; a heavy rain meant acute discomfort for everyone; the hard-pressed mission sisters fell prey to chills and agues, and Butrick grew rheumatic. The first granary was ill built; once a whole season's supply of corn, purchased in Tennessee, shipped down the river to Ross's Landing and overland to the mission at no small cost, was found ruined by mildew. Poor Father Hoyt, as conscientious as he was bungling, gave voice to a lament worthy of Job or Jeremiah. In what way, he asked, had the missionaries offended God that he had punished them thus?

His more matter-of-fact colleagues ascribed such difficulties to the purely human factor of lack of proper attention to detail. Dr. Butler reported that when the corn wasn't spoiled it was wasted. The chore of shelling it fell to the schoolboys, who were languid, having been up since five in the morning at field labor and at school; they let their good friends the mission hogs push into the cabin and help them. When the corn had been ground or pounded and the meal made into pone by the little girls as their chore, the hogs found ways of rooting the loaves from the outdoor ovens.

No one went hungry for all this; the missionaries were in no such plight as their spiritual ancestors, the Pilgrim Fathers. In an emergency a draft could always be drawn on Boston, and was; Father Hoyt worried about Boston's reaction to the size and frequency of these drafts. An early mission farmer, one Conger from New Jersey, who had promised his wife great things by the transfer, threw the mission economy into still further confusion by declining to remain.

In Cherokee eyes, however, Brainerd was a very imposing settlement; there was hardly such another in the Nation. Agricultural life had somewhat decentralized their own communities; with them a "town" was now often little more than a log townhouse for local council and dances set by a river, perhaps a store and ferry landing, and a number of little cabins and corn patches scattered at far remove from each other by spring places in the hills or along the river bottom. Ill pleased in any case with the location at Brainerd, some of them looked at its growth very much askance and asked if the missionaries had come to profit the Cherokees by founding schools where needed or to profit themselves by founding a city.

4.

The Brainerd school opened coeducationally in 1818 and set up a branch exclusively for females the following year. The mission tried to limit the number to sixty, raised it perforce to eighty, and still was badgered by parents who, hearing of the school tardily in the uplands, made the trek down wild trails with their children and would not take no for an answer. If they were full bloods they usually had their way, for the Brainerd missionaries were uneasily aware that one result of settling where they had was that the school was nearly monopolized by half-breeds and some whites.

The first congregation at their meetinghouse had indeed surprised these missionaries to the Cherokees. It was in equal parts white, red, and black, and some of the last were the more literate.

A Brainerd day was arduous; it ran from 5.30 a.m. to

9.00 p.m., the evenings being given to fireside discussions of religious doctrine. When the children were not in the classroom the boys were in the fields and wood lots, and the girls in the kitchen or washhouse. That education contained so much manual labor did not at first please some of the parents, one of whom is said to have offered the missionaries the use of a slave to do his child's share of the work. The work program, however, was designed not only for maintenance of the mission but also as an important part of the child's training; indeed, it was sometimes the only part a child had any real use for. When the parents grasped this fact they became reconciled.

Formal classroom education was conducted on the so-called "Lancastrian plan," a system involving the use of drill and monitors. The curriculum (until Miss Sophia Sawyer came with her lively innovations) was a rather bleak fare of the three R's, with a marked tendency to slight arithmetic by joint consent of teacher and pupil. The classroom itself, in Chamberlin's day, was not a place of silent concentration. The children studied aloud, Chinese style, ran about, and chattered as they pleased. Other missionaries disparaged the uproar, but Chamberlin defended it. It was his method. At least in his classroom listless little boys were not so likely to sink their chins to their books and doze off as they were in other schools where "order" was kept.

The play instinct was little recognized. To some the instinct came under the heading of original sin—notably Moody Hall, a man of many cares, who was horrified when his youngsters at Carmel tore out of class whooping like the savages he began to fear they were, ripped off their clothes, and set to a ball play, boys and girls together, naked as frogs.

But when Miss Sophia came, she would on a sunny afternoon take her little girls to the "crick" and sit on guard on the banks while the children splashed in the water or hunted for blackberries or wildflowers in the brush.

Vacation was another item not included in the original plans. The parents took care of the oversight. As the time for the Green Corn Dance approached in August they came to the mission and rounded up their young. Acquainted with Christian inhibitions by this time, they avoided mention of the dance; watermelons were ripening fast, they said; they needed their children at home to help harvest and eat them.

So first August and eventually most of the summer became vacation time. During the absence of the children the missionaries accorded them a surprised appreciation. On the premises many of them had seemed incorrigible dawdlers, given to daydreaming, playing with dogs and hogs, pursuing rabbits and squirrels when there was work to be done. When they left, however, it at once became clear that they actually had accomplished a great deal. During vacation sometimes the most scholarly parsons had to fall to with hoe and shovel to help in the fields; Daniel S. Butrick found he enjoyed it.

5.

Half-breeds predominated at Brainerd and also tended to dominate the classes. They were quicker and more comprehending; to them were assigned the superior tasks of acting as monitors and writing sometimes in fine copperplate hand a letter of appreciation to the benefactors. Most children were supported in school by a benefactor in the North, or sometimes in Virginia or the Carolinas, who had the privilege of giving the child the name he bore in school (there was a boy named Boston Recorder) and of receiving a periodic report.

The superiority of the half-breeds was due to the fact that education was in English and most of them came from families and communities where English was spoken. Besides this advantage, some of them had already a grounding in reading and writing, either from the Moravian school or from an itinerant schoolmaster.

Such advantages were not entirely unknown to the full bloods; for examples, young John Ridge, his sister Sarah, who had been to the Moravian school at Salem, North Carolina, and their cousin Elias Boudinot. Usually, however, the full bloods came from districts that neither knew English nor had any present use for it. When such a child knew any English word at all, it was "goddam," and the rebuke he had from his teachers and the derision from his smug classmates when he hopefully aired this vocabulary was a blow to his sensitiveness.

Although some missionaries, notably Chamberlin, became fluent in Cherokee, mission teachers in general took no interest in the language. Nor did they see any need for working out any special techniques for teaching English. Miss Sophia used to make children repeat the words of English hymns after her, but in general it was assumed that the children would absorb English from their environment, as indeed some of them did. But it was possible for an attentive child, by following copy sedulously, to make quite beautiful pothooks and to chant the spelling of two- and three-syllable words in chorus, as he might chant archaic phrases at a medicine man's ritual, without the slightest idea of the meaning. Some teachers probably never plumbed the depths of such pupils' ignorance; but the children knew, the hungry sheep that looked up and were not fed.

At first the novelty of Brainerd held the attention of these. They liked the little clicks of slate pencils and the smell of ink and the whiteness of paper. Chanting in chorus was fun; they could here hold their own with even that show-off John Ridge. And there were great wonders to be explored in the mission at large: the pewter utensils with which one ate, the very act of eating at table, a rocking chair, a mirror. A backwoods child went through an extraordinary experience when he came upon his first mirror. It was uncanny, his own face thrust in front of him, staring eye to eye. There was something very private about the event; one must find ways of being alone with the mirror. Some missionaries were disturbed to find such secretive strains in the children.

They were even more disturbed when they found children going into chambers sacred to the mission families to lay prying hands on intimate possessions. Thieving, they said, and expounded the Commandments. But Miss Sophia didn't see it that way; everything was wonderful to the children, said she. She made a point of leaving her boxes unlocked and let the little girls finger her brooches, her plumes, her laces, her velvets; for Miss Sophia, though full of faith and good works, was also wholly feminine, and used to entrust Boston with shopping lists whose details must have raised the eyebrows of the august Board.

But the novelties were numbered and their appeal presently palled. In class those to whom English words were dark languished, and their attention wandered. Squirrel flirted his tail at the window and they wanted to be out and after him with their blowguns. The good smell of woodsmoke came in from the hills where the home folk were burning the undergrowth in the chestnut groves to make the nuts easier to find. How much better to be out helping tend the fires and gather the chestnuts than to sit here useless, submitting to humiliating correction and profiting nothing!

In the cornfields life was better; instruction with shovel and mattock made more sense than the work with books and pens; and the girls hurried through their household chores in real eagerness to get to work on the wonderful patchwork quilt to be sold to a prosperous Cherokee housewife, the proceeds to be applied to the relief of the

Greeks. (The children heard all about the Greeks from Miss Sophia, and regularly mentioned the oppressed Patagonians in their prayers.)

From these tasks there was some real carryover to Cherokee folk life. The most indolent boy did not entirely forget what he had learned of livestock and of harrowing the soil. Little girls who had seemed asleep in school went home nevertheless with a new critique of their mothers' ways; in any case they persuaded the latter to adopt the voluminous skirts prescribed by the missionaries for feminine modesty in place of the old short gowns, and to restrain the babies from running naked under the hemlocks. They had less success with their fathers. The well-to-do might reserve store clothes for great occasions, but the cut and color of white men's pantaloons and waistcoats were too rigid and too drab to appeal to their fluid taste. Long after the womenfolk had learned to please the missionaries, the men clung to their old hunting breeches and homespun blankets draped in classic fashion over one shoulder and under the other. And though the women took to hats as a symbol of propriety, sometimes setting them very oddly on mismatched heads, the men fancied lengths of flowered calico, which they wound around their heads as turbans.

Brainerd thus exerted some influence through even the least responsive children, but for these, none the less, the hours in class were endless and without fruit. They sickened for their forest freedoms. When they sat before the carefully swept hearth at night listening to the missionaries discourse and catechize them on their incomprehensible doctrines, they ached for the comfort of the dear dirty chimney corner of their own cabins or for the stifling atmosphere of the hothouse, where they could lie all day long in winter, crunching on parched corn and listening to the old men yarn about ancient wars and the ways of the bear people.

Meanwhile their parents were brooding over their absence from home. When the least rumor reached them that a child was unhappy or that sickness threatened Brainerd, the parents would return and take their child away. This happened so often that Council passed a law requiring any parent who so interrupted his child's schooling to pay full costs.

Children did not always wait to be rescued. Sometimes a child, oppressed by his failure, smarting under the reproaches his lassitude incurred, quietly made up his own mind and took off.

The missionaries, in writing a child's benefactors, made no effort to conceal a failure. Some young ladies in Charleston received this discouraging report in 1824: "With trembling hand I grasp the hollow tube to communicate a few lines respecting your benefactor [sic], Wheeler Gilbert," a ten-year-old full blood who "has been very unsteady at school, absent several weeks at a time, in all about nine months. His talents appear to be rather below mediocrity, his habits rather indolent."

CHAPTER III

The Chiefs

The attitude of Americans of the day toward the Amerind was various. To one type of frontiersman engaged
in pushing into Indian land, he was a varmint, and to
credit varmints with legal title to the soil on which they
happened to live made as much sense as deeding land to
a bobcat. Moreover, they were a murderous breed of
varmint; one's women and children were not safe so long
as there was one left in the country.

This school of thought, by no means universal even
among frontiersmen, was backed by certain philosophers
who had evolved a comfortable theological doctrine that
justified the extermination of the Indians on the ground
that this had been expressly predestined by God. To this
end God in his mercy had refrained from endowing the
doomed red men with human feelings; pity was lost on
an Indian, for he was by nature impervious to sufferings
that would have been agony for a white man.

Such a theory, with its counterpart that slavery was
justified by the fact that all Negroes bore the mark of
Cain, or else that they lacked souls, was of value to those
whose interest it served. It had a certain vogue among
entirely disinterested Americans who considered it a very
advanced, scientific racial doctrine.

Americans at large, however, particularly in the east,

where all Indian problems had been disposed of more than a century back, inclined towards sentimentality. With them it was "lo, the poor Indian"; if anything could be done for his "untutored mind," they would be glad to help. The proposal of the missionaries, particularly of the powerful American Board, to Christianize these people and raise them to civilized standards of living aroused the liveliest interest. Brainerd was well publicized in the widely read *Missionary Herald*, and since the station was close to the Federal Pike, travelers between Georgia and Tennessee often shaped their course so they could stop off to judge for themselves what success the experiment was having.

A gentleman from Raleigh came frankly admitting his skepticism. He bore the red men no animosity, but in his opinion there was as little likelihood of educating them as of domesticating a mountain lion. However, he was willing to be open-minded, and to this end he spent some hours in the Brainerd classrooms.

These happened to contain at the time the most talented youths in the Nation, some of them soon to become its leaders. They included John Ridge and his cousin Boudinot; also John Arch and the brilliant David Brown, both of whom were to serve the missionaries as interpreters for their Sunday sermons. Leaders among the girls were Sarah Ridge and David's sister Catherine, the latter as comely as she was intelligent, and the joy of the mission. On arrival she had been a vain child, given to jingling bangles on her arms and turning up her nose at lowly chores. Then all by herself through private readings in her Testament she had taken on "a seriousness." Now she was so firm in piety, so advanced in learning, that the missionaries were considering her for teacher in one of the branch stations they hoped soon to open.

The skeptical gentleman from Raleigh watched these

alert and serious young people at work, and his skepticism gave way to a generous enthusiasm. He confessed his change of heart to the missionaries and gave them money in token of his sincerity.

President Monroe, in the course of one of his tours of the United States, dropped in and caught the mission off guard. He was greatly interested and also helpful. He authorized them to apply to the Indian agency for funds to replace with a brick structure the crude log cabin for the girls. Also he advised them: they should concentrate on perfecting Brainerd rather than undertake to branch out elsewhere.

This advice the missionaries disregarded, not without embarrassment. Pressure from the Cherokee chiefs was more urgent than advice from the President of the United States, and the former were insisting on a wider distribution of small schools. Already the missionaries were preparing to open a first outpost, at Taloney, later called Carmel. "Time is precious," John Ross was urging them. "Cold weather is coming on and the sooner the school gets into operation the better for the children." Eventually the missionaries were to open eight schools for the Cherokees: four in Georgia, at Hightower, Carmel, Haweis, and New Echota; two in Alabama, at Willstown and Creek Path; two in Tennessee, Brainerd itself and Candy's Creek.

Cherokee common folk took a personal responsibility for these little stations. Each was built by the Cherokees in a rousing community logrolling and house-raising. Their industry may be judged from the fact that the first timber was cut for Butrick's school at Creek Path on a Friday in April 1820, and that on the following Thursday Butrick was sitting before his first class. This school flourished, and Catherine Brown was presently sent for to take charge of the "females."

2.

Brainerd never lacked for Cherokee guests. The parents of the school children were haunted with anxieties for their young, whom they had turned over to strange white folk, heartlessly ignoring the frightened tears of a little girl, and sometimes even beating a little boy to make him stay. Sooner or later they could stand it no longer. They mounted the family nag, father in front, woman behind, and the current baby blinking solemnly from the carrying-cloth on her back, and made for the mission.

Often such a journey covered forty or sixty miles; naturally they expected to put up at the mission. That they might not be welcome never entered their heads. Among the Cherokees the law of hospitality was universal and absolute; the primal object of industry had been to have enough venison and corn on hand so that the wayfarer need never be sent hungry away. Wherever you happened to be at nightfall you stopped and slept, and whether it was the meanest of little cabins with dirt floor and wooden chimney, or The Ridge's grand house on the Coosa, you were equally welcome.

So arrived at Brainerd, the parents fondled and exclaimed over their children, much to the surprise of the missionaries, who had not expected such demonstrativeness in the supposedly impassive Indians, told all the gossip of the hills, heard all the gossip of Brainerd, and then settled down patiently to wait for the supper bell.

Meanwhile the mission sisters agitatedly directed their charges to lay extra plates, recalculated their supplies, and wondered just where to bed these latest guests. As a matter of fact, the floor would have been quite satisfactory, and the Indians quite relished a comradely crowding and the opportunities for sociability offered thereby. It was the spirit of the hospitality that counted, not delicacy of fare or luxury of appointments.

But even the plainest fare, demanded so frequently, made dismaying inroads on the mission stores. Large-scale hospitality was an item that the careful providers in Boston had not included in their reckonings. At first the missionaries saw nothing to do with the custom but accept it. Later some of them decided that there was no need to take the hint when comparatively near neighbors dropped in at mealtime; this thrifty rule was enforced at Carmel, where Moody Hall early decided that he was being imposed on by loafers. Brainerd also adopted the practice, as Butrick discovered on a visit when he learned that he was expected to break off a conversation with good friends who had come far to see him and eat while they waited hungry. Always sensitive to the feelings of the Indians, Butrick denounced this parsimony; indeed, it did mission prestige little good; in particular it did Moody Hall no good.

3.

Old Pathkiller, the principal chief, brooded over the destinies of Brainerd and its tributaries like a benevolent forest spirit.

Very soon after the arrival of the missionaries he made them officially welcome in a meeting of the National Council. This event took place after the old fashion, about a campfire and under a shelter of green boughs placed on crotched branches. Pathkiller sat in state in the center on a heap of skins and listened with grave attention while Hoyt explained the purpose of the mission and a Cherokee interpreted. The whole council was intensely interested in the missionaries, whose willingness to work among them was a testimonial of the good faith and good will of the white men. When Hoyt asked permission to take the chief's hand, every member of Council arose, anxious to do exactly the right thing, and filed before the missionary, each taking his hand in turn. Pathkiller himself did not forget that the handshake was a courtesy pleasing to white men (Cherokees wanting to express good will grasped the arm above the elbow). When he visited Brainerd he took pains to shake hands with everyone on the premises, including each of the children.

In January 1819 he came to Brainerd, suitably attended, and listened delightedly (though without understanding a word) to the children demonstrate their prowess in spelling and in learning the answers to Emerson's Doctrine and Historical Catechism. When the children sang a hymn in chorus, the old man was overcome. The missionaries saw him lift a corner of his blanket to his eyes; then he gave up and let the tears roll down his weatherbeaten, leathery old cheeks.

"Dear old Pathkiller," observed Butrick, "one can but love him."

Pathkiller stood at the end of an epoch; in choosing him principal chief, the Cherokees had for the last time elected an illiterate who did not even speak English. The connotation of the word "illiterate" may be unfair to old Pathkiller. A certain naïveté in his recorded utterances may derive from clumsiness of translation. Nevertheless, though the Cherokees venerated the old man, the missionaries observed that it was usually the well-educated second chief, Charles Hicks, and aggressive young John Ross who carried on the real business of the Nation.

Pathkiller in these days was troubled by the action of a group of Cherokees led by Chief Jolly, and including Sequoia, who had, without consulting Council, accepted a government offer to exchange Cherokee lands for territory in the Arkansas. Council had now passed a law pronouncing the death penalty on any Cherokees who thereafter made such unlawful land deals, and had protested to Agent Return Meigs the government's willingness to deal with an unauthorized minority.

"I love my country where I was raised," Pathkiller had

said on this occasion. "I never can find so good country and water to what I am used to. I hope you have conscience to let me raise my children in my own country."

The plaintive tone of this appeal, written in a very different vein from later Cherokee protests, confessed to the tremulous apprehensions of the old man. Once in May 1823, after a good supper at Brainerd, Pathkiller opened his heart to the missionaries and expressed his fear that the whites would end by driving his children off the earth.

There were plenty of good whites, that Pathkiller warmly recognized, but he was nevertheless afraid of them as a race. The white presidents from Washington on had always spoken kindly to the Cherokees, but the promises of the presidents were invariably broken by the people. They asked for treaties and land, and after every treaty there would come another president and another demand for land. Now the Cherokees had set their faces forever against further cessions. They had learned to content themselves with little, but this "last little" they must keep.

But a new and powerful force was beginning to press from the south and east: the state of Georgia, impatient that whereas the raw young state of Tennessee had got what it asked from the Indians, the Cherokees should still be allowed to monopolize some of the best Georgia land. Dangerous forces were at work in Georgia; looking in that direction was like looking into a black thunderhead boiling over the hills. Already Georgians had harried and murdered in the Nation, and nothing done about it. The old chief, full of days and near their end, was bowed with dread of what the Georgians might do to his people.

"This grieves me so that I can think of nothing else," said old Pathkiller, and he went on, speaking in parables like an Old Testament patriarch. "If we have a little brother who is poor and does not know well how to take care of himself, I do not think it is right to try to get away from him the little all that he has."

There was something simple and good, something touching greatness like the virgin timber in the Great Smokies, in the character of Pathkiller. Perhaps it was this and not Yankee nostalgia for majesty that made the missionaries call him "the old king." They were the better for his visits. And so was he, for all his hopes lay with the children bending over their slates. He wept when they sang, and was not ashamed.

4.

His second in command, Charles Hicks, was even more frequently at Brainerd than "the old king." He was a man of good sense and integrity; the missionaries came to rely on his judgment. He would tell them candidly whenever they offended Cherokee sensibilities; for instance, by giving voice to a suspicion that a length of cloth missing from the storeroom had been taken by one of the children. He gave all his support to their attempts to give the children not only book learning but training in husbandry and home-making. He urged them also to bring in artisans to whom the children could be apprenticed, particularly blacksmiths, since all the blacksmiths in the Nation were white, profane, and hard-drinking.

The missionaries yielded to persuasion and brought in a blacksmith, one Thompson, and sent him to the new station at Hightower. And such was the prejudice against blacksmiths that while the people were raising him a house a local chief made them stop and would not let them proceed until they had convinced him that this was not as other blacksmiths, but a godly man especially sent by the mission.

Hicks was, in contrast to the older chief, all hope. He too had passed through a time of discouragement when it seemed that the Cherokees had no choice but to move west; but in Hicks's eyes the land had now been guaranteed to his people. The whites had proved their good faith by setting up the missions. Hicks, himself a devout believer, was, in the words of the missionaries, "overflowing with joy and gratitude and praise to God."

5.

Neither Pathkiller nor Hicks was to live long enough to see the founding of the Cherokee republic or the full force of the aggressions of Georgia. Their places were to be taken by John Ross, as principal chief, and The Ridge, whose influence depended less on his various official functions than on his personality and his extraordinary power as a speaker. Of the two, The Ridge resembled Pathkiller; he was, like him, a spokesman of the true folk spirit of the Cherokees in spite of his broad acres, his manservants and maidservants, and his belief in progress. Ross resembled Hicks in that he had a white man's education; his learning was, indeed, sounder, for his father had sent him to school at Kingston, Tennessee, and he was well read in his father's well-stocked library at Rossville.

Ross was a near neighbor of Brainerd. He operated a trading post and ferry on the Tennessee and lived with his father, brother, and his own family in one of the pleasantest homes in the Nation, a two-story house in Rossville, ceiled and washed white within and set about with a comfortable veranda. Miss Sophia visited his family there and thought herself back in New England.

In Brainerd's first days Ross, not yet thirty, was already president of the National Council, an office subordinate only to that of the two principal chiefs. He was a conspicuous figure; Butrick wrote in 1819: "Mr. Ross is rising highly in the opinion of the Nation. He is not in point of influence inferior to any except Mr. Hicks. These men walk hand in hand in the Nation's Councils and are the hope of the Nation."

An event in Council in 1823 gave Ross further standing. The Federal government, as Pathkiller had reported, was pressing the Indians for more land. This time the Federal agent enlisted the Creek chief McIntosh to bribe influential Cherokees, telling them that since they had to give up the land anyway they might as well make money out of it. Ross, being approached, got McIntosh to put his offer in writing and then dryly read the document in open council in the presence of the panic-stricken Creek. The Cherokees were stunned, not so much at the treachery as at the Federal agent's willingness to descend to such trickery. They protested angrily; and they turned to Ross as a leader whose intelligence and integrity they could trust.

A man with many irons in the fire, Ross was not given to haunting the mission to expound his philosophies of civilization like Hicks and Pathkiller, nor did he join the church, though he visited both church and school now and then, especially at examination time, and spoke well of what he saw there. His support was always direct and practical.

It was he who, unasked, saw to it that the Council granted the missions, on exactly the same basis as the Cherokees, the use of the land on which they wanted to build. He helped the mission buy corn and saw that they got it, and when Ard Hoyt ran short of funds Ross was usually ready to advance him a hundred dollars. Such advances were loans and came under the head of business, not benefaction (though he seems to have charged no interest). This fact became clear when Hoyt's account mounted to $400, and Ross, hard pressed himself, exacted a sight payment. Poor Hoyt was in a dreadful flutter about it.

Much later, in 1828, when Ross, having been elected principal chief, was about to move his own family to his new plantation near The Ridge's at the Head of Coosa, and discontinued the post office at Rossville on which the mission had depended, J. C. Ellsworth thought him a hard man and indignantly wrote that he was no friend of the mission. Other missionaries wrote denials of this impeachment, but it was a fact that the nearly white Ross, whose fame was to wax and become exceedingly great, and who was to be known in Washington as "the Indian prince," never commanded such affection among the missionaries as the full bloods Pathkiller and Hicks. It was for the missionaries quite the final straw when he joined the one church of which they were constrained to speak disparagingly, the Methodist.

6.

The Ridge had a personal stake in Brainerd. He had sent a son and a daughter there. One July day in 1818 John incurred the reproof of his teachers, and a busybody saw to it that The Ridge immediately received an exaggerated report that his children were both running wild in school.

The Ridge stopped for nothing; he mounted his tall horse and rode to Brainerd, cutting across country the shortest way, swimming the rivers as he came to them. He reached Brainerd the second day after John's misdemeanor and came straight to the point.

"If my children are wasting their time, I have a little Coosa girl you may have in their place," said The Ridge in his grief and anger, the Coosa girl being one of the orphans of the Creek campaign. Many Cherokees had brought back such orphans as a kind of atonement; Jackson himself was rearing a Creek lad named Lincoy.

But there was no need to provide a replacement for John. The missionaries were well pleased with the boy, who was far ahead of his class, having already studied with the Moravians, and being besides quick and ambitious. It was his very superiority that had given trouble;

a spelling lesson had been cut down to accommodate the pace of the weaker pupils and John had protested too imperiously. Why, he wanted to know, must the intelligent be forced to wait upon the dull? He had, however, properly accepted reproof; indeed, the reproaches of his teacher had reduced the fifteen-year-old boy to tears.

The praises of the missionaries warmed the anxious heart of The Ridge. His son, to be sure, must not be overbearing. "You must obey the missionaries as you would me," he told his children; but in his heart he recognized the justice in John's protest. It was not good that one descended from a line of "beloved men" illustrious in Cherokee lore, and himself inevitably destined to take his place in the Nation's councils, should be held to the pace of the halt. The new order of chiefs must have an education the equal of any white. Brainerd had apparently already done its best for the boy; where could he find something better than Brainerd's best?

It so happened that such contingencies had been provided for by the far-sighted American Board, which had just set up in Cornwall, Connecticut, a school of higher education for promising youths from the Sandwich Islands and the Indian nations. The Ridge had no sooner heard of it than he was sounding out the missionaries. Would it be possible for them to arrange for John to attend?

The request put a responsibility on the missionaries. It was now the summer of 1818; their own school had barely started to function, and here were the Cherokees already pressing for something better. Boston and Cornwall must be consulted; there must be searching interviews with the parents. Butrick found just the right opening when he was sent for to preach at the funeral of The Ridge's married daughter. John, Butrick pointed out, was himself not wholly strong, and winters in Cornwall were severe; were the parents prepared to risk his health and possibly his life?

"I could not," said John's mother simply, "keep him alive if he stayed with me."

So John went to Cornwall in September, and with him two other gifted youths, David Brown, brother of the saintly Catherine, and a young man with a long Cherokee name whose specialty was painting. Later John's cousin Elias Boudinot and some others followed. The Cherokees felt an honest swell of pride that so many should be found worthy, and the missionaries were equally gratified. Butler, the only physician in the country unless one counts the conjure men, urged that a boy be sent especially to study medicine.

7.

The Ridge could not sufficiently express his gratitude to the missionaries for their kindness to his son. His home was theirs in a sense exceeding even the normal generosity of Cherokee hospitality. Butrick spent many happy hours there. Once The Ridge asked him to hold his Sabbath service in the October woods by his daughter's grave, where he had set up benches. The Ridge saw to it that attendance was good and that the congregation behaved correctly; he instructed it to kneel for prayers. Butrick, who usually knelt only for the more private form of prayer, was somewhat taken aback by this papist touch; but he was an adaptable, large-minded young zealot, and rather than shame The Ridge by setting him right, he knelt too.

Butrick lingered in the gracious house and returned for other visits. The Ridge and he walked together under the stars and called their names. It pleased The Ridge that sometimes white man's names and Cherokee coincided. For instance, Butrick pointed out the Seven Sisters; with the Cherokees they were seven brothers, six of whom had made a medicine to go up to the sky to punish mothers

who gave them stone for bread and the seventh of whom,
pulled back to earth, became the ancestor of all pine
trees.

The Ridge had never formally accepted religion, but
just now his heart had been opened by the death of a
daughter and the departure of his son. He looked at the
stars and said thoughtfully, "It's easy to see they never
made themselves."

Then he asked about God. What displeased God and
thus became sin? How did one know?

Butrick told him all about the Old Testament, about
Moses and his Commandments. Then somehow the talk
got around to slavery; Butrick, never quite reconciled to
the existence of the South's most peculiar institution
among the Cherokees, took the occasion to describe how
the slaves were taken in Africa, how bought and sold in
America. And The Ridge, who himself had bought, if not
sold, listened with warm sympathy and presently gathered
some eight or ten of his slaves so that Butrick could preach
and pray with them more directly. Butrick was especially
interested in a woman The Ridge had bought from the
Creeks, and who always prayed with her own children
and sang them the story of the Crucifixion.

> *They crucified my Lord*
> *And he never spoke a mumbling word,*
> *Not a word.*

Butrick rode off to see Chief Hicks, and The Ridge rode
with him on his tall horse. At a "swimming stream" he
made Butrick swap with him, so that the little missionary
would not get wet. And it was he who taught Butrick to
enter an Indian house at mealtime and help himself to
what was on the table without asking or being asked.

"It's as if we had all been one family," wrote Butrick
in both his journals.

For intermittently Butrick kept two journals, one

edited, expurgated, and copied out in careful hand for the Board in Boston in case they cared to insert selections in the *Missionary Herald*, and one for his very private purposes. The revised edition tended to objectivity, was all about what he saw; the original, the matrix journal, was subjective, all about what he felt. Butrick was a very serious, sensitive young man; he had sworn himself to celibacy and all manner of self-denial, but in spite of all that he found himself unworthy of his great mission; he filled his private journal with his self-reproaches.

8.

After The Ridge left him with Hicks, Butrick went happily on to further adventures. A minor chief, The Boot, had him smoke a peace pipe fashioned with a tomahawk head for bowl and silver bands around the stem, and also introduced him to a dish to his taste, black walnut hominy.

He sat beside Pathkiller at Council, this one by night, by a campfire under the stars. He saw some Creeks come shyly up to the fire to speak, and was displeased when the Cherokees laughed at these guests.

He ran across "the great warrior Shoe Boots," and was glad to learn that he had lately sworn off drinking. He wished the same could be said of everyone he met. In these early days it sometimes struck him, as it struck other missionaries, that the innovation of white man that was exerting the most far-reaching influence over the Cherokees was not the Bible but the bottle. He saw disheartening incidents.

On one trip he caught up with the Lighthorse Guard just as they were tying a convicted felon to a tree to flog him for thieving. Butrick noted with approval in passing how orderly the incident was, how well dressed and intelligent the guard appeared to be; but the impression was not to persist. That very evening while he sat in the home of one Grimmel, the same guard, now roaring drunk, burst in and proceeded to horsewhip Butrick's unoffending host. True, one of the number remarked that the act was illegal, whereon, in a tipsy effort to atone, the guards fell to lashing each other. A day or so later the captain came back to the house all in disarray and badly bruised and still exhaling spirits. He explained that some Cherokees had beaten him up as an educational measure, to show him what a beating felt like.

What was really notable about the incident was that it gave rise to no bad blood. The injured Grimmel did indeed interrupt a meeting conducted by Butrick to summon part of the congregation, the Lighthorse Guard, forth to justice, but the Guard cordially admitted their wrong and were forgiven, and their captain took his own lashing as a proper joke.

Once Butrick found the people of a town where he had hoped to preach assembled in their townhouse, stamping out a dance with bloodcurdling yells and a brave rattling of gourds. The bottle was also in evidence, or rather the keg, for at an all-night dance whisky came that way, and the dance lasted as long as the contents of the kegs. Here, thought the eager little missionary, was his great opportunity; he would go right in and denounce the Evil One on his own ground. It was surely what the Apostles would have done.

Butrick, however, was not alone; he had two Cherokee escorts who gently but very determinedly impelled him away from that townhouse. He yielded perforce, but not without stopping to look back at the plight of the poor sinners he had been sent expressly to save. He could not reconcile himself to leaving the neighborhood until it occurred to him that after he had toured the Valley Towns he could return to preach the gospel here, a proposition that his companions heartily endorsed.

The Valley Towns welcomed him enthusiastically.

Long Town sent for him unexpectedly with news that two hundred were assembled to hear him; when Butrick responded he found that the younger men were whiling away the time in a dance; he had to wait for the music to stop before he could begin to talk and his "linkister" to interpret.

His companion on this expedition, Chief Rising Fawn, took him to call on a chief far gone in years, eighty or ninety of them. The interpreter told the old man that Christians wore clean clothes, whereon the chief excused himself to reappear quite magnificently clad in a clean white hunting frock set off with silver bands about his arms and a silver crescent and a silver medal awarded by a president upon his breast.

"Dear old man!" commented the tender-hearted Butrick. "Oh that he might be clothed in the righteousness of Christ!"

He and Rising Fawn rode on and saw wonderful things, especially in the way of scenery. The mountains that separated the Valley Towns from the lower hills of Georgia dwarfed Lookout, dwarfed everything he had known in New England. The trails up which their ponies toiled skirted the perilous edge of grandeur. Once after a long upward pull they came out on an extraordinary prospect, a vast white lake, its waters gently steaming. Butrick was amazed to find so large a body of water so high in the mountaintops, and even more amazed that he had never heard of it. Then the smoking water at his feet subtly parted and he looked down through the gap to a gray abyss and a wooded valley an immeasurable drop below, and the impulsive little man gave voice to the song the seraphim sing, "Glory, glory, glory."

Rising Fawn listened with grave approval; it was the way he felt about the land the Great Spirit had entrusted to the Cherokees; it was the way every proper Cherokee felt.

CHAPTER IV

Young Men of Cornwall

The fact that some half dozen young men had been found worthy of four years of advanced study in a New England seminary was a source of intense pride to the Cherokees. When in 1824 the last of these had returned, their scholastic honors thick upon them, the October Council at New Echota gave their achievements and the participation of the local missionaries therein national recognition.

The most brilliant record had been made by David Brown; this young man, indeed, now had a sounder knowledge of Greek than of Cherokee, he being from a mixed-blood, English-speaking community; to him fell the honor of delivering an address to full Council and of receiving at the close of it the national salute. The missionaries were honored in the person of Chamberlin; he was invited to preach, and John Ridge asked to serve as his interpreter.

After this The Ridge, his heart overflowing with pride in his son, with gratitude to the missionaries for what they had done for him, and to Providence for bringing the boy safely home (for John had been seriously ill in Cornwall, and The Ridge had visited him there), made a speech in which he solemnly urged the benefits of religion on the assembly. Privately he promised Chamberlin that

a chaplain would be appointed for Council and each session opened thereafter with prayer.

He and Chamberlin strolled away from Council together. It was dusk, the soft, woodsmoky dusk of a fine
October, and the people coming away from Council
carried pine knots and candles in their hands. They
were a multitude, coming and going all directions as
far as the eye could see. The Ridge rejoiced at the spectacle.

"It's like Baltimore," he said, for now The Ridge had
seen Baltimore.

Chamberlin did not smile at the comparison or make
the obvious comment that in a day or so New Echota
would revert to un-metropolitan status, a few cabins and
an expanse of trampled pasture land. He too had been
moved, and his pastoral mind read symbolic significance
into the candles. These people were learning to walk in
the light; upon them a great light was now beginning to
shine. The progress of the Cherokees, of which the achievements of the young men lately returned from Cornwall
were only one manifestation, was something to thank God
for.

Actually, however, some things were not going quite so
well as they appeared on the surface. In spite of their impressive appearance at Council, all was by no means well
with the young men of Cornwall. All was not well at the
mission stations. There was a spirit of ill-tempered reaction to white men's pieties and repressions abroad in the
land; the next Council, in August, far from honoring the
missionaries, was to offer them what seemed to be a
studied insult.

2.

It is to be remembered that the missionaries had been
admitted to the Nation not to preach but to teach; preaching was permitted, of course, but only on sufferance. And
though there were many who responded, who sat before

the pulpit of a Sabbath, their broad, freshly washed faces full of sweetness and faith, receptive to the Word, there were others who resented the whole arrangement. Whenever the religious conviction of the missionaries led them into too forceful an attack on Cherokee folkways, some of these reacted with the violence of a young colt being broken to the bridle.

Willingness to adapt themselves to white man's conception of progress did not necessarily imply willingness to become imitation white men. The Cherokees had all manner of ancient customs which they proposed to keep, and it behooved the missionaries to deal warily with what they did not understand.

Sometimes they did move warily, and with wholesome results. An example was the diffidence with which some of them, at least, touched on the problem of polygamy, which though by no means universal was very common and widely at variance with principles of Christian teaching. Butrick ransacked his Testament to see what the Apostles, who certainly must have encountered the practice, had done about it. So far as he could see they had done nothing. The missionaries seem to have exerted themselves to make Christian weddings fashionable rather than meddle with already polygamous households. The *Cherokee Phoenix* was to publish social notes of brides in white cambric and grooms in a "clean Northern domestic suit." This delicacy produced an effect that denunciation probably would not. Little by little polygamy fell out of fashion; the chiefs played with the idea of renouncing it in Council, but foresaw so many complications in their own family life that the issue was perennially postponed.

A similar tolerance to other Cherokee ways might have borne fruit; for instance, a more sympathetic attitude toward such Cherokee rites as the various dances, Green Corn, Bear, Eagle, the ceremony of Going to the Water, ball plays, the New Fire. The missionaries objected to all of these because they involved conjure, and to the dances because they were attended with hard drinking and were productive of brawls. Indeed, they might well have attacked the dances not for their paganism but for their corruption by white men, since firewater was distinctly a white man's contribution.

The spirit of some of the ceremonies, however, was not unlike the spirit of many a Christian ceremony. The Green Corn Festival had some kinship with the Pilgrim Thanksgiving. Going to the Water, except for the conjure man's abracadabra with beads, resembled baptism. In spring, when the Cherokee year began, there was a custom that could have been adapted to Easter. All pious hearths were extinguished on a day in March and rekindled from a torch lit at the "new fire" kindled by the medicine men.

More than a millennium earlier, Christian missionaries to the German tribes won converts by blending their own story of the Nativity wih the rites of the Balder myth and thus created Christmas. These missionaries had a similar opportunity of which they did not make use. Their only concession was to suppress their own Puritanic aversion to the papist rite of Christmas when they found that the slaves, released from their labors in the Twelfth Night season, craved some special observance, and that the Cherokees themselves "set great store by it."

3.

In preaching to the Cherokees the missionaries labored under two heavy handicaps, the more obvious of which was language.

It was the custom for the missionary to preach in English and then sit by while an interpreter "linkistered" for him. This made for services of great length and a degree of inevitable tedium, and it placed great reliance on the intelligence and integrity of the interpreter, who sometimes tried to save the missionaries from unpleasantness by eliminating the more vehement details of the sermons. Most interpreters, young men who had done especially well in school, were reliable; some became preachers themselves. John Huss (The Spirit) was ordained in the Nation, and Stephen Foreman took his orders at the Princeton Theological Seminary.

Some of the missionaries could, without undue effort, have learned to speak to their flocks in Cherokee. Chamberlin had a reputation for fluency; Butrick had such a course in mind: soon after his arrival, with a characteristic burst of enthusiasm he fell in love with the language, pronounced it much more subtle, rich, and beautiful than any other language, classic or modern, and covered pages of foolscap with erudite analyses of the very fluid Cherokee verb. He was, however, bogged down by his own classical grounding; anyone who had been exposed to Boston believed that mastery of a language entailed the memorizing of paradigms and rules of grammar. Cherokee had never been broken to such a harness; its syntactical variety was infinite and elusive. Chamberlin was gently derisive of the efforts of Butrick, "dear man," in this direction. And the word of God was too precious to be pronounced by an amateur. So the missionaries read their chapter, expounded its contents in English, and left the rest to their interpreters.

The second handicap was the rigidity of the religious doctrine of the day. Let there be no condescension in the statement. The missionaries were laborers worthy of their hire. Each had accepted his work for life, and in so doing had made real sacrifice in breaking home ties and forgoing the comforts of his own world. Moreover, for all their human fallibility, their occasional bickering, they were upright men, and many were to show courage in situations nearly as trying as those which faced the early martyrs.

But they had been reared to a stern doctrine, and they laid heavy emphasis on hellfire and conviction of sin. A hymn early translated into Cherokee and then worked back into English so that Boston could judge the result, gives the general effect:

Remember sinful youth, you must die;
Remember sinful youth who hates the ways of truth,
And in your follies boast, you must die, you must die.

Oh sinner, now's your time, don't delay, don't delay.
Now in the gospel day, God's gracious cause obey.

The Cherokees, ever ready for a song in however minor a key, took to the hymn, but conviction of sin came hard. Young John Arch went through so very painful a conviction that he later confessed that for a while he wished he had never heard of Christian doctrine. Other Cherokees, less responsive to suggestion, simply replied to inquiry that they were not sinners and received with reserve the information that by the standards of the white man's God they nevertheless were.

Once three youths, resting up from a drunk, dared each other to submit the patient but undeluded Butler to a derisive catechism on the Fall of Man. The purport of their inquiry was very modern, quite in the spirit of nineteenth-century agnosticism. If God were really a good father, they asked, would he not have fenced off that forbidden apple tree so that his children need never be tempted at all?

There was much difference of opinion between Cherokees and their mentors as to what sin was; The Ridge had asked Butrick in all sincerity how one knew. In the ruder districts little boys and girls came to school entirely unin-

hibited in speech, given to unabashed public reference
to all the coarser facts of life. Shame had to be patiently
inculcated, and even then, though they became modest
and reserved before their teacher or parson, there was no
proof that they didn't revert to normal when they got
out of earshot.

There was, on the contrary, proof that some of them
did. At least two very discouraging episodes occurred at
Carmel. One involved a girl of whom the Halls were
proud; she had been with them three years, had learned
to speak, read, and write English, had after careful training become adept with pen, needle, and skillet. And it
was this model pupil who was one day found to be steal-
ing away from prayer and monthly "concerts" to keep an
unhallowed tryst with a young man.

What was even more disturbing was that some members
of Hall's congregation could not see anything unduly depraved about such conduct. Hall was constrained to make
a public spectacle of burning the cabin and bed, the better to impress the symbol of hellfire on such skeptics in
his congregation. The girl was sent away, followed by
the prayers of the missionaries; she didn't, they were
pleased to hear, turn out so badly after all.

4.

The symbolism of Hall's bonfire was forceful and quite
in the Mosaic tradition, but the Cherokees responded
more readily to the mercy of God than to his wrath, to
the Sermon on the Mount, presently available in their
own language, than to the angry Old Testament. Such an
attitude as Hall's tended to breed friction.

At first the missionaries had difficulty convincing the
Cherokees of the sanctity of the Sabbath. Cherokees helping them build would in their enthusiasm keep right on
when Sunday came, and took offense when deterred.

"One man," a Cherokee in Hightower icily told Thompson, the godly blacksmith, on such an occasion, "must not think to come in and rule the Nation at once."

When it was explained that the white man's God had placed a taboo on the day, the Indians were mollified: taboos were familiar; they had them by the thousand. One Cherokee woman, eager never again to offend the new deity, got the missionaries to help her work out an elaborate system whereby she could know for herself when Sunday came.

But often some Cherokees felt that the missionaries meddled too much, and resentment occasionally overflowed into incident. Haweis, though not many leagues from The Ridge's acres, seems to have been an especially rough neighborhood. Miss Sophia was presently sent there from Brainerd, and though she was deeply afflicted and affronted by the transfer, she did her best awhile, went bravely out with a pupil for interpreter to confer with the parents of miscreants. She ran one mother down into her chimney corner, to be told that she would as soon see her child in hell as in Miss Sophia's classroom.

Another child, Walessa, "a lovely, interesting child," had a bold bad drinking father named Smoke. "Smoke is coming!" the children would cry, and scatter like chickens before a hawk. And Smoke, roaring drunk, would leap from his pony, pound on the mission door, and shout for his daughter. There was nothing to do but hand her over, Miss Sophia trembling for her innocence. A day or so later she would be returned by a Smoke quite unrecognizably sobered off and somewhat sheepish. Nothing, however, was more certain than that the incident would recur, and it was all very difficult for a refined maiden lady, used to the best society and now in her forties and in delicate health. Miss Sophia took to writing wistfully to Boston of her longing for the joys of the new Jerusalem and her expectation of being translated there soon. She was fated, however, to see much rougher events among the Cherokees before that translation took place.

Moody Hall had the most unpleasant experience. One day a dissolute Indian invaded his mission at Carmel whooping out imprecations and threatening him and his wife with a knife. Mrs. Hall was newly a mother, and unwell. She was so shaken by the incident that the next day Hall retreated with her to Brainerd.

This was a great scandal, and what shocked the Cherokees was not the assault, but the flight of the missionaries before danger. It had been especially undignified; Hall dodged one way, and his wife another, thrusting her baby into the arms of a little Cherokee girl as she ran. The Cherokees considered the retreat to Brainerd conduct unbecoming to missionaries and said so to Butrick, Hall's co-worker at Carmel. Did not Christianity, they asked, make Christians brave? Were not Christians supposed to trust to God and endure all things for his sake?

Butrick, it must be admitted, was rather smug about Hall's flight. He himself, he assured Boston, would have died a thousand deaths before showing such weakness, a statement not to be entirely borne out by his later record. He also quoted the Indians as saying that Hall's reluctance to give hospitality had offended. Butrick could have told him so, and had; when Hall came back at last he was appalled by the inroads that Butrick's openhandedness had made in his stores.

Hall returned to Carmel with John Ross's assurances that he would be protected. Later one of the "malicious fellows" of his district came to church and became a convert. But Hall never wholly got over his fright; he wrote an unresponsive Boston that the missionaries would be justified in demanding that the Indian Agency afford them Federal protection; in 1826 he thankfully accepted release from his duties.

5.

The persistence of conjure gave the missionaries periodic concern. In conjure very strange gods indeed were invoked—butterflies, white dogs, turtles. Isaac Proctor was the more shocked when he learned that a member of his congregation who had received communion at his hands on Sunday had on Monday cursed another member of the congregation by conjure.

Butrick, more sympathetic than any other to native folkways—often on a trip to Valley Towns he displayed such a wide-eyed interest in an old chief's account of the Thunder Boys that it was a question who was disseminating which gospel to whom—would by no means countenance conjure. But reproof from him did not always meet with respect; one conjurer told him to stick to his Bible or get out. At one time the gentle but righteous little missionary had nearly half his congregation under suspension, though not from this cause alone. Proctor, who considered that Cherokee progress had been much overrated, reported that Cherokees in his district were guilty of every offense mentioned in the 21st chapter of Revelation, the reference being to "the fearful and unbelieving and the abominable, and murderers and whoremongers and sorcerers and idolaters and all liars." Hall, in short, was not alone in his troubles.

Dr. Butler, still going about the country with his medicine bags (Boston presently advised him to limit himself to teaching and preaching) found conjure a handicap to his practice. Just as Cherokees saw no inconsistency in blending white man's religion with more ancient rites, in illness they sometimes tried to make recovery doubly certain by engaging both white and red medicine men. Butler had safely nursed a woman through pneumonia when she surprised him by taking a sudden, inexplicable, and fatal chill. Between his visits she had been induced by the local medicine man to get up a sweat in a hothouse and then plunge into the icy river.

Once a benevolent physician from Knoxville, one J. C. Strong, vaccinated the children at Brainerd gratis when smallpox threatened and left "cow pox" vaccine with Butler to vaccinate children elsewhere. Here too he was balked by conjure. In one community the conjurer, a shiftless character not ordinarily respected, was raised to such eminence by the threat of epidemic that he gave orders like a king. Part of his subjects slaved over his neglected garden; the rest ranged the hills under his direction, gathering herbs.

He boiled these in a large earthen pot with suitable incantation and administered sips of the brew to the faithful. Then they danced for four days and nights, after which they were pronounced free of disease for the season.

In spite of these precautions, some of the faithful got smallpox. The conjurer was not abashed. The virtue of the ancient medicine, he explained, had been weakened by the work of the missionaries.

6.

That the unregenerate, and even sometimes such of the redeemed as were illiterate, should still hold to heathenish superstitions and practice did not give the missionaries so much unhappiness as the fact that the young men returning from Cornwall failed to set their Nation an example of piety and decorum. Some of them, indeed, got the reputation for downright misbehavior.

Even David Brown, brother of the sainted Catherine, lately honored by National Council, seemed reluctant to settle down to make proper evangelical use of his advantages; the Greek scholar played awhile with the idea of opening a tavern, "New England style." Boudinot did take a school quite promptly, but even there he distressed the missionaries by the highly questionable innovation of playing ball with his boys, and out of school his conduct was such that some missionaries thought it should be reported to the church he had joined at Cornwall. The behavior of some of the other youths was "notorious."

The missionaries, not usually reticent in such matters, gave no details. Perhaps in their disappointment they exaggerated. The young men of Cornwall were supposedly the very flower of Cherokee youth. Expecting great things of them at once, the missionaries did not make sufficient allowance for normal difficulties of readjustment. After all, the young men had been withdrawn for four impressionable years of their youth to another world. They had lived in a prim white New England town studying in company with Sandwich Islanders, Hindus, Bengalese, and some white Americans. The blessings of such a life had been great, but not unmixed; there had been irksome restrictions. Back in the Nation, their first thought had been to celebrate their release from these restrictions.

Also they all had for the time a sense of being lost between two worlds. The orderly town-meeting ways of New England, the companionship of young white women and of boys brought in from lands beyond the seven seas, had suddenly been blotted out; the Cherokee world was not quite what they remembered; they and it had changed. It was difficult to bring old ways and old friends back into focus. So the young men went through a period confusing both to themselves and their friends.

All of this would have been trying enough, but there was a more special and very real cause for bitterness. An incident had taught them that the idealistic North was not so fair-minded and friendly towards the Indians as it pretended to be. A perfectly honorable act on the part of John Ridge had outraged the town and caused many Connecticut editors to denounce him in the press as if he were a criminal.

John had merely got married. In his illness he had been

nursed in the home of Northrup, a steward of the school; when he got well, he married the steward's daughter Sarah. That was all there was to it, a happy, properly chaperoned courtship and a respectable wedding.

But Cornwall and Connecticut acted as if John had committed all the abominations in the Bible. Editors vilified him. His bride became the butt of local wits who wrote verses to the effect that whereas she expected to reign as Indian princess, she was to be a squaw with a grubby papoose on her back. And the American Board, self-styled friend of the Indians, deserted its protégé in this crisis; it countenanced the dismissal of Northrup from the staff of the mission school and presented an unresponsive ear to John when later on he tried to get his father-in-law installed as teacher in a mission school in the Nation.

The bride bore all this calmly. She came to the Nation with John, warmly welcomed by her father-in-law, and settled down at John's new home at Running Water, adapting herself smoothly to the new life. Echoes of this life gave Cornwall gossip a new turn. The Ridge had come to visit John dressed in broadcloth and driving a coach-and-four, and he had impressed the town as he was always to impress white folk, even Governor Gilmer of Georgia. His state was kingly. Cornwall decided to make an Indian princess of Sarah after all. She was, people now said, dressed exclusively in silk, and had been given fifty slaves as her personal attendants. Actually her home life was not so ducal, but it was happy. In time she bore John five children.

Young John could not take the incident as calmly as his bride. It was his race, not hers, that had been affronted, and John was very proud, very sensitive, and very young; it was not quite five years since he had been boy enough to be reduced to tears by reproach. The injustice of the attitude of the New Englanders cut him deeply and rankled long, and this was so with the other young men; indeed, as the story spread, the whole Nation shared his resentment.

Feeling died down presently. The Cherokees reaffirmed their trust in the good will of the local missionaries, at least, by honoring them in Council. But almost immediately afterwards came a second blow, impossible to overlook or forgive. John was not the only Cherokee to captivate a young woman of Cornwall; the boys had cut quite a swath. In 1825 John's cousin Boudinot announced his intention of returning to marry Harriet Gold.

Opposition to John's marriage had been intense but verbal only. Now Cornwall expressed itself in action. There was a rowdy night more worthy of a frontier settlement than of a refined New England village, in which both bride and groom were burned in effigy and Boudinot was told that if he actually came back and kept his promise he would be lynched.

Boudinot was not deterred; he went north as advertised and married Harriet. No one lynched him; and he and Harriet also returned to the Nation and lived happily, though somewhat insecurely, and had many children. But Boudinot was as sensitive as he was courageous; the episode made a lasting impression on him.

Not even this was the end of the matter. The following year, not quite a decade after the opening of the Cornwall School, it closed its doors and sent the remaining students home on the noncommittal pretext that the American Board had decided it was best to train youths in their own lands. Well, the Cherokees had observed what had brought them to that decision. They had seen race prejudice in action where they least expected it, among their friends. And this, so reasoned the bitter, including the cynical young men of Cornwall, was what Northerners were like behind their ostentatious charities and fine talk. It is not surprising that it was about this time that the missionaries noted particularly disheartening cases of re-action.

Even more than resentful, some Cherokees were perplexed. Why all this sudden to-do over intermarriage when the process had been going on ever since the white man reached the Cherokee? Even Georgia, hostile though it was, had never been thrown into an uproar by a mere wedding. Indeed, on the frontiers, Georgia as elsewhere, it was recognized that a penniless young man could hardly do better than find a likely Cherokee girl for a mate. Methodist preachers had married members of their flock; Father Hoyt's son Milo had taken a Cherokee wife. At what point did this white man's taboo take effect? Was it acceptable for a white man to marry a Cherokee woman but against nature for a red man to take a white wife?

David Brown debated this enigma with youths of his neighborhood. The Ridge told Chamberlin that he wanted a plain answer to a plain question. Could the Northerners show any good reason for the opposition to such marriages? Chamberlin assured him that the Bible and President Monroe were on his side.

However, the indignant citizenry of Cornwall had some sympathizers in the Cherokee Nation. There were communities, as The Ridge had admitted to Chamberlin, that resented it when a Cherokee girl gave herself to a white interloper; Council itself, while not forbidding such unions, made them less desirable for a white man by denying him the right to dispose of his bride's property. It was also true that, now that polygamy was going out of fashion, a Cherokee girl could not so easily find a proper young man as in the old days. Unmarried girls did not relish seeing two such eligible youths come home with foreign wives. They particularly did not relish talk, inspired by the superior young men of Cornwall, that Cherokee maidens were not sufficiently well brought up or well educated to make suitable mates.

There was much talk of a National Academy of higher education; John Ross, perhaps with this gossip in mind, told Miss Sophia that it should be a female academy.

7.

One enduring cause of disagreement between the missionaries and the Cherokees was the matter of the national sport, the ball play. To the missionaries it was an abomination; they exhorted their congregations to keep away from the heathenish spectacle and gave a stern refusal to little schoolboys who asked to be excused from class so that they could attend.

And they had very ill success. Even church members in good standing would not always keep away from the sport; sometimes really model schoolboys, being denied, played truant and saw the game anyway.

As a matter of fact, the ball play was a noble game, ruled at its best by exacting ethical standards worthy of a more sympathetic study by the missionaries. The most respectable men of a community were given supervision of the local ball play to make sure it was honestly conducted; honesty was a quality demanded of its players. The conjure involved in preparing for a game was of the disciplinary sort—going to the river, observance of such taboos as avoiding women and all food except parched corn and water, enduring all-night vigils, and strenuous preparatory dances.

The game itself (since tamed into lacrosse) involved tremendous back-breaking wrestling matches between paired adversaries, and pursuits in which not even the onlookers were safe, since the game, though bound longitudinally between goals, might burst off the field laterally at any time, embroiling spectators with the players. It was indeed nearly as rousing, as male, as dangerous, as the warpath. It had been formerly allied with the rites of the warpath and still remained for the Cherokees a moral equivalent of war. They did not propose to let white men take it away from them.

For the missionaries, these moral considerations were eclipsed by the excesses of the game, its violence, the use of conjure, the gambling that attended it. Yokes of oxen, home furnishings, one's best store clothes, were staked on the favorite team; and so that bets might be placed scientifically, people flocked to the conjure men to procure a divination by beads—people who certainly should have known better, chiefs in National Council, even church elders.

Most ball plays were neighborhood affairs, but on August 7, 1825, just as the sensation caused by the burning of Boudinot's effigy in Cornwall was coming to a head, there was a national ball play. What was worse, it was held at New Echota in conjunction with a special called-Council, and on the Sabbath. And the chiefs, well aware of the attitude of the missionaries, instead of setting an example by keeping away from what Moody Hall called the "scene of national iniquity," attended almost in force.

This was backsliding into heathenism on a grand scale, and some of the missionaries took it very hard. It looked almost as if National Council had deliberately designed to insult them.

Even missionaries who did not take the event so personally were distressed by the attendance of one young man from whom they had hoped better things. The Ridge's nephew Boudinot, unlike most of the other young men of Cornwall, had used his education to a serious purpose. Such was his ability as teacher and interpreter at Carmel that the missionaries had been corresponding with Boston about the wisdom of entrusting him with a high responsibility. But Boudinot attended that ball play and visibly enjoyed it as much as any other heathen.

CHAPTER V

Sequoia

It was during this very time of reaction, so disheartening to the missionaries and so uncomfortable for everyone, that a very wonderful leaven began to work among the Cherokees. At the exact moment when the Indians were wondering if even the North could be trusted, when ominous signs from Georgia were casting a shadow over the last days of old Pathkiller, who too well read their meaning, something happened that sent a ground swell of joy and hope through the Nation.

Disaster was close to the Cherokees now, in 1825, but before disaster came they were to have a renaissance.

Now renaissance is a high-sounding word to apply to anything that happened visibly to the Cherokees. Their nearest approaches to Florentine or Periclean splendor were their homespun blankets and occasional patchwork quilts, and the architecture of the proposed new Council House and courthouse at New Echota, sawn wood instead of split log. Nevertheless, something of the light that once shone on Athens rested for a moment on the Cherokees, like a late afternoon sun blazing down on the hills before being closed in by heavy clouds. And what was most remarkable, no missionary, no Cherokee who had been to school to the missionaries, was responsible for this dawn of learning. It was the work of a stubborn Cherokee who couldn't even speak white man's language, much less spell out his letters. An illiterate taught his nation how to read and write.

And the full bloods who had sat so dumb in school now came into their own; and so did the parents and grandparents who had hitherto watched with helpless incomprehension while bright young people paraded white man's learning; and so did the conjure men, and all the humble, disregarded folk.

For this was not a renaissance of princes; it was a manifestation of the Cherokee folk spirit. It was to be the truest claim of the Cherokees to distinction, for no other people in history has ever had anything quite like it.

2.

When the Indian territory of the West long afterwards attained statehood, the Indians proposed a name for it, Sequoia. The Indians, as usual, did not have their way; the state became Oklahoma. But the name was given to the great trees that of all American living things come the closest to possessing immortality, and that was suitable, for the Cherokee who first bore the name belongs among the immortals. Sequoia, a plain man who lived and died without pretensions to grandeur, belongs in a category beyond ordinary historical fame. His place is not far below that of those primal geniuses who made civilization possible by inventing the bow and arrow and the wheel, by discovering that fire can be kindled and controlled for pleasant purposes. Sequoia is such another as Prometheus.

He was a modest Prometheus, indeed one of the most modest of Cherokees. His life was simple, and all the recorded facts about him are plain and forthright, like the recorded facts about Shakespeare.

Sequoia was probably born some years before the American Revolution. His mother was of good family, his uncle being a "beloved man" in the tribal councils; his father was white. According to tradition that father was an itinerant peddler; according to Grant Foreman, he was Nathaniel Gist, a white trader to the Cherokees and a friend of George Washington; on official occasions Sequoia always called himself George Guess or Gist. In any case, the father drifted back to his own world, and the boy remained with his mother, grew up in the customs of the old hunting economy, looked like a full blood, and never learned the language of his father.

It is remembered of his early youth that he was clever with his hands. Even as a child he is said to have contrived for his mother a very superior sort of springhouse. Later he learned silver smithy and became something of an artist. He made his own brushes, ground his own colors from berries and roots, and, when he could, got paper on which to paint animals. His horses were particularly well spoken of.

His impluse to work out a Cherokee writing was not entirely spontaneous; this too was a spark struck off by contact with white man's civilization. Inspiration is said to have come from a manuscript that a friend took from the pockets of a captured white man, and over which he pored with Sequoia, trying to penetrate the mystery. Sequoia's companion thought white man's marks to be a kind of spell cast on paper, enabling it to talk to another man distant in time and space; but Sequoia insisted it was no magic, but invention, and no more mysterious than the invention involved in the construction of their rifles. The Cherokees were as capable of inventing a writing as a white man; he himself could do it.

"Let's see you then," said the friend, and laughed when Sequoia traced a mark on a whetstone with his knife.

This incident is said to have taken place about 1800, when there were still no schools, and books were a great mystery held to be suspect by the medicine men. Sequoia was perhaps about thirty, an active hunter, very hand-

some, much admired by women, fond of convivial sessions of storytelling and prodigious feats at the bottle.
These were not factors calculated to induce prolonged
semantic experiment.

The Creek Campaign of 1813–14 was the real turning
point of his life. Either he was injured in the fighting or
he suffered an aggravation of an old illness or hurt, for
he returned partially disabled, and thereafter walked
with a limp. He was, moreover, already well along in
middle life. Activity was losing its attraction; he could
the more easily settle himself to a life of contemplation
and research on the question that had been teasing his
mind for a decade.

Now the Cherokees of that day had had mighty warriors and hunters and wise old chiefs. They had medicine
men who conducted profound researches in the properties
of herbs and the identification of spirits who afflict the
flesh with ills, and in the ways of the Thunder Boys and
the Little People. They even had some budding scholars
at the mission school at Spring Place, to say nothing of
some budding saints.

But they had never before had a contemplative philosopher or a native scientist; they had never had a Sequoia,
and they in no way knew what to make of him.

The enlightened and the ignorant both scoffed at him.
The former asked why, if he wanted to write, he didn't let
the missionaries teach him how. The invention of writing
had taken place some time before, they pointed out; why
did Sequoia feel obliged to repeat the process?

The ignorant were afraid of him. To them he was a
kind of Faust of the forest, up to no good. More and more
he was spending his days in a little cabin, leaving his
farm work to his incensed wife and to his sons, while he
grunted and muttered over the cabalistic marks he made
on paper. Plainly he was making medicine, and not a good
medicine, since no accredited medicine man could make

head or tail of it. He was practicing some peculiarly obscure and sinister form of witchcraft. If a cow died in calving or hail cut down the young corn or a mother had pains before her time, more likely than not the craft of Sequoia had something to do with it.

His friends, who thought he had gone mad, tried to reason with him. Sequoia heard them out politely, sucking on his long-stemmed pipe, and then placed the spectacles back on his nose and turned again to his work.

"You're making a fool of yourself," said Turtle Fields.

"Maybe," replied Sequoia, "but what I'm doing will not make fools of the Cherokees."

What went through his mind as he bent over his papers, painting his symbols with fine brush strokes? Probably he was taken in part by the lure of the puzzle, yielding to the same impulse that causes strong men to put all their evenings on cryptograms. He was, in military parlance, trying to break the white man's code. But that a wider vision was dawning on his mind is indicated by the philosophies that he expounded to admirers who sought him out in his honored old age.

A word, he told one of them, was like a wild animal. White men had learned how to catch these animals, to tame them and put them to work on paper. And in this act lay the whole secret of white man's apparently superior understanding. Red men also had wise men among them, but a red man's wisdom often died with him. Parts of his sayings were forgotten; parts were misunderstood and remembered in corrupt form, so that a red man could never be sure he had possession of the true wisdom of his fathers. When a writing was made for red men, then it would be possible for their dead to speak to their unborn; then no wisdom need be lost, and the red men would be as strong in understanding as the white.

Sometimes Sequoia went to Spring Place and prowled about the classroom, peering over shoulders into the mysterious books of the white men. The good Moravian Brethren had no natural sympathy for his project; they were to tell Butrick that Cherokee was so clumsy a speech that it was not even adequate for the simplest practical purposes, like giving directions. (They had probably got this impression by observing a collision between the two major Cherokee dialects.) If they grasped Sequoia's intentions at all, they must have urged him to relinquish the superhuman task in favor of the simpler one of learning the writing white men used. But though Sequoia happily accepted the gift of a speller, it was only for purposes of reference; white men's writing wasn't good enough for him, since it could be applied only to the white man's language. The red man must find a way to write his own tongue; there was no other solution. Quietly, patiently, stubbornly Sequoia persisted in his research.

His study of linguistics went through the metamorphoses of recorded language. He began much as did the Chinese and Egyptians, by inventing a character for each word. This was simple and delightful work, for his hand was skilled and his mind inventive. The little pictures multiplied under his busy hands.

But presently he came to a full pause; the pictures multiplied indeed; they multiplied like the leaves in the forest, but what man born of woman could hope to remember all the leaves of the forest? Messages that he had put together at the time of the Green Corn festival were no longer intelligible to him in the Moon of Falling Leaves. While he invented the new characters, the old faded from his mind. And if he himself could not retain the characters of his own writing, what hope was there that other, less devoted Cherokees could do so?

It was about this period that his neighbors arranged a witch hunt. Cherokees then took their witches seriously; when the new missionaries arrived shortly after, they ran across a miserable woman whose whole family had been put to death for witchcraft, and she spared only because she was pregnant. Sequoia was spared because for all his vagaries he was a quiet, untroublesome neighbor, and also, perhaps, because his wife, whom he later left, was involved in the plot. She decoyed him from his cabin and signaled the neighbors, and together they burned it down and with it all his years of work.

"Well, now I must do it again," Sequoia is reported to have said. But it was probably less native sweetness of disposition than acceptance of failure that gave him his patience. He did not do it again on the plan his intelligence had already rejected, and before he tried a new one, he moved out of the Cherokee Nation in search, perhaps, of more forbearing neighbors. In 1817 he joined Chief Jolly in making the treaty with Jackson that so enraged the Cherokees, and in 1818 left for new lands in the Arkansas country with a party of 331.

3.

A journey at the right moment may serve as a decisive stimulus to the creative imagination. It was so with Sequoia. Three years later he was back in the Nation for a visit. He had with him a gift, and the purpose of his visit was to induce his people to accept it.

The gift was a bundle of papers. One paper contained some eighty-six characters of odd appearance. To the puzzled Cherokees they looked like so many pheasant tracks crisscrossing each other in light snow. To a white man a few looked like English letters, some of them in reverse; some might have been Hebrew characters, or Greek, and some Egyptian or Chinese, and some looked like nothing at all hitherto conceived by the fevered mind of man. Other papers contained these cabalistics in combinations that, according to Sequoia, expressed the sentiments of Arkansas people to friends back in the Nation. In proof thereof he spelled out the messages.

Sequoia, however, had been an object of ridicule for too long; even John Ross smiled at him. His part in the treaty with Jackson had not enhanced his prestige. The Cherokees were difficult to convince. They received the messages gladly enough, but were skeptical of Sequoia's claim that these were contained in the marks made on the papers. Sequoia could easily have remembered what he had been told.

Even when Sequoia demonstrated by taking down testimony in a court case and having his six-year-old daughter, who had not been present, read it back, the chiefs listened stolidly. They were not impressed; there was a trick in this somewhere. And Sequoia retired disheartened.

But next morning, so runs the account Payne recorded only fourteen years after the event, one of the witnesses, Big Rattling Gourd, sought him out.

"I couldn't sleep last night," he told Sequoia. "Yesterday by daylight what you did did not seem remarkable. But when night came it was different. All night long I wondered at it and could not sleep. Sequoia, show me those characters."

And this artless confession, more than the silver medal Council ordered struck for him in 1824, more than the pension, the salt lick in the Arkansas later conferred on him by a grateful people, was perhaps Sequoia's greatest reward.

4.

Sequoia remained in the East only until his syllabary had been accepted, understood, and mastered by a few. He selected several youths, gave them instruction, and then held an examination which according to the *Cherokee Phoenix* of July 29, 1829, was a very exciting occasion, followed by a feast. Then he returned to the Arkansas. Thanks to his early departure, he missed a rare experience, the renaissance among the Cherokees.

In the final stage of his long experiment Sequoia had hit on the principle of finding all the basic syllables in Cherokee and adopting a symbol for each. Once he had this idea he finished his work quickly, within a month. He might profitably have spent more time, for some of his characters are needlessly complicated, and latter-day philologists have discovered that his ear did not always discriminate accurately between sounds. Nevertheless he had worked out a very successful system of Cherokee phonetics. Learn his characters and the sounds they represented and you could write full-fledged Cherokee forthwith with no nonsense about spelling or syntax, if, that is, you were a Cherokee born and bred.

Cherokees whose understanding was quick and whose memory was retentive could master the syllabary and thereby bridge the gap between illiteracy and letters in the span of a single day. To everyone concerned such accomplishment was little short of miraculous. Pathkiller used to recommend four years as the time needed to accomplish this feat the white man's way. Children, white no less than red, could drone away at their books year after year and still not read easily enough to have pleasure in it, or write well enough not to be ashamed before a teacher.

Until now attendance at school had cost too many dusty hours away from sunnier pursuits; and when you had served your time with a Miss Sawyer or a Mr. Ellsworth, what had you? Merely the ability to construe a lot of fossilized talk about white man's exploits and philosophizings, most of it quite irrelevant to a red man's proper interests.

But now came a new kind of school, such a school as might have been designed by Socrates or Comenius. There was no stuffiness or cramped confinement in this classroom; all the bright winds of the mountains blew through it; and its walls were the billowing frontiers of the Cherokee Nation. For the whole Nation had become one great peripatetic Attic academy.

Attendance involved no sitting on rows of benches under the sharp eyes of a Yankee schoolma'am. You went to school in odd moments, whenever you found a bit of paper, a smooth bit of bark, or a knife in conjunction with a beech tree, and a wayfarer to go over your lesson with you.

Nor was this learning a prerogative of the young, though little boys took time off from hunting down the squirrel with blowgun and bow to work out a joyous assignment in youthful obscenity. Mothers big with young, or girls in menstruation, lightened the tedium of the taboos enjoined on them by working out the syllabary on the logs of their cabins. Garrulous old men, addicted to spinning long yarns in their hothouses, fell into the silence of concentration while they got the characters from a passer-by. Farmers worked at it while resting their horses from the plow. And sleek young men, hitherto contemptuous of white man's book learning, worked at this new thing as arduously as they practiced for a ball play, and then journeyed over to yonder side of the mountain to one of white man's more distant post offices so that they could write a letter home, indulging thereby in the swagger of speaking to the maidens of their choice by long distance.

The really remarkable thing about this event was that no principal chief, no government agent, no Great White Father preached at the Cherokees from aloft urging them so to apply themselves. Indeed, such people seem to have been the last to discover that the new learning existed. So literate a man as John Ross had no need of this invention. The Ridge, imbued in these earlier, happier years with the Cherokee folk spirit, apparently never got around to learning the syllabary, for in 1828 he was still affixing his mark to official documents.

No, this was unlike the other revivals of human learning; the scholars, the princes, had nothing to do with its springs. It began as a river does, simply, modestly, naturally, as with the dripping of bright drops from a mossy rock.

5.

Isaac Proctor of the Hightower mission was not one given to exaggerating the achievements of the Cherokees. The presence of conjure, the fact that many Cherokee farmers, having put in their corn and potatoes, settled genially down to wasting the winter in idleness and "frolic," made him skeptical of the nation's much-advertised progress.

Nevertheless it was Proctor who, in January 1825, announced in all seriousness that the American Board need send no more teachers; all the Cherokees needed to become entirely literate was an adequate supply of paper and ink.

Proctor had first mentioned Sequoia's invention in November 1824 apropos of a confession that his school was falling off badly and that parents were ill pleased with the progress of their children. He cited the disappointment of one father who operated a center where white men traded with Cherokees for livestock. This man had sent his boys to school in the expectation that within a month or at the most a year they would be able to act as interpreters and to keep records for him. On the contrary, a term or two at school had left the boys approximately where it found them; now came Sequoia's invention, and in one day the apparently unteachable dullards had learned to read and write. The father withdrew them from school, and Proctor could not blame him.

The real teachers of that community were not the missionaries but some church members who had gone to Willstown to learn the characters from an authority there and returned triumphantly literate in less than a week. The whole community flocked to them and besieged

Proctor with demands for writing materials. Letters passed in all directions; Proctor himself received one and had to get a pupil to read it for him.

A little boy who had never been sufficiently roused from his apathy to learn a word of English now labored in class over a whole sentence in Cherokee, held it up for all his schoolmates to see, and shone with pride when they read it back to him, "The Turtle is my friend."

Few hymns had been rendered into Cherokee; every good church member knew the repertoire by heart; repetition was making them tedious. This did not deter the young men from writing them all down in Sequoia's alphabet and passing them out in church, where people held them in careful hands, following the texts as eagerly as if everything were now fresh and new. It gave his congregation, said Proctor, "quite a literary appearance."

Proctor wanted new songs to be given his people in the wonderful new writing, and all missionaries looked forward to having the New Testament translated and transliterated and placed in Cherokee hands. "The knowledge of Mr. Guess's alphabet is spreading—like fire among the brush," said Chamberlin in October 1824. "If Christians neglect the duty, Satan will no doubt furnish reading for the Cherokees."

Butrick was already experimenting hopefully in that direction. He himself, in the first flush of his enthusiasm for the Cherokee language, had worked out a system of transliterating Cherokee into English characters and had published a Cherokee Speller in Knoxville. The little volume had aroused no interest; apparently neither missionaries nor Cherokees had found any use for it, and all Butrick's later references to it were shamefaced.

Butrick now threw himself into organizing a complete Cherokee New Testament. David Brown was the translator; his Greek was excellent, his Cherokee poor, so his text was to be corrected by Major Lowry, John Huss,

Hicks, and Boudinot. The task of transliterating into Sequoia's alphabet was first assigned Huss, then The Whirlwind, known as the most accurate writer in the Nation. He was also a Methodist, a doctrinaire detail that worried Butrick. Nevertheless the latter asked the American Board for $40 for expenses of board and white paper for the workers, who would accept blankets and clothes as pay.

The translation was actually finished, right through to Revelation, but alas, like so many of Butrick's eager projects, it was ignored. The authoritative text of the Gospel to the Cherokees was to be achieved under the direction of a newcomer, a missionary recently ordained in Boston and sent to the Nation at the height of all this ferment, young Samuel A. Worcester.

6.

Worcester reached the Cherokees late in 1825, hard after the October Council wherein the chiefs, who no longer ignored Sequoia's invention, had voted an epoch-making innovation. They had earmarked $1500 of the national annuity funds for the purchase of a press and type in Sequoia's alphabet.

This Council had also ordered a silver medal struck for Sequoia, and had approved the establishment of a national academy and museum. Under the pressure of events nothing was to come of the last two measures, though people did rummage through their possessions for buffalo horns, wampum, and ancestral peace pipes to be delivered to Boudinot, assigned to the collection of such curios, and a gesture was made towards starting a subscription to finance the Academy. It was the national press, however, that was the immediate and urgent desire of the Cherokees.

Although Sequoia had achieved in a decade what it had taken the white race (without benefit of previous models) centuries to accomplish, and the Cherokees were now actually anticipating the American concept of universal education, not even Sequoia was able to recapitulate the history of human progress to the extent of inventing movable type. To set up a press the Cherokees must depend on the help of white men.

It was providential that a newcomer so intelligent, sympathetic, and aggressive as Worcester arrived in the Nation at exactly this juncture. To Worcester was entrusted the responsibility of getting the type cast in Boston and negotiating to that end with the American Board, who must supervise the undertaking on the spot and arrange the purchase of the press.

Boston, or at least the American Board, was electrified by these developments. That aborigines should be capable of self-improvement to so radical an extent had never entered their calculations. In spite of the fact that they had sponsored the eminent philologist William Pickering in devising a system of transliteration suitable for all Indian languages, they were ready to aid the Cherokee venture. Or at least they were until the syllabary itself, meticulously transcribed in Worcester's hand, reached Boston.

At this point the whole proposition suddenly looked preposterous. Certainly the alphabet did, an incoherent garble of outlandish characters, and not a manageable twenty-six, but eighty-six of them. The learned Bostonians were conversant with Hebrew and Greek; many could even construe Sanskrit and Arabic; but Cherokee was a language little known on Beacon Hill, and there was no one to recognize with what skill these odd characters represented Cherokee sounds. The Board was surprised at Worcester; what had seemed an unusually level-headed young man had obviously let himself be swept away by a premature and ill-judged enthusiasm.

They therefore wrote back that having given the matter

their mature consideration they found it impracticable. The Cherokees indeed should have their press, but Worcester must induce the chiefs to accept Pickering's system of writing instead of Sequoia's.

Worcester did no such thing. It was only Butrick who tried to persuade the chiefs on the ground that the Board, having lavished so much on Pickering's system, would get "discouraged" if they couldn't use it. Worcester, his fighting instincts aroused, bent all his efforts to win over the Board.

"Their enthusiasm is kindled," he wrote back. "They are circulating hymns and writing letters every day. . . . At National Council they have listened to a proposal to substitute an alphabet like Mr. Pickering's and have rejected it. They have talked much of printing in the new and famous characters. . . . Tell them now of printing in another character and you throw water upon the fire which you are wishing to kindle. . . . In the meantime a crisis in the Nation is passing by, and when at such a crisis such an enthusiasm is kindled, it must be cherished, not repressed, if you would save the Nation."

The Bostonians were just men. They still had their misgivings, but after all, the Cherokees were spending their own money. They delivered the order for the Cherokee type to a Boston house and printed Worcester's eloquence in defense of the syllabary in the *Missionary Herald*.

Worcester had designs of his own on the press. Not that he proposed to meddle with the newspaper; that was Cherokee business. But a press once set up can put forth all manner of publications. Worcester proposed that these include translations of the gospel, religious tracts, and hymnals. This suggestion had the blessing of Council, not only because in the main the chiefs approved Christianity, but for the strictly practical reason that given such an interest in the press the Board would aid in its upkeep. The Cherokees knew that the appropriation of $1500, one fifth of the national income, was insufficient to carry out their full plan; indeed, Boudinot, who was going North anyway to marry Harriet, had been authorized to appeal for money in the North. The press had not been the inspiration of white men, but it could not go far without white man's help; the Cherokees were grateful for the presence of the dynamic young Worcester.

Worcester, for his part, was no less in need of Cherokee help for his translation. He had plunged into the study of Cherokee, had in his turn encountered the protean Cherokee verb, had, or thought he had, identified 170 forms in the present tense alone. For all his scholarship, he could not in a lifetime of study hope for mastery of such a language or expect to make translations single-handed. What he needed was a collaborator with an expert knowledge of both languages, and such a man he found in Elias Boudinot, who was also being considered as editor of the Cherokee paper.

There were difficulties in using Boudinot. Boston did not raise the issue of his marriage, but it did question his attendance at the Sabbath ball play and other evidences of backsliding. Boudinot himself was reluctant to accept not only the mission offer but also the editorship of the paper. It irked him that though the chiefs originally proposed to pay a printer $500 they thought $250 enough for the editor. He had returned to his people with an alien wife, a white man's education, and the problem of supporting a family that was to grow rapidly. Whatever occupation he adopted, it must befit his dignity and be lucrative.

Worcester, however, had been won at first sight by the young man's ability. He would not consider parting with him, and he overrode every difficulty as fast as it arose. With the help of Butrick he persuaded the Board that in spite of Boudinot's recent shortcomings he was worthy of this trust. Butrick thought Cornwall's cruelty sufficient explanation of Boudinot's wavering: Worcester pointed out that his serious young wife was of such stuff as good missionaries are made of and was now a steadying influence. The Board was induced to augment Boudinot's editorial salary by a grant of $100, a figure it was ultimately to triple.

One further difficulty arose: Worcester's headquarters was at Brainerd, a spot that Boudinot, worried about his health just then, considered unwholesome. His home was New Echota, the capital and the site chosen for the new printing shop; here, not elsewhere, would he work with Worcester. And Worcester accepted the condition; as the date for the arrival of the press drew near, he set to work building him a mission at New Echota.

This circumstance, so trivial on the face of it, was to have far-reaching consequences for Worcester, for Boudinot, and for all the Cherokees. Indeed, the Board had some well-founded misgivings about the lengths to which their newest apostle's zeal was carrying him. To begin with they wished he could have been content with a log house instead of one of expensive sawn wood. And David Greene, sent from Boston early in 1828 to supervise the setting up of the new press, foresaw other complications.

New Echota, the capital, had been so chosen not because of its size, but because of its accessibility; it was almost at the mathematical center of the Cherokee population. Populous only during Council, it was otherwise a deserted hamlet in rather barren uplands where only four or five families then lived. These did not pretend to an interest in religion. Worcester's congregations on Sundays were microscopic; he was lucky if beyond his own family and Boudinot's there were half a dozen present.

What deduction, asked Greene soberly, were the Georgians and others hostile to the Indians going to draw on seeing Worcester leave the school and church at Brainerd to settle in the "place where the press is but there is no school, no church, and no mission work for him to do?"

Georgia was not slow in drawing its conclusions, and they were exactly what Green anticipated, but the American Board, willing to adventure much for its faith, did not interfere with Worcester.

7.

By late 1827 all difficulties had been adjusted. Boudinot's editorial salary had been revised upward to equal that of the principal chief, and the printer's downward: editor $300, printer $400. Boudinot had accepted his double responsibility, and two printers were found in Tennessee, the profane and contentious Harris and the mild-mannered John F. Wheeler. A log cabin had been built to house the press; the name of the paper had been chosen and approved. It was to be *The Cherokee Phoenix*, in Cherokee something like *I Will Arise*, a title suggested by Worcester. Now all that was needed was the arrival of the press and type from Boston. To the Cherokees, raging to see themselves in print, it was rather like waiting for Christmas.

Boudinot, having composed some very stinging editorials on Georgian policy (which Greene read with a sinking) and having translated the new Cherokee constitution for serial publication, set to work with Worcester on St. Matthew, while waiting for the press to finish its journey by sea from Boston to Savannah and overland through Georgia. The printers tried to familiarize themselves with the contours of Sequoia's syllabary. That is, Wheeler did; Harris made a preliminary attempt, and then with many oaths declined to touch the Cherokee columns of the paper. A Cherokee youth stood by as apprentice, and as soon as such youths could be trained as printers, the Cherokees proposed that the paper should be wholly an Indian publication. Much of the paper was to appear in English, for it had a double purpose: to acquaint the

Cherokees with the state of the nation, and to acquaint the world at large with the Cherokees. Already subscriptions were coming in response to a prospectus printed in Tennessee; one came from Germany, from a friend of William Pickering, Baron von Humboldt of Berlin.

Early in 1828 the wonderful press actually lumbered up the wagon trails from Savannah and was installed under the eye of David Greene, with more eager Cherokee hands to help than were necessary. No paper, unfortunately, had come with it, but paper was rushed up the Federal Pike from Tennessee. By February the first issue of the *Phoenix* was ready for Boston, for the Berlin baron, and for the Cherokees; and to the last that modest four-page journal was more precious than the Gutenberg Bible and more wonderful than all seven wonders of antiquity.

An itinerant peddler, such a one as is by some alleged to have fathered Sequoia, had perambulated the Nation just before the *Phoenix* came out. His pack contained a consignment of spectacles. The clear-eyed Cherokees had fitted these over their noses and, finding that the prospect pleased, had gone in for spectacles in considerable numbers.

When the *Phoenix* began to come out in weekly editions, and after it St. Matthew, a hymnal, and a tract on temperance, the Cherokees put on their spectacles, settled down in the chimney corner if it were cold or out under the hemlocks by the spring place if it were warm, and, thus owlishly outfitted, pored over their reading.

Many of them sought out bilingual friends to construe the information in the English columns, especially as these comprised from half to three quarters of the paper. Thus all manner of news penetrated the hills: tidings from Petrograd, Turkey, and Greece; a sentimental account of a suicide in France, the story of a nine-year-old Cherokee shot by an arrow, and that of a dissolute old woman in Hightower who burned herself to death while drunk; anecdotes of George Washington as recalled by Custis; information about an imminent collision between the earth and a privateering comet; Cowper's "Pity the Poor African"; instruction on how to exterminate cockroaches and cure colic. The Cherokees, in short, had many of the advantages that the tabloids offer the straphanger in the subway.

The Cherokees also read matter of more relevant and pressing interest. The *Phoenix* reprinted *in extenso* everything that it found in its exchanges of what was being done in Congress and Georgia relative to the Cherokees. Such facts now came straight to the people without distortion by rumor-mongers. They gave this information such detailed and intelligent attention that it is doubtful if there was any section in America where the general public was better informed on questions affecting its own welfare.

For years the Federal government had been harrying the Indians with agents sent to induce them to remove. Among these there were periodically some to whom the task looked easy, like buying Manhattan for a string of beads; any white man could beguile a simple forest folk. But this forest people, never easily beguilable, now displayed a grasp of relevant current history very disconcerting to such agents; in fact they were often better informed than the white emissaries.

Nor was such knowledgeableness confined to the chiefs. The hill people read their *Phoenix*, too. Judging by its columns, one of the most wide-awake communities of all was the Aquohee district on the Hiwassee on the southern flanks of the Great Smokies, well away from the paths beaten through the Nation by the white men. These people gathered in district councils where the latest problem presented in the *Phoenix* was analyzed and zestfully discussed. Their findings were often recorded in a letter that, though it might be intended for a chief or for Congress, usually received publication in the *Phoenix* on its way.

Could the enemies of the Cherokees have foreseen the effects of the press on the Cherokees, they would have saved themselves much trouble by seizing it on its way through Georgia. For the *Phoenix* was to play an important part in unifying and heartening the Cherokees in the long ordeal that lay ahead of them.

8.

The first edition of the *Phoenix* probably caught up with Sequoia in Washington. He had gone there early in 1828 as one of a Western delegation sent to treat with the government. This delegation did not cover itself with glory; sent merely to make an adjustment on annuities, it let itself be persuaded to commit the Arkansas Cherokees to removal yet farther west. This result profoundly impressed the Eastern Cherokees, confirmed them in their judgment that the white men were insatiable and that wisdom lay in making their stand where they were happy, in the East. The Western Cherokees were ill pleased with their delegates, talked of trying them on their return. The reputation of Sequoia, however, seems not to have suffered.

Sequoia was now a celebrity. Distinguished people sought him out, and his portrait was painted, pipe in mouth, a flowered turban on his head, one lean finger pointing to his syllabary.

He was, however, a celebrity of modest habit. Back in the West, in his home on Skin Bayou, he was no more conspicuous than his fellows. He and his children worked his farm, his salt lick, and every so often Sequoia saddled him a pony and rode off to the nearest post office to get the latest issues of the *Phoenix*. These he read with profound satisfaction.

Even in the West distinguished travelers occasionally

found their way to his home. John Howard Payne ("Home Sweet Home"), who happened on the Cherokees at a crisis of their history and became very much involved therein, was one day to have a two-hour conference with him. Sequoia talked at great length, his voice warm with eloquence, his eyes alight; but unfortunately his discourse was in Cherokee. A "linkister" was present, but he put off Payne's requests for enlightenment, saying: "Not now. What he is saying is wonderful . . . wonderful. Later you shall hear." But when Sequoia, exhausted at last, limped off to bed, the linkister said: "Now it is impossible to tell it. There was too much. I would say it wrong. Wait until I can ask him again." And there was somehow no opportunity for the linkister to do so.

It was a pity. Sequoia was an accessible character living in historic times, and yet because of accidents like these he has somewhat the status of a myth. His life might have been known in homely detail, the nature of his thinking understood, for he is said to have kept a diary in his own writing. But that diary, and with it the secret of Sequoia's genius, has been lost.

One dream imputed to him is worth noting. Although Sequoia invented his syllabary for the Cherokees, he reached out beyond the needs of his own people to the needs of all the Indian peoples. It was probably the impact of his new environment in the Arkansas country, where dozens of nations jostled each other, that gave him the idea. Quite early he worked out an adaptation of his syllabary to the Choctaw language, and he proposed that Indians of all tribes be made literate through this device.

There was something of the vision of Tecumseh in this plan; indeed, could the genius of Tecumseh and Sequoia have worked in conjunction, the great plan of the former might not have failed. But Sequoia's achievement came too late to shape the fate of the red men. His people, after standing for a moment in the light of history, were to be thrust aside and forgotten, and his work with them. The Cherokees were not to forget their writing or their press, but both were to become merely local phenomena, presently little more than curios.

As for Sequoia himself, defeat never touched him and old age did not wither him. In the early 1840's, when he was at best over seventy, he undertook an expedition into Mexican territory, now Texas, for the scientific end of discovering a fabled lost tribe of Cherokees. On this adventure he died.

CHAPTER VI

The Georgians

Unlettered old Pathkiller had in his simplicity a more clear-eyed view of Cherokee destiny than some of his more sophisticated colleagues who were carrying on the real business of government for him. All during the third decade of the nineteenth century, when the Cherokees were reacting to the stimulation of Sequoia's invention, setting up a national press, and planning great things— in particular a new written constitution that would prove to the white men how enlightened and progressive they were—Pathkiller had his eyes on one stubborn fact, the entanglement of Cherokee affairs with those of the state of Georgia. In 1828, the year when the *Phoenix* began publication and the new constitution went into effect, these difficulties suddenly came to a head.

But Pathkiller was spared the details; the old man had died in January 1827.

The situation between the Cherokee Nation and the state of Georgia in relation to the Federal government was rather like one of those myths of classic antiquity in which mortals of divergent views pray to their favorite gods about the same situation, and the gods, without mutual consultation, give affirmative answers to quite incompatible prayers. Both Cherokees and Georgians had prayed for legal title to the same territory; both had been confirmed in the possession thereof.

The prayer of the Cherokees had been answered by treaties that assured them their country "in perpetuity." This was all they asked; they had no further prayer to make.

But the state of Georgia had also been saying its prayers. In 1802, in return for the Federal government's promise to extinguish Indian titles in Western Georgia as soon as this could be peaceably arranged, it had relinquished its claims to the land on which Mississippi and Alabama were created. This promise, contradicting the earlier one to the Cherokees, who had not been consulted in the new arrangement, had thus far been only partially kept. By 1828 Georgia had waited more than a quarter of a century for its rights; it was now becoming clear to Georgia politicians that if the state was ever to have satisfaction, it must act with no less vigor than the Tennesseeans, who had settled territory to which they had not even a pretense of a legal claim.

Georgia's waiting, to be sure, had not been entirely unrewarded. The treaty of Fort Jackson in 1814 had virtually cleared the state of its Creek incumbents. Jefferson's offer of an exchange of lands in the West had met with some response from the Cherokees, who had now a sufficient number in the Arkansas country to organize themselves as the Cherokee Nation West. But after a good beginning such migrations had become sporadic. Emigration could go on for a century at its present rate without perceptibly diminishing the population in the East. Also, since 1819 it would do Georgia no good, for the law of 1819 forbade Cherokees to make independent land cessions on pain of death.

Until now the Federal government had shown little sympathy with Georgia claims against the Cherokees. Monroe had said in his message to Congress in 1825: "I have no hesitation to declare it as my opinion that the Indian title was not affected in the slightest circumstance by the compact with Georgia, and that there is no obligation on the United States to remove the Indians by force."

Adams had not only taken a similar view, but refused to continue to press the Indians to remove. It was not he but Congress that in 1828 was persuaded by Governor Forsythe and Senator Lumpkin of Georgia to send Colonel Hugh Montgomery to the Cherokees to induce them to go west. The maneuver was in any case not a success. Its failure convinced Georgia officials that a very different order of persuasion was needed to get the stubborn people out of the country.

They now pinned their hopes on the election of Jackson. The treaty of Fort Jackson had proved the soundness of his attitude on Indian affairs. If elected, he, a frontiersman, could be counted on not to let petty legalities stand in the way of Georgia where the Cherokees were concerned.

2.

The Cherokees intensely resented the pressure applied to them in 1828; John Ross, now acting chief, had to make a tour to dissuade the Cherokee patriots from laying violent hands on Western Cherokees who had been involved in the unauthorized 1817 land deal and had now been induced by Colonel Montgomery to circulate in the Nation adding their voice to his. To be seen in the company of one of these agents was enough to ruin a Cherokee reputation. William Hicks, interim assistant chief (for Charles Hicks had died two weeks after Pathkiller), lost his chance at re-election because a relative had enrolled and rumor had it that Hicks too was interested. At the October Council, Chief Ross gave for the Nation a forthright refusal of Montgomery's proposals.

The Federal government had insulted the Cherokees by the timing of its new offer. It had urged them to accept land where they could again become hunters at the very moment that the Cherokees had announced their political coming of age by the adoption of a written constitution proclaiming them "one of the sovereign and independent nations of the earth."

The Cherokee Nation was now a republic, just like the United States. (Independence Day, 1827, had been selected for the ratification of the constitution as a gesture to the big sister republic next door.) It had a president, a bicameral House, though these were still called chief and Council respectively; it had a supreme court, and it had a body of laws now codified as once suggested by Thomas Jefferson.

The Cherokee constitution was, however, no blind imitation of the American model; in some ways, indeed, it was an improvement, or so thought the Cherokees. The Americans, for instance, had somehow failed to recognize their prevailing religion. The Cherokees, under the necessity of proving how very advanced they had become, certified themselves as a "Christian" nation. The constitution incorporated a law of 1826 providing that "no person who disbelieves in the existence of the creator or reward and punishment after death [is] to hold office or testify in court." Ministers of the gospel, however, were pronounced ineligible for office either as principal chiefs or as members of Council.

There was also one prime oversight in the new Cherokee government: the lawmakers had given no attention to setting up an independent fiscal policy. A national currency was not even thought of; when people needed cash they would continue to use notes and scrip issued by the banks of neighboring states. Taxation consisted of an annual poll of fifty cents a family, seldom collected. It was not new; early Brainerd had received intermittent help from Cherokees wanting to earn enough to pay off their obligation.

The Cherokees received from the government from old land sales a yearly income of $7500, and this sum, paid to the national treasurer, was the real fiscal basis of their government. Expenditures were as of the present moment mostly in salaries—the modest stipend of the officials, the $2.00 per diem for members of the upper house and $1.50 for the lower when Council was in session; the expense of the October Council of 1828 was reported as $5,105.48¾.

In their reliance on their annuity (a term suggestive of retirement and of old age pension) lay a real weakness of the Cherokees, a challenge to their right to the words "independent and sovereign." For all the healthy town-meeting atmosphere of their local councils, they were not nationally self-sustaining. Just as most of them depended on Northern philanthropy to support their children in school, their government depended on the sufferance of the whites for its maintenance. Significantly, the least responsible of Cherokee public officials was the treasurer, John Martin, who, indignantly wrote "A Cherokee" in the newborn *Phoenix*, was never to be found on duty in New Echota. "A seat of government without a treasury may be called a coat without a pocket," said "A Cherokee." "Adorn a naked metropolis with its treasury."

Before the Cherokees could do so, a hostile administration in Washington City was to discover this Achilles heel in their economy.

3.

The Cherokee constitution had not been achieved without birth pangs. As always, there was a strong reactionary element that bitterly opposed such aping of white men. To these, the lip service the constitution paid Christianity was an outrage against the faith of their fathers. The death of Pathkiller and Hicks in January 1827 set off the period of ferment and protest known as "White Path's Rebellion."

This phenomenon really frightened the missionaries.

They saw the townhouses become the scene of passionate oratory, of rump councils called to denounce the proposed constitution, the preaching of the missionaries, the prevalence of the new soft ways, and to demand a return to old customs. It was at times almost a ghost dance. Strong leadership and an intelligent sense of direction were lacking, however, and the Cherokee leaders were undismayed. "A noise which will end in noise only," John Ross reassured the alarmed Worcester. And indeed, a Council called to conciliate the disaffected bore quick results. The constitution was ratified without further incident on July 4, 1827.

It was not to take effect until the following summer. Before that time it was published in the *Phoenix* in both English and Cherokee. The word was made manifest to the malcontents in their own tongue; they could examine it at their leisure. And such was their reverence for the new Cherokee writing that the very act of publishing it invested the document with a kind of sanctity. Also, viewed at close range, it presented no startling innovations after all; the form of government was merely a consolidation of trends that had been clear for two decades; the laws were only those which had been passed in Council from about 1819 on.

So the fever passed. And when some of the missionaries, including Proctor, were asked to help superintend the elections held *viva voce* in the district council houses in 1828, they were agreeably surprised by the order and sobriety that prevailed and the general good character of the candidates chosen. "There was nothing of that intrigue and unfairness which is to be seen at elections in some of the civilized states," wrote Proctor.

4.

One purpose of the adoption of the constitution was to make a good impression on the outside world. In this the

Cherokees had some success, especially in the North, where the *Missionary Herald* gave generous space to the details of the new government. It even became discussed abroad, in England, for instance, where some editors were to denounce proposals to oppress Indians capable of such enlightenment in exactly those terms reserved by writers of a century later for Hitler's treatment of the Jews. Editorial approval came from so near a neighbor as Alabama.

But there were others who took different views. Even the just John Quincy Adams looked askance at the document and disturbed the Cherokees with a notification that his agent Montgomery would visit them to point out flaws. This conference, however, was, in Boudinot's words, "a pleasant surprise." Adams merely wished to emphasize the fact that the terms "sovereign and independent" must not be made to apply to Cherokee foreign relations; their government was, he said, to be considered as of "purely municipal character." Relieved, the Cherokees assured the agent that they had no intention of becoming independent of their treaties with the United States. They did not relish, however, the phrase "municipal." "Hold your great father, the president, by the hand," the agent had exhorted the chiefs in a reversion to the paternalistic terms now disappearing from such negotiations. "Don't move a single step in any direction without his counsel and advice."

No approval at all came from the neighbor the Cherokees most urgently needed to placate. Officials of the sovereign state of Georgia, reading the audacious document, decided that the time for conciliatory measures had passed, that they must now take matters into their own hands. They waited only to see how the presidential elections would turn out. When Jackson won, they took his victory as national endorsement of their own claims.

In December 1828 a bill was passed in the Georgia legislature extending Georgia authority over all Cherokee territory within its chartered limits. All Cherokee laws were declared to be null and void, and no Indian could testify in a court case involving a white man.

Such a rule, if enforced, would indeed make the new constitution a mockery. It was not, however, to go into effect until June 1830. Even Georgia preferred peaceable adjustment to the use of force. It was simultaneously agitating in Congress for the passage of a removal bill applicable to all the Eastern Indians; there was hope that before the new laws need take effect this bill would have passed Congress and the Indians would be propelled west by Federal action.

5.

The new attitude of Georgia sounded the death knell of Cherokee hopes in the East, but of this fact the Cherokees at large were oblivious. The notion that they might be dispossessed of the land on which they were now doing so well was fantastic. They were good neighbors to Georgia; a white man could pass through their nation in perfect safety and enjoy Cherokee hospitality on his way. They were even helping feed the Georgians; it was no uncommon sight to see prosperous Cherokees driving wagonloads of grain and droves of cattle or hogs down to Georgia market.

They took the new laws seriously enough to send Ross to Washington with a protest signed by 3095, in which they reminded the government that they had never been party to the agreement with Georgia and had never surrendered their rights. Then they went on about their affairs, awaiting developments calmly. The white man's law was on their side, a fact that Washington City had never once failed to recognize. Even at worst the Georgia laws would not go into effect for nearly two years, and in two years much could happen.

The *Phoenix* had curiously little to say in this crisis, the significance of which was obscured for Editor Boudinot by preoccupation with his own troubles. Never able to overcome his mortification that Printer Harris, who in Worcester's words was "ignorant—disagreeable—and a Methodist," drew $400 to his $300, he had resigned just at this juncture. Ross tried vainly to get David Brown to take the job and then won back Boudinot by raising his salary to $400 and letting him fire Harris. This last took a bit of doing; Harris, muttering innuendoes about Worcester's purpose in "sneaking about" the printing shop, had finally to be ousted by the national marshal. Thus distracted, the editor let the issue with Georgia pass for the moment almost unnoticed.

It was the vigilant Aquohee district that editorialized the Cherokee point of view on the general question of removal. Apropos of Montgomery's visit they had written in September 1828 that they were tired of being "teased to part with our inheritance just as we are rising out of obscurity and are beginning to occupy a respectable standing in the estimation of Christians who know us."

In April 1829 they hinted slyly to Georgians agitating for their eviction: "Our white brethren have more knowledge than we have, and they are better skilled in traveling and commencing new settlements; why then do they not go and possess that good land for themselves?

"We are governed just as we wish to be. . . . We hold the power in our hands and whenever it becomes necessary we will use it to redress our grievances. . . . A great portion of our people can read and the *Phoenix* furnishes them with useful information every week."

Their lot and their land contented them, these simple people of Aquohee. It was a land as lovely and various as any area of similar size on the face of the earth. They had no intention of leaving it. If force was threatened against them, all that was necessary to be maintained in their rights was to address an appeal to the conscience of the American people.

Such faith should have moved mountains. Indeed, it was to come close to doing so. Georgia itself was by no means impervious to the appeal to conscience. The Cherokees had friends there. One, R. Campbell of Savannah, in 1828 and 1829 wrote frequently to the *Phoenix* declaring that the Georgians had land enough and that the state owed the Cherokees a debt of gratitude for fighting with them against the Red Stick Creeks. The proposed removal he compared to the partition of Poland and said that it would entail on Georgia "the odious charges of being Faithless, Covetous, Ungrateful and Inhuman."

Campbell printed a memorial embodying these sentiments in pamphlet form and sent it to the Georgia legislature. Two pages were read to the Senate, whereon that body declined to listen further.

At no time were visitors to Georgia to find its plain citizens seething with lust for conquest of the Cherokees; such seething as went on was confined within the legislative halls. But if agitation in Georgia was almost exclusively political, it was also true that there was no influential state politician to take a stand against it. In time the political ferment made some impression on general consciousness. A popular song expressed the concern of the public:

> *All I ask in this creation*
> *Is a pretty little wife and a big plantation*
> *Way up yonder in the Cherokee Nation.*

And by evil chance, about the time that the Cherokee constitution went into effect, something happened that made the ownership of Cherokee lands of passionate interest to Georgians with no political leanings at all. Gold was discovered at Dahlonega, in that portion of the Cherokee Nation claimed by Georgia.

CHAPTER VII

Gold Rush

Man may not have progressed, but at least his interests have changed. Quite recently a chapter in Cherokee history was reopened; a fresh deposit of gold was struck at Dahlonega, now indisputably Georgia territory, and the incident had no repercussions on national affairs. This seems to indicate that gold, an attractive metal of only moderate utilitarian value, whose symbolic aspects American Indians from the Incas and Aztecs down to the Cherokees have had cause to execrate, has begun to lose its power over the imagination of white men. When we push people around today, we do so for the sake of elements of more practical use: bauxite, tin, or plantations of rubber. The emotional voltage of one ancient abstraction is clearly on the wane, and that waning may be progress.

But in the late 1820's, where gold lay, there lay El Dorado; where El Dorado was, there white men also desired to be. Furthermore, many Cherokees, who had been picking up white men's symbolism along with other aspects of civilization, desired to be there too. On the gold fields of Dahlonega came the first real collision between Georgia and the Cherokee Nation.

Gold was said first to have been discovered near Dahlonega by a boy at play in 1815; his mother sold the nugget to a white man but refused to say where it was found. The deposit was rediscovered in 1828 or 1829, and this time the discoverer was less discreet; by early 1830 some four thousand whites were reported crowded into the gold fields. Luckily for the Cherokees these were in the extreme southeast of the Nation, and though the invaders brought with them some rough characters and copious kegs of whisky, they were not the menace to the Nation at large that might have been expected so long as they confined their activities to the fields.

The missionaries were less troubled by their presence than by the disposition of the Cherokees to join them. Some of Dr. Butler's parishioners at Haweis, a station close to the fields, neglected their farms and all the hard-won improvements thereon in the hope of getting rich quickly at the mines. On the reverse side of the medal were two members of Butler's congregation, one a notable rake, now reformed, who voluntarily undertook the task of visiting the fields of a Sabbath to hold religious meetings. And though they preached in Cherokee (with interpreters), large congregations of Georgian fortune hunters crowded around them and listened with respect.

The deposit near Dahlonega, though no Klondike, was also no flash in the pan. In the first nine months of 1830 gold from these mines to the value of $230,000 was reported received in Augusta. In later years a United States mint was for a time maintained in Dahlonega. A new lode was discovered in recent years. Could the Cherokees have had full control of their mines, they would have had ample means for endowing their press, their proposed national academy and library, and all manner of improvements.

Curiously enough, though all Cherokee land was communal, not individual property, though Cherokee citizens as prominent as William S. Coodey, Ross's nephew, and Elijah Hicks, member of Council, were actively interested in the mines, the possibility of working them for Cherokee public interest seems not to have occurred to General Council. Cherokees participated in the general scramble and that was all. Council, already faced with the first consequences of Georgia's new laws, could give even these little protection.

The discovery of gold had given Georgia officials excellent impetus for their plans. Such discovery was proof positive that the state was being unrightfully deprived of property of untold value. It was an excellent talking point. Plain folk who ordinarily didn't care who held the country upstate could be made to see the urgency of the issue once it was demonstrated that the disputed hills held gold.

In June 1830 Georgia's laws took effect; Georgia militia was promptly sent to the mines to round up Cherokee gold diggers. By good fortune, on their march to jail the first group met with Federal troops on the road; Federal law was with the Indians; in the spring the Indian agent had made a gesture of warning white intruders off the land. To the joy of the Cherokees the military arrested the Georgians and took away their firearms.

At the local command post, however, the Georgians outtalked the Cherokees; the Federal troops, evidently hitherto ignorant of the Georgia legislation, released the Indians but warned them that they could not hope for Federal protection. On June 24 one hundred members of the Georgia militia paraded back to the Cherokee mines in fine fettle, smashed mining apparatus, and according to the *Phoenix* made a great show of drawing up a platoon to fire on a tin milk-strainer in the springhouse of a hapless Cherokee milk-woman.

They made no arrests, but in July Governor Gilmer served writs of injunction on eleven Cherokees and two Tennesseeans found working in the mines. Most of the Cherokees left, hiring Georgians to work their lots in their absence. Other Cherokees not only persisted, but had the temerity to order white men out of their way. Their aggressiveness may be inferred from the plaintive tone of a warning written them in August by nine Georgians: "The place where we are diging has been left by you and we have come in Peace and have not molested any of your People where you are diging. Therefore we recommend you to be friendly. We are gentleman your friends."

In October the Cherokees found an unexpected advocate in Georgia. Judge Clayton of Gwinnet County, not in the main friendly to Cherokee pretensions, refused to pass sentence on the Cherokee gold digger Cunatoo in these words: "to consign a weak and defenceless race to the gloom of the dungeon by night . . . for no other crime than taking gold from their own land and the land of their fathers will incur the condemnation of all civilized nations."

Governor Gilmer, somewhat harried at this point, asked the Georgia lawmakers for special legislation to regulate the mines.

In October, also, the Federal troops took definitive action—definitive at least so far as the Cherokees were concerned—by seizing the whole mining area. The soldiers charged the miners at Pigeon Roost "with considerable shouting and clashing of firearms." The whites fled across the Chestatee, but the Cherokees, while offering no resistance, stood their ground, and were marched off to camp, where all their gold was confiscated, even their pockets and moccasins being searched to this end. At the fields the soldiers destroyed equipment, burned cabins, and ordered all work suspended until the issue could be settled.

The whites, after a day or two of watchful waiting, straggled back across the creek and resumed operations. Ross protested to the Federal authorities, only to be told that the latter could no longer intervene in the controversy between the Cherokees and the Georgians.

2.

Skirmishes at the gold fields were comparatively harmless, however, and many a Cherokee would gladly have relinquished any claim to the gold in exchange for an uncontested right to enjoy more modest holdings in peace. The gravest aspect of the gold rush was that it called the attention of hitherto disregardful Georgians to the charms of Cherokee country. Men balked in their hopes of striking a rich deposit looked about them and liked what they saw: good acres of cotton and corn, orchards, herds of beef cattle, and sometimes blooded horses. The less offensive of them began to stake out land for themselves, sometimes at the outskirts of the gold fields, and settled down to farming on Cherokee soil. Others moved around, laying hands on livestock left unsufficiently guarded. Bands of horse thieves known as Pony Clubs began to harry the borders.

Essentially this was nothing new. Old Pathkiller had fretted over his helplessness in the face of such depredation a whole decade earlier. But now it took place on an increasingly wider scale. It was contrary to Federal Law; the Intercourse Act gave the Cherokees the right to dispossess such intruders. John Ross, in no mood to wring his hands helplessly as Pathkiller seems to have done, availed himself of this right.

During October Council of 1829, discussion had turned to this problem. At Beaver Dam at the south of the Nation, close to the Georgia-Alabama line, lived a settlement of eighteen white families who had moved into cabins left by Cherokees enrolled in the 1828 migration. The newcomers had come in without permission, in defiance of Cherokee rights, and were said to be a bad lot, hard-drinking and given to thieving corn and livestock from their neighbors.

In practice the Cherokees had usually depended on the

agency to oust intruders; in this case they had received no satisfaction. General Coffee, an old friend of the Creek campaign and an intimate of Jackson's, was just now in the country to take testimony on a dispute raised by Georgia on the old Creek-Cherokee line. He told Ross, or so the missionaries heard, that it was his duty as chief to get rid of the intruders; and the National Council gave him the authority to do so.

Some sixty Cherokees, headed by The Ridge, were entrusted with the mission in early January 1830. The whites claimed that the Indians bore down on them in ancient war dress and war paint, whooping and yelping. Perhaps they did; such theatricals were effective, and besides the release of action after waiting so long for the Federal government to do something was very stimulating. The enemy further deponed that The Ridge, dignified lord of a manor, owner of a coach-and-four and a broadcloth suit, and father-in-law of a white gentlewoman, went into action wearing a buffalo forehead and horns by way of headdress. And maybe that was true also; he had run across several such items in his search for material for Boudinot's museum.

However the Cherokees dressed for the event, they set out on January 4, gave the white families time to load their belongings into carts and get started down the road to Alabama, and then burned the cabins so that there would be nothing for them to come back to. They returned punctually and unscathed, all but four.

That four did not was their own fault and an act of insubordination. Ross had expressly forbidden them to loiter, and above all had told them not to meddle with any kegs of whisky they found lying about. But the kegs were there, and the four, their mission completed, saw no good reason why they should not give The Ridge the slip and celebrate.

Next morning twenty whites, coming back to reconnoiter, found the four all drunk as lords. They beat them, loaded them on to ponies, and set off for the Carroll County jail; when they got there, however, they had only one captive. The body of the sodden Chewayee had kept sagging off the back of the horse where they had slung him; repeated beatings had no effect on it; presently they discovered that it was a dead body and let it lie. Two others, The Wagoner and Rattling Gourd, sobered up as they neared jail and, though badly mauled, managed to cut loose and get to John Ross with the story. Only Dan Miller reached prison and he languished there several months.

Now came some very exciting times for the Cherokees, especially those who lived near the homes of Ross and The Ridge at the Head of Coosa. Mounted bands of whites were on the prowl in the country, claiming to be authorized by Georgia to make arrests. Sometimes they fired on wayfaring Cherokees, and the latter, taking cover, returned the fire. Luckily for everyone's peace of mind, all shots went wild.

The Cherokees were roused to fighting pitch. On January 10, when Chewayee was buried, the Cherokees poured down from the hills with their rifles, not only to attend the funeral, but to offer their services as guards about the homes of their threatened chiefs.

There was a faint thrill of the old warpath in all this, and the situation was reported in this vein. "War in Georgia," read Boston, and sent posthaste to the missionaries for details. But the "war" was not very glorious, and its results were unsatisfactory for the Cherokees. Their one little act of initiative accomplished nothing; the Indian agent reprimanded Chief Ross for having taken matters into his hands and did not prevent the intruders from returning, and Federal authorities showed languid interest in demands that they apprehend the murderers of Chewayee.

There might be hotbloods in the Nation who dreamed of fighting off the Georgians, but their sober leaders recognized that such hopes were futile. Ross never again risked an overt incident. As relations with Georgia worsened, he saw that the Cherokees would thereby merely give Georgia officials the excuse they craved for taking over by violence. Thenceforth he counseled the Cherokees to endure insult and deprivation with stoic patience while their battle was fought on another front.

In July 1830 Ross sought and obtained from General Council authority to carry the case of the Cherokee Nation versus the State of Georgia to the Supreme Court of the United States.

CHAPTER VIII

"*Nine Wise Beloved Old Men*"

The Cherokees were famous by 1830. The reputation of
Sequoia, the publication of their own *Phoenix*, had already made them well-known. Now events were making
them sensational: a gold rush, the unprecedented spectacle
of a band of Indians undertaking to challenge an American state before the Supreme Court, the fact that they and
other Eastern Indians were made the subject of a prolonged and bitter debate in Congress. Their faith that the
"American conscience" would be stirred by their plight
had been justified. People in New England and the Middle States who had never seen an Indian were holding
public meetings on the plight of the Cherokees and demanding that Congress rescue them. The plain people of
America were aroused as they were not to be again until
the publication of *Uncle Tom's Cabin*.

The July Council of 1830 that had authorized Ross to
carry the contest with Georgia to the Supreme Court also
addressed an appeal "to the people of the United States."

"Let Americans," read the memorial, "remember the
great law of love, 'Do unto others as ye would that others
would do to you.' Let them remember that of all nations on the earth they are under the greatest obligation
to obey this law. . . . Their forefathers were . . .
drawn from the old world. . . . The winds of persecution

wafted them over the great waters and landed them on the shores of the new world where the Indian was the sole law. . . . Let them remember in what way they were received by the savages of America. . . . The Cherokees have always fulfilled their obligations, have never tried to reclaim what they surrendered at Holston."

There were American readers of this appeal who were deeply moved that a group of erstwhile "savages" could stand in dignity and integrity before the great sister republic and plead their cause on the basis of the teachings of Christ and of the example of the Pilgrim Fathers. There was beauty in this gesture; it was proof of the soundness of the American idea that even Indians could embrace it and make their appeal on the moral basis of the American republic.

The moral aspects of the question involving the Eastern Indians in general and the Cherokees in particular had already received eloquent and exhaustive public discussion in a series of twenty-four scholarly letters published in the *National Intelligencer* in 1829. These letters, signed "William Penn," were by Jeremiah Evarts, courageous secretary of the American Board of Foreign Missions, who had come honestly by his knowledge of the Cherokees, since he had not only visited them, but was also kept in intimate touch with their affairs through his voluminous correspondence with the missionaries.

In the series he analyzed the Treaty of Hopewell, pointed out the fidelity with which the Cherokees had carried out the ensuing obligations of permitting transit through their country and refusing to harbor outlaws; he maintained that they could not be coerced under the 1802 agreement with Georgia, since they had not been a party to it; he eloquently described their progress and forecast the destruction of both progress and national integrity if they were forcibly removed. The legalistic argument that a state could not exist within a state he countered by saying that the arrangement inconvenienced no one except in the imagination of Georgians.

One statement imputed to Evarts (though not found in the collected William Penn letters) was so inflammatory that Lumpkin of Georgia was presently to quote it before the House as a sample of what America might expect if the claims of Georgia were not met. "Better that half the states of the Union were annihilated," Lumpkin quoted Evarts, "and the rest left powerful in holiness, than that the whole nation should be stained by this guilt. We would rather have a civil war, were there no other alternative, than avoid it by taking shelter in crime. . . . We would take up arms for the Indians in such a war . . . as confidently as we would repel an invader." Lumpkin, citing this passage, need not have tried to strengthen his argument with dark hints that such writers as Evarts were "well paid for 'their labors of love' to the cause of Cherokee sovereignty." The mere suggestion that the contentious states of the gangling, loose-jointed young republic might come to blows over the Cherokee issue was enough to dampen moral fervor in some quarters.

To many Americans, however, conscience took precedence over caution and expediency. The letters, widely reprinted (the *Phoenix* ran them all, and the grateful editor named his third son William Penn), had a tremendous influence in arousing public opinion. Evarts's plea that Congress be petitioned to give justice to the Indians brought fervent response. Farmers in Pennsylvania, New Jersey, New York, townspeople throughout New England snowed Congress under with their appeals. Some ladies in Hartford reinforced their petition with a poem, "The Cherokee Mother."

> Here *on our souls a Saviour's love*
> *First beam'd with renovating ray.*
> *Why should we from these haunts remove?*
> *But still you warn us, hence—away.*

Child, ask not where! I cannot tell.
Save where wide wastes uncultur'd spread
Where unknown waters fiercely roll,
And savage monsters howling tread.

Will a crush'd nation's deep despair,
Your broken faith, our tear-wet sod,
The babe's appeal, the chieftain's prayer,
Find no memorial with our God?

These literary contributions were little appreciated by Georgian Congressmen; they demanded that Congress refuse to entertain them. How would New York have taken it, demanded Foster, if a few years earlier Georgians had tried to meddle with New York's regulation of its own Indian affairs?

But the petitions, many of them published in the *Phoenix*, warmed and cheered the anxious hearts of the Cherokees. The Aquohee district spontaneously expressed its gratitude to William Penn, to friendly Congressmen, and to the authors of these petitions in a memorial drawn up by one Chostosa and signed by John Wickliff, Sweetwater, Kaneeda, and others.

At the mission schools the children were beginning to turn their attention from the problems of the oppressed Patagonians to those of the oppressive Georgians. "If the white people want more land," one little girl asked her Cherokee Sunday School teacher, little Nancy Reese, "why don't they go back to the country they came from?"

Nancy herself reported to her Northern benefactor her naïve reassurance on hearing that "a seriousness" was increasing in Georgia, that Georgians too were becoming converted to Christianity. "I did not know that there were so many that were Christians. I do not think these Christian people wish us to remove. I think they wish us to be civilized and to live like other Christian people."

So reasoned Nancy, who could not imagine that one could be a Christian and not live by "the great law of love" in the name of which the Cherokees were appealing to America.

2.

A bill proposing to remove the Eastern Indians to the west of the Mississippi came before Congress in the spring of 1830. Georgia had long been agitating for such action; a report by Governor William Carroll of Tennessee, sent to the Indians in 1829 to persuade Cherokees and Creeks to emigrate, had emphasized the indispensability of some such measure.

On the face of it, Carroll's report might have been written by a partisan of the Cherokees. He had been instructed to go about his work secretly, to meet influential Indians privately in an attempt to divide them. This maneuver had some success with the Creeks; with the Cherokees it was a flat failure. A people so intelligent, so well posted on current affairs, said Carroll in his candid report to the War Department, could not be so easily deceived. And the Cherokees intensely resented the attempt.

The Cherokees won Carroll's admiration. He had been, he said, "astonished beyond all measure" at their advance, at their orderly farms stocked with cattle, sheep, hogs, and fowl, at homes that sometimes had not only comforts but luxuries; at their advance in religion, morality, and general information. But the nature of some of their information he deplored, for he was after all, though an honest reporter and observer, working for Jackson and Jackson's plan for removal. Cherokee chiefs had been led by friendly Congressmen to believe that Congress would support them against Georgia. Until Congress had given unmistakable proof that it had no such intention, it was useless, said Carroll, to talk to the Cherokees of removal.

Congress acted on this hint. The Removal Bill, drawn up in harmony with the Indian policy announced by

Jackson in his first presidential message, was duly brought
before Congress, and was passed late in May, just before
the Georgia laws went into effect. It was not, however,
passed easily; reputations were risked and made on a
passionate display of oratory that was further to rouse the
country at large.

The political line-up revealed a prophetic pattern of
division between North and South. Forsythe and Lumpkin presented the case for Georgia. The former angered a
Cherokee delegation present to follow the debate by referring to them as "poor devils." Lumpkin attacked the
missionaries for their "self-centered" support of the Cherokees and advocated the bill as a humanitarian measure
to save the Cherokees from the confusion about to fall
upon them by their being held accountable under three
sets of conflicting laws: Cherokee, Federal, Georgian.

The Georgia contentions were answered by several
Northern senators and representatives, among them Senators Peleg Sprague of Maine, Theodore Frelinghuysen of
New Jersey, and Representative Edward Everett of Massachusetts, and by one Southerner, David Crockett of
Tennessee. Sprague quoted Shakespeare in demonstration
that Georgia was a kind of Shylock demanding its pound
of flesh; but in this case, he maintained, it was the Cherokee Nation, not Georgia, that held the bond. "Who can
look an Indian in the face and say to him, 'We and our
fathers for more than forty years have made to you the
most solemn promises; we now violate and trample on
them all, but offer you in their stead another guarantee.'"
He said further that in the West, offered to the Indians
as a land of promise, Indians were dying of famine.

Frelinghuysen's speech made him famous. It went on
for three days with sundry interruptions for Senate business. He said that the partition of Poland had been an
act of humanity compared to what the Removal Bill
would do to the Cherokees; prophesied that the identical

conflicts between white man and red would arise all over
again in the West, pointed out that Georgia had made no
complaints of the Cherokees when they were savages, but
found them intolerable only when they became literate
and Christian. The situation, he added, represented a
crisis in American history that involved the honor of the
Republic.

In the House, Edward Everett, later to share the platform at Gettysburg with Abraham Lincoln (just then
setting out to take part in the Black Hawk War), cited
statistics on the phenomenal advance of the Cherokees.
"These, Sir, are your barbarians . . . whom you are going to expel from their homes . . . and you will do it
for their good! In the West you grant the same land two
or three times to different tribes. . . . What is the population of Georgia where there is no room for these few
Indians? It is less than seven to the square mile; we,
Sir, in Massachusetts have seventy-four to the square mile
and space for a great many more. . . . The subtleties
which satisfy you will not satisfy the severe judgment of
enlightened Europe. Our friends there will view this
measure with sorrow and our enemies alone with joy. And
we ourselves, Sir, when the interest and passion of the
day are past, shall look back on it, I fear, with self-re-
proach and a regret as bitter as unavailing."

A representative of Jackson's own state stood out also
for the Cherokees. This was that lovable Tennesseean,
the half-fabulous Davy Crockett, another veteran of the
Creek Campaign and a frontiersman who had spent much
less time in school than had most of his Cherokee auditors.
There was nothing of the smooth politician about David
Crockett; he had originally run for Congress on a dare
and now admitted that he spoke for no considerable number of his constituents; but knowing from personal experience that most Cherokees preferred death to removal,

he felt it his duty to speak for his conscience rather than his constituents, and to vote against the Removal Bill.

Crockett paid for his honest speaking; his constituents did not return him to the next Congress. He came back, however, at the next Congress but one, still an undaunted friend of the Cherokees, and in their behalf introduced a bit of satire into Congressional proceedings: a bill for the removal of whites in eastern Tennessee beyond the Mississippi lest they impede the territorial designs and sovereignty of the state of Gorgia.

A Cherokee delegation intently followed these proceedings. When the bill, in spite of Frelinghuysen's efforts, passed the Senate in April, one member indignantly wrote the *Phoenix* that though "the unfortunate people . . . who nobly fought the battles of Georgia are now repaid with ingratitude and oppression, they are not yet vanquished." The bill still had to pass the House; when Everett defended Indian rights before that body, some of the Cherokees were seen to weep.

There were also feminine observers. Some were frivolous, described by Fanny Kemble as in "pink and blue and yellow bonnets" and given to "a tremendous bustle and waving of feathers and silks . . . a jumping up, a sitting down, a squeezing through and a how d'ye doing and a shaking of hands."

But some were serious, and one of these was that keen and caustic observer, Mrs. Trollope, who was in town at the time of the passing of the Removal Bill and felt very strongly about it. In the Englishwoman's eyes the proposed removal of the Indians epitomized everything despicable in American character: the immense gap between what Americans professed as their ideals and their actual behavior.

Evidently Mrs. Trollope missed the eloquence of the Northerners and was vague about fine points of procedure, for according to her the bill "was finally decided by fiat of the president." She continued: "If the American character may be judged by their conduct in this matter, they are most lamentably deficient in every feeling of honor and integrity, treacherous and false almost beyond belief in their intercourse with the unhappy Indians. . . . It is impossible for any mind of common honesty not to be revolted by the contradiction between their principles and practice. . . . You will see them with one hand hoisting the cap of liberty, and with the other flogging their slaves. You will see them one hour lecturing their mob on the indefeasible rights of men, and the next driving from their homes the children of the soil, whom they have bound themselves to protect by the most solemn treaties."

Mrs. Trollope was amazed to find in Washington young Frenchmen who, having in Paris visualized America as a Utopia of liberty, equality, and fraternity, came over to see for themselves and found exactly what they expected. The Englishwoman couldn't for the life of her see what these ardent young Frenchmen were looking at. Yet probably the caustic Englishwoman and the believing Frenchmen shared something of the truth between them. There were honest, impassioned idealists in America for young Frenchmen to talk to; and there was also abominable practice for Mrs. Trollope to deplore.

The Cherokees were now in serious difficulties. The Removal Bill had passed, Governor Gilmer had proclaimed Georgia law in force over their territory. But unlike Mrs. Trollope, the Indians were slow to despair of American idealism.

In July they gathered at a called Council to hear Ross summarize the situation in a solemn but unterrified address. The act of Congress he ascribed to lack of true information about the Cherokees, but the bill itself contained one hopeful clause: "provided that nothing in this act shall be construed as authorizing the violation of any existing treaty between the United States and any of the Indian tribes." The question of Georgia's jurisdiction would be carried to the Supreme Court. The Cherokees were meanwhile not to despair, "for in the appearance of impossibilities there is still hope."

3.

In the days of Washington, official correspondence with the Indians was flavored with poesy. Negotiators on either side were called "beloved men"; the Indians first heard of the function of the Supreme Court in a reference to "nine wise beloved old men" appointed to guide the president in difficult decisions.

In the days of John Quincy Adams such endearments began to fade from the records; their text became more businesslike; and when the Cherokees appealed to the Supreme Court they wasted no energy coining phrases about "beloved men"; they retained the best counsel they could find, William Wirt of Philadelphia, to draw up their brief for them. They sued for an injunction against the laws of Georgia.

The case reached the docket early in March 1831, and it was lost. The decision, which had two dissenting votes, represented a triumph of legal abstraction over human sympathy; the ruling of John Marshall was that the Cherokees could not so sue before his body because they were not a foreign, independent state, but a "dependent domestic nation." Therefore, whatever the sentiments of the justices, the injunction must be denied.

This decision was not the body-blow at the Cherokees that might have been expected. In the first place the tone of the decision was warmly sympathetic. "If the court were permitted to indulge its sympathies, a case better calculated to excite them could scarcely be imagined."

And Justice Johnson, supporting Marshall's denial in a separate opinion, remarked apropos of the invasion of Cherokee territory by the Georgians "this is war in fact, though not being declared with the usual solemnity it may perhaps be called war in disguise . . . a case in which the appeal is to the sword and to the Almighty justice and not the courts of law and equity."

Such phrases as these, added to Marshall's own term, "domestic, dependent nation," gave the Cherokee delegation present in Washington at the time the impression that they had won. They were rather naïvely taken aback to learn that President Jackson thought otherwise. He called them in next day to point out the futility of their struggle and to scold them for putting their trust in lawyers. "I have been a lawyer long enough to know how lawyers will talk to obtain the client's money."

Even the president was not unsympathetic. He reminisced of his comradeship with the Cherokees in the Creek campaign, and admitted that he did not blame them for trying to preserve their liberty. "But I blame you for suffering the lawyers to fleece you."

The delegation, John Ridge among them, walked away from Jackson's study not so much cast down as thoughtful. The decision still seemed favorable to them; the phrase "domestic, dependent nation," though it lacked the fine ring of "sovereign and independent," was recognition still. The Court had by no means denied the justice of their cause; it merely denied its own power to do anything about it. And Justice Johnson felt so strongly that he had actually by implication suggested that they go to war with Georgia.

The Cherokees did not act on this subversive suggestion, nor were they disheartened by the decision. Before it had been handed down they had received encouragement from another quarter. Events were shaping themselves to provide the Americans and the Cherokees with a true *cause célèbre* that would dramatize their plight as nothing else could.

John Marshall had not heard the last of the Cherokees; the verdict of March 5, 1831, was not final.

CHAPTER IX

Of Paul and Silas

It is a tribute to the moral force of the Cherokee cause
that the four denominations of missionaries established
among them, each with its own peculiar theology and
ritual, were able to come to unanimous agreement on one
article of faith, the question of justice for the Cherokees.

The various sects, indeed, had had surprisingly little
trouble with each other, considering the strong doctrinaire
emphasis of the religion of their day. In fact there had
been no trouble at all, beyond normal personality clashes
between missionaries of the same denomination and some
feeling against the Methodists. The latter, it must be
added, did not participate in the conference the Moravians, Presbyterians, and Baptists held at New Echota on
December 29, 1830, to consider how they could best defend the Cherokees. The Methodists, however, absented
themselves not because they disagreed with the proposals
under discussion, but because they had already taken such
action independently.

By this time the missionaries had seen some of the early
results of the extension of Georgia's laws. They had seen
pony thieves make away with the livestock of hard-work-
ing Cherokee farmers; they had seen whisky peddled
among the Indians in defiance of Cherokee law; they had

been warned by friendly Georgians that notes were being forged against the Cherokees to take advantage of the statute that forbade an Indian to testify in court against a white man; they had seen unoffending Cherokees, among them Judge Martin, who kept a public house by the toll-gate on the Federal Pike, arrested by the Georgia Guard and haled into court on frivolous pretexts. This they had seen, and they knew that when Georgia carried out its plan to survey Cherokee land and redistribute it among its own people by the proposed state lottery, far worse was coming.

Proud of the development of the Cherokees in which they themselves had participated, the missionaries had not been able to observe these things with cold dispassion.

There is something peculiar about Cherokee nature, some special quality of warmth and sympathy. Few honest people have at any time been able to live on terms of intimacy with a Cherokee community without learning to love their neighbors. Jackson was later to be inconvenienced by the fact that no matter how hard-bitten an Army officer he selected to impress his will on the Cherokees, the officer ended by becoming pro-Cherokee.

The missionaries were under no illusion as to the faults of the Indians, but they loved them. And now, drawn together by a generous surge of sympathy for their troubles, they unanimously subscribed to a series of resolutions in their defense.

The bulk of the statement was a description of the advance of the Cherokees set forth in detail in the hope of counteracting lies about them published elsewhere. (Lumpkn's favorite *mot* was that nineteen twentieths of the Cherokees were too ignorant and depraved to know what was good for them anyway.) The report made no extravagant claims. It stated that though all Cherokees had shown some improvement in their adaptation to civilized standards, they were still in all stages thereof, from those who already lived like well-found whites to those who were just making a clumsy beginning to better themselves. Education was still at a low level; only two hundred were known who could read or write except in Sequoia's alphabet. But the people were industrious; few went in want; public opinion was making effective an otherwise unimplemented law against polygamy; intemperance had been controlled under "wholesome" laws to such a degree that the orderly Cherokee elections and court sessions presented a favorable contrast to such events in white communities. Their new government was working effectively; it was democratic and provided freedom of speech, though the latter was somewhat under restraint on some issues owing to "an overwhelming torrent of national feeling in opposition to removal."

The objectivity of the missionaries may be gauged from the fact that they by no means attributed all this progress to their own efforts. Government agencies had helped too, and so, most importantly, had intermarriage with and proximity to the whites. In defense of their theory that intermarriage made for progress, they cited the fact that, though whites had no voice in the government, all responsible positions had been filled (by election) with mixed bloods.

This testimony was of particular interest in view of the fact that the friends of removal had made much pious talk about the necessity of placing the Eastern Indians safely out of the way of contamination by the whites. The missionaries admitted that harm sometimes resulted from such propinquity, but maintained that on the whole the result was a happy assimilation of cultures. As for the widely current notion that intermarriage made for degradation, they declared the exact reverse to be true.

The resolutions were signed and sent forth into the

world. They went to Boston and were printed in the *Missionary Herald*. They went to Georgia and were probably not reprinted. But official Georgia took full and immediate cognizance of their import.

2.

In the middle of January 1831 two anxious missionaries, Isaac Proctor and Daniel S. Butrick, collaborated on a letter to the Prudential Board in Boston appealing for advice. Each had received notice that it would be a penal offense for a white man to remain in Cherokee country after March 1 unless he took an oath of allegiance to Georgia and obtained a special permit from the governor. This information had been conveyed in a marked copy of the *Georgia Journal* of January 1. What were they to do?

Butrick had matured somewhat since his early impulsive days; a change had come into his life in 1827, when the Cherokees were in an uproar over their new constitution. Butrick's mind was just then hardly on the Cherokees at all. He was writing the Board an agitated letter, which he asked them to destroy, asking their opinion as to the wisdom of his keeping an early vow of celibacy.

The Board had hardly time to deliberate this problem when it had another letter presenting them with a *fait accompli*. Late in April Butrick had passed through Carmel on his way to the Valley Towns and had found Sister Elizabeth Proctor all alone with her scholars at the mission. "Dear loves, said I, how can I leave them immediately alone in this wild desert?" So he stopped there, lodging with the boys in their cabin.

A question of propriety then arose. Butrick decided to continue his journey, but his horse had run away. He sought lodging with a neighbor; there was no room. There was only one other way to protect the fair name of the young woman: marriage. To his happy surprise Butrick found that Sister Proctor welcomed this solution. The surprised Chamberlin was summoned and duly performed the ceremony.

For a time Butrick's letters made frequent artless reference to "Elizabeth"; then she became, more decorously, Mrs. Butrick, and his associates began to detect changes in him, a swing towards conservatism. He no longer, reported one observer, insisted on taking in every Indian loafer who hung around the mission for a free meal.

Now Butrick was collaborating with his brother-in-law on a letter asking what they had better do about the new Georgia law ordering them out of the country. The frightened Proctor thought they had better obey it; he also hinted that his services would now be much more valuable if he were in Boston, or anyway not in Georgia. Butrick merely asked for instruction.

He was, however, ready to suggest what form instruction should take. He came out for obedience to the state in things temporal; to disobey was to take a political stand, and to meddle in politics was not part of a pastor's duty. (The missionary resolutions of December 29 had expressly disclaimed any political purpose.) In the long, frightening days that Butrick and Proctor waited for word from Boston, Butrick went through his Testament very thoroughly, seeking guidance from God. He found it in the Acts of the Apostles. Many times had the Apostles found flocks suffering from political persecution, and never had they undertaken to work out such political questions, for the Kingdom of Heaven is not of this world.

The Cherokees respected Butrick's point of view, did not construe it as cowardice or desertion. But Worcester, who took the contrary point of view, and was nerving himself to dare all things for the sake of his flock, was much afflicted by Butrick's opposition.

3.

The spirit of Jeremiah Evarts, though he himself was then in failing health, still dominated the American Board. One who had been publicly quoted as saying that civil war was preferable to national dishonor was little likely to advise his missionaries to give way before the unconstitutional demands of Georgia. Word came from Boston that the missionaries were to stay where they were, and though it was phrased as a recommendation, the missionaries obeyed it as an order.

The cautious Moravian Brethren sent their menfolk across the border, leaving their women, who were not affected by the Georgia ruling, to manage the mission. But the Presbyterians and Congregationalists, reluctant martyrs though some of them were, went about their affairs as usual and grimly awaited the first of March.

Waiting was unpleasant. The Georgians continued to arrest the Cherokees on various pretexts, and the treatment of these in Georgia jails foreshadowed what the missionaries might expect. One Beanstalk, carried off by a Pony Club, spent four weeks in jail in bitter cold, having no covering but his own cloak and saddle blanket, and being prevented from approaching the fire. Also, though now and then someone came to his cell with charitable intent, he was more often the butt of derisive visitors. The missionaries well knew that Georgians in high place, Governor Gilmer for one, regarded them as so many pious frauds; they could expect no more gentle treatment.

Almost worse than reports of actual events were the rumors of what was impending. Worcester suspected that Georgians started most of them in the hope of frightening both missionaries and Cherokees into submission. He made an illuminating discovery. Georgia was taking pains to avoid publicity about its new laws. Separate editions were printed of papers intended for outside circulation, and from these the text of the laws was omitted. Hence news of Georgia's intentions filtered slowly into the country at large and public opinion was not aroused. The missionaries faced their ordeal alone.

But within the Nation there were courage and support for their stand. To be sure, Cherokees privately told Butrick that they saw no reason why he should stay to suffer indignity, but Chief Ross himself was all for their staying. In a letter to Boudinot he pronounced the Georgia ruling "ridiculously absurd" and added: "I do hope that our white citizens will not be so ignorant of their own rights as to be frightened out of their true interests and expatriate themselves by licking the usurper's hand."

These words were written with white citizens of the Nation in mind, rather than the missionaries; but the latter also heeded them. They did not "lick the usurper's hand," did not offer oaths of allegiance to Georgia, and did not apply for permits to stay. They simply stayed.

And on March 12, ten days after Worcester had sought counsel for such contingencies, the arrests began.

4.

The unhappy Proctor was the first victim of the Georgia Guard. His arrest, however, was by no means so unpleasant a function as his anticipation of it; it preserved the amenities. To be sure, a pang of terror passed through hearts at the Carmel mission when the Georgia militia came riding up and fell into rank outside. But the three officers who came to the door were mannerly. They inquired politely for both Proctor and Butrick. The latter, who had waited with Proctor on the first of March for the expected arrest, was just now on a visit to the Valley Towns in the shaggy Carolina end of the Nation, where no extension of Georgia law could touch him. Mr. Proctor had to go off alone.

He was not long alone. The party spent the night at a

near-by public house, conducted by the Cherokee John Saunders, and next morning, which was Sunday, Proctor was allowed to say good-by to his family before leaving on the forty-mile ride to New Echota. The militia reached the capital just before sunset and picked up several white men. These included Worcester, the mild-mannered printer Wheeler, and a few expatriate Georgians. Again the amenities were preserved. Worcester, to whom a third daughter had been born, was permitted to go home to see his wife Ann during the evening.

On Monday the party rode thirty miles farther to Hightower to arrest the blacksmith Thompson. On Tuesday they marched their prisoners into headquarters to the sound of fife and drum. On Wednesday, March 16, they delivered their prey to the civil authorities at Lawrenceville. In the whole proceeding there seems to have been no unpleasantness and only one irregularity: all the arrests were made without warrant.

At Lawrenceville the missionaries encountered not only courtesy but the warmest of sympathy. Two prominent citizens, the Reverend Mr. Wilson and Dr. Alexander, gave personal security for them, that they might be released from the Guards. An Athenian of note and a member of the bar, General Edward Harden, spontaneously defended them in court, an act for which he asked no reward, though the grateful missionaries, learning that he was in straitened circumstances, later each made him a gift of $15.

Worcester also gathered that the public sympathized with the prisoners and to some extent with the Cherokees. He found to be sure, that most of them favored jurisdiction of Georgia, and he heard some loud talk of resisting the Federal government by force if it tried to interfere. But his impression was that the oppressive new laws were unpopular. "Jurisdiction, but not oppression, seems to be the prevailing cry," he wrote.

Underwood and Harris, two Georgia lawyers who were also retained by the Cherokees to defend Cherokee citizens arrested during the controversy, acted as counsel for the missionaries. To Judge Clayton they applied for habeas corpus, and this was promptly granted. The missionaries, Worcester, Thompson, and Proctor, were released on the ground that since they acted as postmasters at their respective missions, they were Federal agents and therefore not subject to the law of Georgia.

Worcester went home in good spirits. He suspected that the whole affair had been arranged merely to intimidate. Well, intimidation hadn't worked; the law itself had vindicated their stand; now they could go on with their work secure against such unseemly interruptions.

But Worcester's rejoicing was premature.

5.

It took Governor Gilmer exactly two months and some correspondence with President Jackson to untangle the legal knot that had restrained him from imprisoning the missionaries. By May 16 he had succeeded. He wrote the missionaries severally that they had been relieved of their duties as postmasters, that having been so relieved they were no longer Federal agents, and being no longer Federal agents they must get out. His letters had a nasty ring; he gave them ten days.

When the next wave of arrests began, the rule of decorum was not so meticulously observed. Governor Gilmer had written of the "criminal" behavior of the missionaries; evidently this view was also impressed on the Georgia Guard, who on their next rounds handled the missionaries accordingly.

But during the spring, before all this happened, several other events were in the making.

One was a bit of rough buffoonery. Early in April three members of the Georgia Guard, idling on horseback to see a group of Cherokees receive baptism, suddenly announced that they too felt the spirit. They ordered the dripping converts out of their way, charged into the river, and baptized their horses with full rites. The *Phoenix* editorialized the blasphemy.

Early in May, Elizur Butler, who had somehow missed the March arrests, had his own encounter with the Guard. They took him at Haweis, but let him go when he explained that his young wife (formerly Lucy Ames, teacher at Brainerd) was expecting an early confinement. Sergeant Brooks of the Guard remarked that he had heard of the circumstance and had hoped to be spared a painful duty by finding Butler not at home; the two had so pleasant a conversation that, as Butler later remarked, he quite forgot he was a prisoner.

It was arranged that he would surrender himself when his wife was out of danger. This he did early in June, presenting himself to Colonel Sanford at General Headquarters. The latter, apparently more annoyed than gratified by his scrupulousness ("A metaphysical point," he called it), declined to accept the captive, but took the occasion to denounce the missionaries. He called them political firebrands engaged in trying to unite church and state; if they wanted to prove their piety, he asked, why didn't they try living in caves clad in goatskins?

Butler went home to his wife, but not happily. In releasing him, Colonel Sanford had promised an early arrest. Butler saw himself marched off in chains, and his vision was accurate.

But no one needed more courage than Worcester. He was in special disfavor with the Georgians because of his intimacy with Boudinot. David Greene had correctly anticipated that Worcester was inviting trouble when he left Brainerd, in Tennessee, for New Echota in order to be near the Cherokee editor. Indeed, the ink on the first issue of the *Phoenix* was hardly dry before Worcester was accused of writing it. The Georgians, infuriated by out-spoken editorials and the response they were drawing from Northern readers, had no intention of letting Worcester slip through their hands.

Worcester, who had much of Evarts's spirit, had no intention of escaping, but he was worried and very lonely, for most of his colleagues were inclining to Butrick's view. Even the blacksmith Thompson was saying that perhaps the president of the United States had the right to order the missionaries to leave. Butler, obsessed with family cares, had little to say. Worst of all, the indomitable Evarts had fallen silent. He had gone to Havana in an attempt to mend his health, and in May he died there. Worcester could not so soon have heard of Evarts's death, but the mere withdrawal of his leader was hard enough. No one else on the Board had quite his uncompromising courage.

Worcester grieved over the desertion of his colleagues, but clung to his own stand. He would leave only if the Board specifically ordered him to do so. "And if all my brethren forsake me, I am willing to bear the burden alone. Only let not God forsake me." And he mentioned the possibility of carrying his case before the Supreme Court, a contingency that had already been reviewed in Boston. Worcester believed that such a case could not go against him, but declared that he would stand by his convictions even without such hope.

There was an even deeper affliction in store for him. Late in May, after the order from Governor Gilmer, his wife Ann had fallen dangerously ill. Doctors summoned from Tennessee could not come; Worcester cared for her as best he could, but she was so ill that she could not sit up without fainting. And Worcester, holding to his beliefs, suffered the anguish of knowing that the shocks and stresses he thereby incurred might well kill his wife.

On June 23 the Georgia Guard fell to work again, and

this time the missionaries were not allowed to preserve their dignity. Thompson, the captive of the day, was taken on a two-day ride in a rough wagon heaped with gear and greasy sacks of provender, and at night was chained to his fellow prisoners, a white man and a Cherokee, though he was feverish and in pain. When the cavalcade came in sight of headquarters on June 25, the prisoners were marched into camp on foot.

After such discomfort, Thompson was more than exasperated when Colonel Sanford released him after delivering another denunciation of mission activities. The journey home was ninety miles.

Worcester, taken early in July, was at first treated with consideration, at least to the extent that the commanding officer, Colonel Nelson, expressed regret for having to force him to leave his sick wife. But the courtesy of Colonel Nelson ended there. Two Methodist ministers happened by at just the wrong moment, and their comment so enraged the Colonel that he arrested one of them, McLeod, and kept all the prisoners, Congregationalist, Methodist, and two gold-digging Cherokees chained together by their ankles at night.

Even worse indignity befell the honorable Butler. Taken on July 8, he was forced to walk chained by the neck to the neck of a guardsman's horse. But Butler had his unpremeditated revenge. When after dark he was unable to keep his footing, he was allowed to sit on the horse behind his captor. Then the horse fell, and though the captive was unhurt, the captor broke two ribs. Thereafter it was Butler who rode, and the soldier who walked, leading his horse and lifting a burning pine knot to pick out the forest trail in the rainy dark.

Butler slept that night in bed at a nameless stopping place, and he was chained by the ankle to the bedstead.

There were two days more of this journey. The Methodist McLeod fell ill of colic, as later did Butler, and

Proctor, who had a horse, let him ride it. The soldiers, not on the whole an unfeeling lot, let the missionaries ride on horseback and in the wagon awhile, but for this they were roundly cursed by Brooks when he caught them at it.

They were marched into Camp Gilmer in traditional style, to the sound of fife and drum. The sergeant indicated the jail with a flourish. "There is where all the enemies of Georgia have to land," he declaimed, "there and in hell."

It was a most unpleasant little jail, and it was crowded, for a white man with a Cherokee family had meantime been added to the party. The place smelled; there was no furniture, and no place to sleep except on the dirty floor of split poles. However, no one was chained, food and blankets were plentifully provided, and the missionaries were not restrained from improving ventilation by enlarging some holes in the daubing of the walls.

The prisoners were held there until their hearing in Lawrenceville, Saturday morning, July 23. Their treatment varied. The guard who brought them their meals liked to mock their religion. "Fear not, little flock," he would say, flinging open their door. When they asked Colonel Nelson to hold a service for the guard and neighborhood generally, he denounced their request as impertinent. But insults, the missionaries were careful to report to the *Herald*, were not characteristic; there was also kindness.

At Lawrenceville, Worcester again found the sympathies of the public with the captives. He heard less talk of armed resistance to government intervention than on his earlier visit, and met people outspoken enough to denounce the claims of their state on the Indians. That the courageous stand of the missionaries was swinging public sentiment to the side of the Cherokees was suggested by a debate held by a literary society on the eve of the hearing. The question was "Ought the Georgia Guard to be continued in the Cherokee Nation?" and the negative won, nine to three.

Harris and Underwood, the lawyers retained by the Cherokees and missionaries, were prevented by the illness of the one and commitments elsewhere of the other from representing the missionaries at this hearing. Obliged to find a new lawyer, Worcester's choice fell on one Elisha W. Chester, a Vermonter, now practicing in Lawrenceville. Even at the time the choice was questionable. Chester was on record as convinced of the unconstitutionality of the new state laws in their present form, but equally convinced that Georgia had an essential right to occupy Cherokee territory. When it came time to argue the missionary case, however, he reversed his stand on the second point and argued so well that Worcester believed he had convinced himself. Impressed by this apparent conversion, Chester's legal knowledge, and his careful attention to detail, Worcester decided to retain him permanently. This decision did little credit to his judgment, and was to have the gravest consequences in his relations with the Cherokees.

However, Chester ably defended the missionaries at the hearing; they were released pending their trial before the Georgia Supreme Court in September.

6.

Back in New Echota, Worcester's situation demanded all his fortitude. The trial had been set for September, but he had no assurance that the Guard would not indulge in several punitive excursions in the meantime. His wife's condition was still precarious; she was far too ill to bear a succession of such shocks or to be removed to safety outside the Nation. In desperation he wrote Colonel Sanford that he would consent to leave the country if he could have permission to wait until his wife's health improved. Sanford's reply was contemptuous; he should, said the Colonel, have thought of his wife before.

When in mid-August the Guards next came for Worcester, they followed close on the heels of death. It was not, however, Ann who had died, but the baby daughter whose birth had occasioned so much suffering. Worcester, summoned from a pastoral visit to the mission at Candy's Creek by news of her illness, got home too late, but not too late to receive a call from the Georgia Guard. It was a friendly call; a member of the Guard came after dark and in disguise to warn him that a third arrest had been scheduled for the following evening. And Worcester was taken again, but Colonel Nelson, hearing of his bereavement, let him visit his wife. "We wish not to oppress," he said, "but to execute the laws of Georgia."

On September 16, Worcester and ten others were tried before the Georgia Supreme Court in Lawrenceville. This time he and his fellows had full counsel, Harris, Underwood, Chester, and the magnanimous General Harden, who this time flatly refused to accept a fee. Of the eleven, all but Worcester and Butler took the oath of allegiance to Georgia and were released; the latter were sentenced to four years' hard labor and were committed to the penitentiary at Milledgeville.

Ann Worcester, left behind in the Nation, was now doubly bereaved. But if something of the strength of martyrs was given Worcester, the faith of the saints was given Ann. Now that the final blow had fallen, she renewed her strength, in the words of the Psalmist, and mounted up on wings as eagles. With the help of the unquenchable Miss Sophia Sawyer she undertook the management of the mission school at New Echota. Not even visits from the Georgia Guard, for there were more, could dismay her. Far from being crushed by the humiliation that had come upon her husband, she was borne up by faith in the cause for which he suffered. No letters in the vast collection of the American Board breathe so sweet and fervent a spirit as those which Ann wrote to Boston in the years when her husband lay in the penitentiary.

One act of courage makes the whole world braver. The example of Worcester and Butler sent a glow of faith and hope through the Cherokee Nation. The Christian God was a merciful God; he had sent his saints to live among the Cherokees in their need; he had sent Paul and Silas. The Cherokees, unable to visit their cells, treated their womenfolk with reverence.

On an October day in 1831, Lucy Butler and Chamberlin were riding down the Pike on their way to pick up Ann in New Echota for a visit to the penitentiary when they were overtaken by some Cherokee horsemen riding home from October Council. One of these let his fellows ride on ahead while he lingered to inquire after the prisoners.

Then abruptly he dug his heels into his horse's flanks and galloped away, cutting through the woods to head off his friends.

At a turn in the road the mission folk were surprised to find the whole cavalcade lined up waiting for them. They had a presentation to make; the lone Cherokee had been taking a collection for the prisoners. "They are suffering for us," he explained, "and this is all we can do for them. We will go home and exert ourselves to get more."

It was very little indeed, only $2.12½, for the councilors could no longer draw pay for their services. But how that came to pass, and how it happened that this Council had sat on camp-meeting ground at Chatooga* instead of in the cavernous new capitol at New Echota, is a story for another chapter.

* The modern spelling is Chattooga.

CHAPTER X

New Star

While the missionaries were undergoing their ordeal, life had not been standing still for the Cherokees. Georgia's new laws, that had once seemed like a bluff, were now in operation. Worse, though hitherto the Federal government had protected the Cherokees, Jackson not only refused to interfere in the controversy with Georgia, but actually helped the latter. Though the Cherokees had not yielded one inch, they were already a government-in-exile. Georgia, exasperated by their refusal to heed a warning sent to their October Council in 1830, refused to allow Council to meet again within Georgian limits.

This was a sore affliction. The Cherokees had always made much of their right to meet in their own capital, had many a time annoyed Federal agents by refusing to hold Council at the agency, insisting that the Federal representatives come to them instead. They had lately spent treasure and much pains to improve what had been disrespectfully called a "naked metropolis." Besides the *Phoenix* office, there was now a two-story Council house with raised platform within, and its timbers were in Cherokee eyes more excellent than the marbles of the capitol at Washington City. In some respects New Echota was not unlike the latter, whose noble plan was in those days still obscured by the fact that its magnificent reaches were punctuated with settlements of mean little hovels and many mudholes. There were no mudholes in New Echota in fine Indian summer weather when Council met; the cabins were decent, and when a true Cherokee looked at all the carefully marked vacant lots noted by the unimpressed David Greene, he saw not vacancy but splendid projects—the National Academy, National Library, National Museum.

Also the place was more settled than it had been. Worcester's mission was an improvement. Another home now had a piano; sometimes children from the school were allowed to look at it, touch its keys, and sing gospel songs around it.

In 1830 the chiefs had come to New Echota for the last time, though that they mercifully did not know. Some came lightly on foot down woodland trails, accompanied by their women, their dogs, their young, and some of their neighbors. Some came on ponies, and more youthful chiefs liked to race each other down the last lap of the road. Sometimes a whole family came in riding one sorrowful nag. The patriarch rode ahead, got up in his colored turban and blanket like a beardless prophet out of Samuel Worcester's Bible; his woman behind him had her skirt of printed calico hiked up about her knees; a child clutched her from behind, and from the unbleached cradle cloth on her back looked out the solemn Mongolian eyes of a Cherokee baby.

These would be the humbler folk from outlying districts, hill chiefs such as The Fire, Robin Muskrat, or Ball Town George. Some of the well-to-do from the rich bottom lands came in style in hacks. Old Going Snake wore a frock coat and cockaded hat, and rode a blooded mare.

The town was all cheerful bustle at this season. Ponies stamped and worried their bits at the hitching posts. Dogs scuffled and scratched in the road; hogs on the loose scrambled out of the way of cantering hooves and of the blowguns of small boys. Cherokees went about paying calls and settled down *en famille* in the homes of kinsmen and clansmen, to visit as long as Council should last. Ann Worcester found extra blankets for guests at the mission; Elias Boudinot, always worried about money, was afflicted with a plague of country cousins.

Then Council began. The men moved into the Council House, and some women came too, taking special seats reserved for them. For though only men had a direct voice in government, the women were deeply interested and on occasion composed a memorial of their own. Other women lingered outside with their youngsters and dogs until such time as they must lay tables and prepare venison and turkey and corn for the community feasts that punctuated the Council sessions.

There was a guest at the October Council of 1830. He said he was Colonel John Lowry, a representative of the Federal government, but he had come uninvited and unannounced, and the purport of his visit was not clear. The Cherokees eyed him suspiciously, but since a government representative cannot be turned away, they made him welcome, let him eat at their board and sit at their deliberations, which, being in Cherokee anyway, were hardly enlightening to a white man. For days this went on, the visitor dumbly in attendance, the Cherokees puzzled and distrustful. Then on the eleventh day, October 20, the stranger addressed the Council.

The day was lovely, too lovely for Cherokees to remain under cover. The chiefs lugged their benches outside and sat in the sun to hear Colonel Lowry. But his message cast a shadow over the bright day.

John Ridge, who had been rising fast since his return from Cornwall and was now president of Council, served as interpreter. He read in translation the formal document that Lowry had brought with him in writing from the Secretary of War. It was a disturbing document. Embodied in a routine appeal to the Cherokees to conform with the Removal Bill was confirmation of what had hitherto been merely a rumor. Georgia, impatient to possess its property, was to survey Cherokee land and distribute it, gold mines and all, among its citizens by lottery. And Jackson would not interfere.

"What then," asked Lowry, looking into the impassive faces before him, "will become of you?"

The faces remained inscrutable, but they masked anger and dismay. Not before had Washington descended to threats. Was there a chance that the whole thing was a Georgian trick and Lowry an impostor? The Ridge demanded that his credentials be read. But the papers were in order. The colonel had really been sent by the War Department, whose new chief, Secretary Eaton, had recently displayed the obsolescence of his acquaintance with Cherokee affairs by asking them how they hoped to live when the game was gone from their hills.

The Cherokees replied to this message by sending a new delegation of protest to Washington. Warm-hearted Davy Crockett busied himself to see that they met the right people there. Congress, he assured them, was already ashamed of the Removal Bill. He showed them new memorials from the North, Pennsylvania in particular, petitioning Congress to deal justly with the Indians.

Even Jackson, receiving them the day after the Supreme Court decision on their suit, was unexpectedly friendly. To be sure, he gave them no satisfaction; they went home empty-handed. But they were in good heart, and so were most Cherokees. The brave stand of the missionaries seemed to promise that what the Cherokees could not do for themselves, white men would do for them.

Georgia authorities, observing all this, resolved not to dignify the Cherokees further by sending representatives to plead with them before Council. Simpler to order the Councils discontinued; and it was so ordered.

2.

Jackson had joked with the Cherokees about their giving money to the lawyers. He had already taken precautions to see that this should not recur. In 1830 the War Department had seconded Georgia's attempt to make Cherokee self-government impossible by announcing that henceforth the Cherokee annuity would be paid, not into the national treasury, but to each Cherokee individually. The annuity had already been paid for that year, but when in 1831 Treasurer Martin reported to collect the year's accrual of funds, he was told that each Cherokee must come personally to the agency to collect his share.

Thus was the weakness in the Cherokee economy uncovered and attacked. Federal funds until now had financed Cherokee resistance, their Councils, their embassies to Washington, the hiring of such eminent counsel as William Wirt. Payment of funds was discontinued in the expectation that without revenue the government would collapse. The agency was instructed to wean the Indians from their leaders by pressing upon them the funds of which John Ross had been depriving them.

Jackson's measure did succeed in embarrassing the Cherokee government. Councilors had to serve without pay, and to hire counsel and pay for journeys to Washington the Cherokees presently had to borrow. But as a means of shaking Cherokee faith in their government, the device was futile. To accept the bounty, the Indians had to come to the Indian agency on the Hiwassee, for some a journey of a hundred and eighty miles. And when they got there the reward was $0.44 a head, though the agent was empowered to raise this largesse to $0.50.

Some Cherokees took the money. Some of the more ignorant, who happened to drop in on the agency on other business, were too ill instructed in the principle involved to reject the little windfall. There were also a few shiftless Cherokees, the sort who liked to go begging in white communities and thereby give the whole Nation a reputation for improvidence; who had no principles anyway and never refused a handout. These too accepted the annuity.

But that the vast majority of the people, poor as well as rich, scorned the offer was admitted by the agent himself. The *Phoenix* had charged that he had been profiting by the transaction by giving the Indians rations of corn from his own fields and pocketing their money. The agent indignantly retorted that he had given full measure of corn and that in any case only $130 of the funds had been disbursed. This sum represented less than two percent of the total—260 out of a population of 16,000, and probably not more than fifty families.

Too well informed of the issue at stake to accept their due on any such beggarly basis, the Cherokees allowed the annuity funds to accumulate in the banks at Nashville, served in office and Council without pay, and raised loans to cover unavoidable expenses.

The most evil effect of the new arrangement was that word got around that the Cherokees were about to come into some ready cash, and white merchants prepared to profit thereby. The most salable article they knew was whisky; they imported it by the barrel. As early as October 1830 the *Phoenix* estimated that fifty to a hundred retailers (some of them Cherokee) were selling the stuff in Cherokee country.

Such sales were in violation of both Cherokee and Federal law; they had, however, the blessing of Georgia. The Federal authorities would not drive out the whisky peddlers; the Cherokees at present dared not.

In recent years the Cherokees had made marked progress in sobriety. Local judges made a real effort to enforce the ruling against selling whisky in the Nation, and hunted down and destroyed private stills. It was found possible, as the *Phoenix* reported with satisfaction, to have wholesome fun at a logrolling without broaching a cask. By keeping temptation well beyond their doors the Cherokees had achieved a general sobriety superior to that of white frontier towns.

But once whisky was available again, in sales uncontrolled by their own authorities, many could not keep away from it, and they did not hold their liquor well. Young men went on drunks and committed follies for which the Georgia Guard could virtuously arrest them. Even the dignified John Martin overdid it and made remarks for which the Guard took him into custody. "Shame on me for being drunk," he said. "For a man who is drunk is not a man at all."

Women, good sisters of the mission churches, sampled the drink, sometimes because it was urged on them as a medicine. Some of them could then be led simpering into the woods by white men, particularly one Tennesseean. Recovered, they stayed away in shame from their churches. "The dear people," commented Butrick, "cannot bear to have us see them when they are in this condition."

Not all Cherokees were so unwary. Some refused the whisky as resolutely as they had refused money. Councilors in particular met soberly and took vows of temperance as an example to the Nation. Parents co-operated with the missionaries to keep children out of the grogshops. Nevertheless "brutal intoxication" among "all ages and sexes," to quote the *Phoenix*, became an increasingly grave problem and threatened to demoralize a people who had valiantly resisted other temptations and all threats.

Some thoughtful observers, white and red, watching these signs of degradation, aware that the Cherokees were powerless to prevent it without help from the Federal authorities, began to wonder if the Cherokee stand was after all practical.

3.

On the southwestern frontiers of the Nation there was another special cause of disorder. Georgians were not the only invaders on Cherokee soil; refugee Creeks, at one time an estimated 2500 of them, were haunting the borders, seeking food and shelter from their Cherokee neighbors.

The Cherokees, it must be remembered, were not the sole target of the Removal Bill, though so able was their defense and so great their fame that some Americans had that impression. Five nations were affected: the Cherokees, Creeks, Chickasaws, Choctaws, and the Seminoles in faraway Florida. All of these had in some degree caught the contagion of white man's civilization, though none had it in so advanced a stage as the Cherokees. Immediately after the passage of the Removal Bill, Jackson himself had visited the Choctaw Council Grounds to confer with both Choctaws and Chickasaws. Both had agreed to treat under the terms of the bill and to remove in 1832. The Seminoles were as stubborn as the Cherokees and geographically far less vulnerable. The Creeks were divided.

Division among the Creeks went back to the Red Stick campaign, which had been not only an invasion but a civil war. Such dissension had made the Creeks an easier prey to pressure from without than the Cherokees. Jackson had exacted half their land in 1814. In 1825 certain of their chiefs, yielding to bribery, had signed a fraudulent treaty ceding the entire country. Their Council immediately exposed and denounced the deal, and Adams had honored their protest. Now in 1831 a similar situation prevailed in aggravated form. Another treaty had been signed, but again by a faction only, and the Federal government would not provide transportation to the West until the issue had been conclusively settled. So there was misery among the Creeks, who were already dispossessed of their lands without having anywhere to go, and this misery overflowed the Cherokee borders.

It is a striking fact that during all this period when the "Five Civilized Nations" were being pressed to remove against their will it apparently never occurred to any of them to unite in concerted action. United, they might have put up a formidable resistance; at the very least they could have demonstrated to the American people that the problem was not local, the contest of one state with one tribe. It had been tragic for the Southern Indians that Tecumseh's message had been completely misunderstood; appealing for unity, he had in effect merely precipitated some fanatics into civil war. The Cherokees, in spite of their eager imitation of the American constitution, had not grasped the principle of federation that held the American Republic together. Indeed, Americans themselves still had an imperfect appreciation of that principle, which had not yet had a decisive testing: Rhode Island had stood out against federation; New England had very recently considered renouncing it; and now South Carolina, apropos of the tariff, and Georgia, apropos of the Cherokees, were challenging it with the principle of nullification.

It would have been interesting if the red men had been so much wiser and better disciplined than the whites. Could the Indian nations have united in the 1830's in so intelligent a plan of resistance as that conducted by the Cherokees singlehanded, a federation of white states might have been able to solve certain difficulties in the 1860's without bloodshed, and a federation of states of varying colors might in the 1930's have averted global disaster.

But this is expecting a great deal of the Cherokees. Tecumseh had died, and they had never understood him anyway. The Seminoles were preparing for war, but, said John Ross, "I never saw a Seminole." The Cherokees were in regular contact only with the Creeks, and by 1831 the Eastern government of these was already in process of dissolution. For all practical purposes the Cherokees now stood alone. A great opportunity had gone by default.

John Ridge, who had taken over his father's former duties as a kind of ambassador to the Creeks, kept the *Phoenix* informed of difficulties on this border. In June 1831 he relayed a report that the Georgians had murdered twenty Creeks on the Cherokee frontier. "Who now are the savages?" he demanded. "No pity or shame seems to go with their design, as if we were wolves or boa con- strictors."

This emotional commentary was small comfort to the harried Creeks. One of them, who signed himself "A Creek, Old Ned," wrote an abusive reply in which he hinted at earlier gestures of co-operation. "If you are ever caught about this place, your d— —d throat shall pay for it," wrote Old Ned with excisions by Boudinot. "You are a cursed scoundrel and a liar. . . . You have been the cause of Georgia treating us as she has. . . . If we had listened to our good chief McIntosh we would have been happy, but it was through you and some other d— —d scoundrels that we have done wrong."

McIntosh was the Creek chief who had tried in 1823 to bribe John Ross. It must not be forgotten that less than a generation before, the Cherokees had contributed to the glory of the now reviled Andrew Jackson by helping him annihilate a Creek faction. During this later crisis Creeks and Cherokees had conferred, but any practical measure of collaboration between them had been thwarted by old scores, old rancors.

4.

The Cherokees were meanwhile making a heroic effort to keep their own house in order. It was Ross's policy that no acts of reprisal must be taken against the Georgians; no matter how great the provocation, the Cherokees must wait on the processes of the law for redress of their wrongs. It is a tribute to Cherokee self-control that this policy was largely successful.

Provocation was very great. Illegal arrests continued. David Vann, as responsible a citizen as John Martin, had been jailed for sowing rye in a field abandoned by emigrants to the Arkansas. The harrying of the Georgia Guard was supplemented by the raids of the Pony Clubs; horse thieves from Carroll County had made off with an estimated total of 500 head of cattle and horses from the southern part of the Nation.

They were a rollicking lot, these Pony Clubs. One band, unable to find any proper plunder in the little farm of an old woman, set fire to her grove and sat in their saddles laughing to see her scramble to save her fence. Another band had a literary character among them; he was bestirred by the plight of another old woman to write a poem to her in the cadence of Burns:

> *The white man's your Joe*
> *O, Coquo! Go.*
> *Our venom then can't grip ye,*
> *If once you'll roam,*
> *And make your home*
> *Beyond the Mississippi.*
>
> *Go, nature's child.*
> *Your home's the wild,*
> *The Indian here is droop'd;*
> *His doom's here weav'd —*

O! I am griev'd
Thus to see the wild beast coop'd.

White men might behave like that; red men would not.
They couldn't afford to. They were not "wild beasts,"
they were not "nature's child." They would prove to the
world that they were an orderly, civilized people standing
on the law for their rights. They would shame the white
man's savagery by their own discipline.

That, at least, was the official doctrine. Individual
Cherokees, savage or not, were human. National honor
was endangered by the fact that two white men were
killed in the country late in 1830. Of these, to be sure, one
was only "probably" white, since when his body was
found in a wood just before the October Council all that
was left of him was a skeleton, pantaloons, and a hat. But
the hat contained a certificate awarded to one "John" for
good conduct as a stage driver between East Court House
and Augusta. It is a safe guess that John was white. As
the Cherokees had an agreement with the Federal government to turn over killers of white men to the agency for
trial, it was incumbent on Cherokee honor to investigate.

Shortly before the discovery, there had been a ball play
in the Rabbit Trap and Dirt Town neighborhood, followed by a townhouse dance. Four young men in their
cups had been overheard in loud talk.

"I'm much of a man," James Graves had bragged.
"I've killed a man."

That was nothing, said the others; they had too.

But Graves said that he had proof of his prowess: if
they would look near the spring behind the old ball
ground on the Salaquoyee-Cooseewaytee Road, they
would find the body of his victim. They looked and they
found it, but the find only increased their derision, for
the body had been there a long time, a fact not consistent
with the details of John Graves's bragging.

The joke got about, and soberer Cherokees thought it no joke at all. A jury of six, headed by The Ridge, was called to summon the braggarts to an accounting. Nothing, however, could be proved. The drunken talk had apparently been sheer fantasy, a wistful harking back to the brave old days when men were men and ready with the tomahawk. "John" was not even demonstrably white; the skeleton was noncommittal and the certificate might have fallen into other hands. The youths could not be convicted of anything worse than tall talk; they were not delivered to the agency.

The trial had aroused keen interest, had been almost as well attended as an off-season council. In dismissing the case The Ridge, who had headed the jury of six, gave the crowd one of the speeches for which he was famous. Their interest, he said, would be an indication to the United States that Cherokees were determined to prevent violence against the whites. He solemnly charged his people with the necessity of showing good will to white men traveling among them. "Let them be safe in our houses and on our highways," he said. "Even if we are mistreated by *some*, we will treat them *all* as brothers."

That was the Cherokee answer to oppression, an impressive answer. When shortly afterwards a Cherokee shot and killed a white man riding away with his horse, the *Phoenix* deplored the incident and urged Cherokees to refrain "from every rash measure in defending their property from thieves and robbers. Let our horses and other property go, but let not human blood be shed."

5.

In the summer of 1831, while the missionaries were being arrested, released, and arrested again, Editor Boudinot of the *Phoenix* had trouble of his own with the Georgia Guard.

His editorial policy had been liberal. After John

Ridge's piece "Who then are the savages?" he had printed the abusive rebuttals not only from Old Ned, but also from one Ralph Scrugg of Gainesville. The latter addressed Boudinot's distinguished cousin as a "d——d little frog eater and wasp destroyer" and expressed a desire to cut strips from his back for use in making a horsewhip, and added: "If you don't mind, I will sell you as a Negro, for you favor one more than a d——d Indian."

But to offset such screeds, Boudinot pursued a vigorous editorial policy that drew upon him the displeasure of authority. The Indian agent, offended by the charge that he had profited by the annuity deal, wrote a protest; the agent's son-in-law, John Hardin, denounced as a lie "the remarks of your little editor" to the effect that he had been digging gold on Cherokee property. "I have never seen one of his papers without one."

He referred to Jackson as "our false and faithless father," and he had the temerity to attack the Georgia Guard. In August 1831 Boudinot was twice summoned before Colonel Nelson, of ill repute even with Governor Gilmer, to answer for his "abusive and libelous articles." The first time he was threatened with a whipping. The second time Nelson had him marched into camp by an armed guard, but inasmuch as he had then made his final arrest of Worcester and Butler, and therefore considered that he had the situation well in hand, he dismissed the editor with nothing worse than a lecture.

He didn't, he explained, condemn Boudinot, whom he knew as "a peaceable, passive, inoffensive man, not possessed of sufficient talents to write." Boudinot was to be blamed only for letting the missionaries dupe him into permitting them to use his name. Well, that wouldn't happen again; Boudinot was free to go.

Such an exoneration was little to the taste of the proud and sensitive Boudinot. He might have endured more cheerfully the promised whipping. He protested that he alone was the author of the offending articles. But Nelson knew better; no Cherokee was that intelligent.

Boudinot went home to the penning of further denunciations of the Georgia Guard.

Late in November, it was only by spurring their horses at the right moment and taking flight down the dusky woodland road that Chief Ross and his brother Andrew escaped assassination at the hands of a loud-mouthed North Carolinian named Harris, who had picked up with them at The Ridge's store. A companion named Onehlaty put a knife into the aggressor before making his own escape, but did not kill.

Although there was evidence that not only Harris but a Tennesseean with a large red mustache, one Looney, had plotted the attack, the assailants appeared to be casual horse thieves and the assault without special political significance. Ross reported the matter in the *Phoenix*, but apparently made no attempt to apprehend the miscreants.

6.

The attack on Ross had taken place about the time when the returning members of Council had collected $2.12½ for the relief of Butler and Worcester. He too had just left October Council at Chatooga, where the Cherokees held Council in October 1831 when Georgia forbade them to assemble within its limits.

Compliance with Georgia law was a departure for the Cherokees and came hard. As late as September the executive committee, headed by Ross, had voted to meet in New Echota as usual, the state of Georgia notwithstanding. In answer, Judge Clayton, who, though he defended Cherokee rights to dig gold, had already denounced the Cherokee Supreme Court suit as a piece of impertinence and was not taking any legal tricks from the Indians, charged the grand jury of Gwinnett County to find a true bill against Ross for calling Council, and to order his arrest. Also in September Worcester and Butler were consigned to four years in the penitentiary like any common criminals. At this point the chiefs decided to reconsider.

Georgia meant business, and it was patent that nothing would please Governor Gilmer more than an excuse for ordering the wholesale arrest of the Cherokee Council, locking up every chief in the Nation until kingdom come, and leaving the people leaderless in the crisis. Galling as it was to show less boldness than the missionaries, it was in these circumstances good sense. In any case, thanks to the courage of the missionaries and the generosity of the American Board, Georgian acts of oppression were about to receive a clear retesting before the Supreme Court. Best to practice discretion while awaiting that decision.

In October 1831 the Guard did make a raid on the Council House at New Echota. But there was no one there. The Council was holding its deliberations on the bad manners and the customs of Georgians safely over the border on the Alabama side of their territory.

Chatooga was an uncomfortable location for Council. From all the more populous parts of the Nation the distance was considerable. On rainy days the chiefs had no better protection from the weather than branches supported on crotched sticks. Squatting thus under cover was not in keeping with the dignity of the Cherokee government, and since this government was very jealous of its dignity, it did not meet in Chatooga again.

But meeting at all in the face of the combined efforts of Washington and Georgia was a moral victory. Undivided and undismayed, the chiefs listened to the annual message of Chief Ross.

Ross was no orator. He did not speak in the grand manner of the old chiefs, who without moving their arms from their sides could so address a multitude as to melt their hearts. The Ridge was of the old tradition, but not Ross. The latter's talks were concerned mainly with prosaic facts and figures, and on this occasion with a summary of the year's events.

In spite of the year's trials, Ross saw hope ahead. National unity had been demonstrated by the Cherokees' refusal to consider mass emigration or to accept payment of the annuities on the new, beggarly basis. Even in Georgia a voice had recently spoken out in defense of the Cherokees, at least so far as their right to dig gold was concerned—Judge Clayton's.

Towards the end of his speech Ross made a significant statement. Progress in the Nation continued in spite of the obstacles. Thanks to that progress, continued Ross, "the happy period" will "be hastened when an incorporation into the great family of the American Republic" will "be greeted by every patriot."

For maintaining him through many discouragements, Ross had a dream that one day, not far off, a new star would be added to the flag of the United States, and that star stand for a state the like of which had not yet been received into the Union—an Indian state, the State of Cherokee.

In the conviction of such glory ahead one could wait, one could accept suffering patiently, for the suffering would endure but a day and the glory would last as long as the Union itself.

The sovereign state of Cherokee of the United States of America. The day would come when Georgia would be no longer an enemy, but a sister.

CHAPTER XI

A Sun Rises

On Washington's birthday in 1832, when snow still stood on the mountains, Smoky and Jaybird and Little Turtle and Daylight and Macklemore got together with Jesse in the latter's well-set-up cabin to write a round robin to the prisoner they knew best, Dr. Elizur Butler.

Some of them could have with less labor raised him a new house. They bent flat broad faces over white paper, clutched the slim pen in powerful hands, and grunted. It was not easy to translate the warm affection they felt for the missionary into the pothooks recalled from their schooldays. Only Jesse, who liked checking the Cherokee version of St. Matthew with the English, was really fluent with the pen.

"Letters are writing," Macklemore put down, "and I wish to write you a few words." But what words? Butler had of his own will assumed the burden of the Cherokees; he had accepted imprisonment that they might go free. Because of him there was new hope in the Nation. But could you say all that in English? Macklemore couldn't. "It's a Methodist brother who salutes you," he wrote, and told Jesse that he was done.

On Little Turtle's face as he worked, there was something of the sweetness that shone from it when he read in the Cherokee St. Matthew of the white man's Jesus. "I

[163]

am not afraid of what the Georgians are doing," he wrote. "I do not feel sorry that you were willing to go to prison, for you have done no wrong, and I do not think you will be unhappy."

The six read their letters aloud, and Jesse examined them and made emendations. Then he sent the lot to Milledgeville, where they warmed the heart of Butler. The Cherokees had sent the prisoners other gifts. Besides the $2.12½ collected by the unknown councilor for Mrs. Butler, the chiefs had made substantial contributions. But none of these meant more to Butler than the affection behind these labored documents. He kept them.

As Little Turtle had surmised, Butler was not unhappy. From the very first stage of the controversy with Georgia he had longed to defend the Cherokees, had written Boston that if it were possible he "would go trembling like Esther to the president . . . and plead with him by the prayers and tears of that dear saint whom he left in Tennessee to have compassion on these dear immortals, for whom she would no doubt now be willing again to live and suffer and die."

Like Butrick, he had questioned the propriety of the missionaries' taking a stand of political implications; unlike Butrick's, his conscience had been put at rest by the Prudential Committee's decision that they should. After that he had been prey to purely human fears, reluctance to leave his young wife, so recently a bride, and their newborn baby, fear of being dragged off in chains.

Every one of these fears had been realized. He was parted from his family (his elder children by his first wife enclosed letters with the Indians' beginning "Dear Pa"), chains had chafed his limbs on the way to the Lawrenceville jail, and now he was committed for four years. But in prison he was at peace. He the shepherd had suffered all things that had been required of him for his flock; his conscience was clear; his fate was in the hands of God and the Supreme Court, and he had faith in the justice of both.

Also, prison life had turned out to be unexpectedly pleasant. The workshop gave him cheerful extrovert occupation; he was learning to be a shoemaker, a good one. He had leisure for the first time since he came South to bring his medical reading up to date. And such was the kindness of the warden, Mills, that on Sabbath and midweek he and Worcester were allowed to hold devotions for such as cared to attend.

Worcester also worked in the shop, at carpentering, but he did not find so much comfort there as Butler. He was the intellectual, the scholar, far more deeply grounded in theology and casuistry than his companion. He was troubled now by afterthoughts; where Butler had questioned the propriety of opposing the Georgians before the event, Worcester questioned it now. While he worried, his hands grew clumsy, his tools slipped; the Board smiled at the sample of his workmanship that he sent them, a box that did not lie quite true to line.

2.

The six in Jesse's house had probably addressed themselves to Butler alone just because they knew him better. But it was a fact that a rumor circulating about Worcester had caused much uneasiness and even a sense of alienation.

It happened that Boudinot and Charles Reese had a distant cousin in Georgia, one Dr. David A. Reese of Monticello, who, unlike most white men, neither scorned nor tried to conceal his Indian relationship; in fact, he was bringing up a Cherokee boy in his own household. He was a rather important connection, for he was a member of the Georgia legislature, where he had to some extent befriended the Cherokees, insisting that if they were made to remove they should have adequate compensation for their lands. Perhaps if he came to the Nation and saw the situation for himself he would become altogether an advocate.

No one, therefore, held it against Boudinot and Reese when late in 1831 they entertained the Georgian in their homes. The affair was in any case purely private and social; the Georgian had not come to harangue Council; he merely rode about the countryside paying calls. The Cherokees, delighted to meet a friendly Georgian, talked to him without restraint, confided in him the hope that they now placed in the case of Worcester versus the State of Georgia, soon to come before the Supreme Court.

Then a coolness came over this relationship. Reese smiled at such confidants compassionately and told them they were trusting too much in the missionaries; Worcester was already changing his mind in prison. He knew; he had it from an unimpeachable source.

It was left to Ann Worcester to discover the identity of this source. The Cherokees consulted her as one who might know her husband's mind rather better than the eminent Dr. Reese, and Ann confronted the latter. The source, it seemed, was Governor Gilmer, and the governor had his facts from a Dr. Alonzo Church, president of the University of Athens, who had twice visited Worcester in prison and on the second visit found him "less fiercely convinced" than on the first.

Ann, devoted to her husband, even proud that he had risked her own life in order to stand up for principle and the Cherokees, knew that Gilmer and Church had put a false construction on her husband's moods. That Reese should go about making such talk angered and also frightened her; he had talked thus to the removal agents, who were making capital of the report to persuade the Cherokees to emigrate. She lost no time in reporting the incident to Boston.

In point of fact, Dr. Reese's visit had been no more

inspired by simple sociability than had Colonel Lowry's. Governor Gilmer himself had picked him for what was in effect a disguised mission. There had been correspondence between the Secretary of War and the Hiwassee agency as to where Reese should go and whom he should see.

3.

Reese's visit coincided with another visit even more disturbing in its effects. For the first time since the passage of the Removal Bill the Cherokees were confronted with the possibility that the government would attempt the strategy of "divide and conquer," the device that had brought about the ruin of the Creeks.

While Reese was making his rounds of calls, while a few Cherokees shamefacedly, secretly, listened to the inducements of the latest enrollment agents, members of a delegation from the Cherokee Nation West, appointed by Chief Jolly, called on their Eastern kinsmen on their way to Washington.

Usually visitors from the Arkansas were made welcome back home in the hills, but not particularly representatives of Chief Jolly. As a leading figure in the unauthorized land cession of 1817, he commanded little respect among the Eastern Cherokees. To prevent a recurrence of such deals they had revived the old blood law in 1819, and had written it into their constitution in 1828, making such acts punishable by death. Some of them now wished the law could be made retroactive; for the visit had been inspired by Federal agents who promised advantages to the Cherokee Nation West if its representatives would influence the Eastern Cherokees to remove.

When Jolly's delegates moved on to Washington City, they took two recruits from the Tennessee and North Carolina end of the Nation, the Aquohee district—John Walker and James Starr.

This pair had as much right in Washington as any

casual sightseers and no more. So far as their own government was concerned, they had no credentials and no official standing whatsoever. The Aquohee district expressly
repudiated them. But when the authorized delegates appointed by National Council reached Washington City,
they found their activities hampered by the presence of
the free lances. The latter were cutting a figure in Jackson circles; Jackson himself, who ignored the official
delegation, was receiving Walker and Starr because they
were willing to discuss what the authorized delegates
would not—removal.

The result was that the two delegations canceled each
other out. Walker and Starr could achieve nothing because they had no authority; the official delegates could
get no hearing, except with proven friends who were
sympathetic as always but had no influence with Jackson.

Within the Nation a slow fire of anger burned against
Walker and Starr. Such action was close to treason; it
must not happen again. It was not good to give Jackson
the impression that division was possible among the Cherokees.

4.

After Reese had gone home, Boudinot left the *Phoenix*
in the hands of his brother, Stand Watie (to whom he
sent frequent and detailed editorial instructions), and
went out into the world. He had two objectives: to educate the American public to the significance of the Cherokee situation, and to raise money for the government and
for the upkeep of the *Phoenix* by a series of lectures. It
had never been hoped that the paper would be self-sup-
porting: it was to be a subsidized government organ. Now
that the source of the subsidies had been cut off by Jackson, it was necessary to find other resources.

The happy hunting ground of lecturers in those days
was the reportedly scholarly and humanitarian New England. Boudinot was New England–bound, but first he

stopped off in Georgia. He wanted to see his friend Worcester; he owed a return call to Reese; and he wanted to judge for himself the temper of the Georgians.

On the latter account he was agreeably surprised. After his experiences with the Georgia Guard it took courage for him to visit a state whose population appeared to be in a state of uproar on the Cherokee question. He discovered that the alleged uproar was confined almost wholly to political circles. Plain people, at least those whom he met in Athens, cared very little who possessed the Cherokee country.

This was encouraging—or was it? Everyday people were indifferent to the whole situation, but general indifference hardly constituted championship; in the end it might be the most dependable weapon in the hands of the oppressors. Boudinot, however, was at the moment surprised and encouraged.

In New England he met the people who counted, the Beechers for instance, and thanks to such influence found many a congregation or lyceum ready to give him sympathetic attention and collections sometimes mounting to $800. He was especially well received in New Haven, where John Ridge took time out from his duties as delegate to Washington to share the platform of the Center Church with his cousin.

The missionary case had again focused public attention on the Cherokees. The news that the facts were to be presented by two scarcely less spectacular actors in the drama than Worcester and Butler filled the town with the liveliest interest. These were the two young "savages" who had not long ago roused the sedate town of Cornwall to mob hysteria by making off with two respectable white women. New Haven very much wanted to hear from the Cherokees, particularly these Cherokees.

On a day in February, about the time when Jesse was assembling his round robin, people crowded into the church with a subdued rustle of silks and crinolines. They filled the floor, then the gallery, and finally the space around the pulpit.

Those who expected something outlandish were disappointed. The young men, well educated, well groomed, very much at home in the great world, outlined the Cherokee story simply and impressively. The editor of the New Haven *Religious Intelligencer* was surprised to discover that the "clear and melodious voice" of John Ridge bore not a trace of accent. Only in the color of their skins was there a touch of the exotic; they were red men, Boudinot somewhat more obviously so than his tall and slender cousin.

In Boudinot's speech there was more emotion than in his cousin's reasoned analysis of the facts in the case. Boudinot began quietly enough with an account of George Washington's advice to the Cherokees. "You gave us good advice. We followed it. We were happy." But when he came to the oppression of the Georgians and Jackson's refusal to intercede, he rose to a climax that may have troubled the more reserved of his auditors. It was a moving climax; its emotion was understandable, yet it suggested something close to hysteria; it was as if there was something not altogether stable in this young man.

"What shall we do?" Boudinot had cried. "We are distressed. . .we are distressed!"

The news that New Haven was later to hear of Boudinot was very distressing indeed.

5.

The new year wore on, the year of 1832. The missionaries had been cobbling and carpentering in their quarters at Milledgeville for four months, then five, and six, and still the Supreme Court had not been heard from.

In the Nation there was only one mind as to what the

Court would say, must say. Missionaries who had at first thought Worcester was carrying his defiance of Georgia too far now swung over to his point of view—all but Butrick. Butrick still believed that one must render unto Caesar the things that were Caesar's, or anyway Georgia's.

Butrick had escaped the September arrest by complying with the letter of the Georgia law; both he and Proctor, following the example of the Moravians, took up nominal residence in Tennessee, a device that enabled them to "itinerate" in Georgia at will.

In spite of this solution and his own fierce and rather ungenerous refusal to see any virtue in Worcester's conduct, Butrick now had very little peace of mind. The sound of a bugle was enough to throw him into panic; at the sight of a white stranger his throat became so dry that he could barely return a greeting. He alone of the missionaries in Georgia had escaped arrest entirely; God, he wrote in his private diary, had preserved him from "the mad dog." But not all his righteousness or his conviction that he was doing exactly what St. Paul would have done could exorcise his fantasies.

His position was uneasy in other ways. The opposition did not appreciate the spirituality of his decision. Indeed, Enrollment Agent Curry accused him to his face of profiting by deals with the Cherokees and of using Cherokee money to pay the lawyers of the missionaries.

From the other side he was harried more gently but very persistently by Ann Worcester and Lucy Butler, and sometimes by Chief Ross himself. Ann pleaded with him to take "the larger view." Butrick listened patiently, kindly, but stuck to his convictions; an apostle should not meddle with such unapostolic matters as politics. When he heard of the wickedness of Jackson and the cruelty of Georgia, he confided in the Board, he felt a desire to weep "but no disposition to join in the conversation."

Georgia had "grievously transgressed," yet "she is still a dear sister and I sometimes fancy I almost see tears on her cheeks."

He preoccupied himself with the care of his flock, just then a sad, shamed little flock, for Georgians had opened grogshops in his neighborhood too, and the "dear people" could not always keep out of them.

6.

Worcester had one champion whose identity must have surprised him: that stormy petrel, Miss Sophia Sawyer. These two had never seen eye to eye, to put it mildly; there had been differences between them, highly emotional differences on Miss Sophia's part. But when Worcester went to prison admiration extinguished her resentment. She devoted herself to helping Ann manage the mission, particularly the school, and when the Georgia Guard stopped by to interfere she faced them down in the name of Worcester and the Supreme Court; and the Guard retreated from the gaunt New England maiden lady, saying "Yes, Ma'am."

Worcester, all too well acquainted with Miss Sophia's powers of expression when she was aroused, must have felt a secret twinge of sympathy for the Georgia Guard. It was a judgment on that organization, created expressly to harry the Cherokees and not too highly regarded even in Georgia, that when they undertook to harass the mission womenfolk they ran right up against Miss Sophia.

Miss Sophia was a Yankee schoolma'am from Rindge, New Hampshire, who had come to teach the "females" at Brainerd in the early twenties. Even then past her youth, it was not her fortune to find romance like Lucy Ames, who married Butler, Elizabeth Proctor, who married Butrick, or Delight Sargent, who was presently to marry into Cherokee aristocracy. Miss Sophia herself was by no means unresponsive to masculine charm in her blameless, schoolma'am fashion, but the response was never mutual. She was afflicted with an angularity of both body and mind that made her difficult to get along with. Her colleagues until now had found her impossible.

The Cherokees, on the contrary, were much attached to her. Their shrewd simplicity grasped the real root of her difficulties, an ardently emotional nature with no natural outlet. They endured her fantasies of temperament kindly, seldom protested her correction of their children, respected her talent. For Miss Sophia was a gifted teacher. Even Worcester admitted that.

Life was interesting in her classes, for though she did not neglect the three R's, she and her children ventured far beyond them. They learned celestial geography together, and, outgrowing their prosy readers, subscribed to *Parley's Magazine* and learned what went on in the world. Sometimes Miss Sophia even managed to get them a *Youth's Companion*. Nor was she afraid to face the less maidenly facts of life in their behalf. Some of her charges were big girls, apt to afflict her by unseasonably early marriages, and exposed to worse temptation. Once when she scented danger she read about the Lewd Woman of Proverbs to some of the older girls. She made a profound impression. One girl came back from summer vacation asking to have that passage pointed out to her again. Her mother wanted to hear it.

Miss Sophia had ideas about education in general. Although she had been happiest at the boarding school in Brainerd, she believed boarding schools of dubious value for Indian pupils. True, the children learned more quickly there, but they returned half aliens to their own communities and usually became backsliders in self-defense. In the day school, though progress was slower it was surer, for here the child, living at home, did not become a stranger from his natural environment, and his parents, by following his daily progress, in some measure grew with him. In New Echota in 1832 Miss Sophia was testing this theory (which anticipated government educational policy in Indian affairs by a century), for most of her children came from the neighborhood.

A stormy history had preceded her arrival. She had started at Brainerd, had been exiled to Haweis, and thence had precipitately fled to New Echota. She had made one brief return to Brainerd, just in time to see it burn on March 15, 1830, and though the missionaries were rebuilding it in answer to an appeal from Chief Ross as a sign of their confidence in the future of the Cherokees, Miss Sophia was now reasonably content elsewhere. She had friends at last—Harriet Boudinot and Sarah Ridge; in fact all the Ridge family, whose home at Running Waters she sometimes visited.

During all these trials she had poured out her heart to the American Board in voluminous diary letters, often poetic, poignant letters, for Miss Sophia excelled at self-expression. It was, indeed, this very gift that.had been her undoing; it was what Worcester had objected to, her habit of expressing herself out of season and out of reason. The lady, being frequently unwell, had a temper, and being gifted, had a tongue with much sting to it. When she desired to denounce her superiors, Worcester for instance, she did so, no matter who else was present, without reserve, at great length, and with maddening eloquence.

The best of missionaries could not always preserve a saintly concord under the stresses that are inevitably engendered in any small, intimate community placed in an alien environment. Mission people were thrown to an abnormal degree into each other's company; everyone had an uncomfortably detailed acquaintance with everyone else's business. Lack of privacy and natural collision of temperament made it possible for even missionaries of the highest principle to bicker sometimes, and tempests to brew in the teapot. In fact, the higher the principle, the more certain the bickering. Butrick, who had recently had with the blacksmith Thompson a falling out so serious that it required the mediation of Boston, was now, as has been seen, at odds with nearly everyone. And Miss Sophia had been driven from one station to another.

"Oh how *tired* I am of Republican government!" she once wrote apropos not of politics but of such difficulties as these. Teapot tempests may be the most destructive of meteorological disturbances just because the teapot is so small; under stress it can only explode.

But now Miss Sophia had the cleansing experience of conflict on a higher plane. On March 16, 1832, when Worcester and Butler had been six months in the penitentiary, there came a knock on the door of the Council House where Miss Sophia now held her classes. She opened it, and there was the Georgia Guard. She invited them in.

7.

The members of the Guard docilely sat where Miss Sophia directed them, on the raised platform resigned for the executive council, and listened while the children droned away at their books, with only an occasional swift glance of appraisal at the Guard of great and terrible fame. There were twenty children, all the older children of the Ridge and Boudinot households, the Wilson young people whose father had moved his family to New Echota expressly to give it the benefit of Miss Sophia's teaching.

Conspicuous among the sleek blue-black hair and severe aquiline profiles stood out the curly pates and softly rounded features of two little black boys. And everyone knew that it was because of these, Sam and Peter, that the Guard had called.

The two were children of slaves of the community; it is a commentary on the character of slavery in the Nation that no Cherokee thought it amiss that the slave children should attend class and mix in the rough-and-tumble of their own youngsters.

Of the two, Peter was the more regular attendant. The eight-year-old Sam could come only when he could be spared from his duties in an unidentified kitchen, usually half a day at a time. But there he was on March 16, and he too knew why the Guard had come.

Late in January Miss Sophia had had an anonymous note warning her that teaching colored pupils was a violation of Georgia law, punishable by arrest. But she was not the sort to be intimidated by a threat. She traced the note to Dr. Reese and then ignored it and the others that followed. The only effect on her was to warm her emotional heart to the plight of young Sam and Peter. She redoubled her pains with them; if they were to be taken from her, at least they should know how to read their Bibles first.

So she knew why the Guard had come, and though she received them with self-possession and went on with her duties, she found she was trembling. She needed to pray, and since St. Paul says it is not meet for a woman to pray before men, she asked the Guard to withdraw so she could do so.

"Yes, Ma'am," said the Guard, and bashfully obeyed. They had brought their best manners. They sat under the trees where the Cherokee chiefs had lately listened to Colonel Lowry and waited while Miss Sophia led her children in an appeal for strength and heavenly guidance. They waited until she gave them permission to return.

This time only one came in, the officer, hat in hand and smiling. Looking about at the children he complimented her on the fine work they were doing; he seemed not like a Georgian at all, but like any friendly visitor. But then he lowered his voice, and everyone knew why. Those "Nigras" over there: didn't she know it was Georgia law, punishable by fine of $1000 to $5000, to teach "Nigras"?

Yes, Miss Sophia knew about Georgia law; with the eloquence that Worcester so well knew she expressed herself on the iniquity thereof in this particular. Then she inquired what it had to do with her. This was the Cherokee Nation, not Georgia; the Cherokees were too civilized to pass such laws.

"No, Ma'am," said the officer firmly, but keeping his manners, "this here is Georgia."

"That," said Miss Sophia, "is for the Supreme Court to decide. And until the Supreme Court decides it in your favor I will not yield to the law of Georgia."

The Guard warned her that he must report her to General Coffee. Then he made a mannerly leave-taking that was in effect a retreat. Miss Sophia, left tingling with the excitement of the encounter, and always susceptible to good manners, involuntarily reflected that even Georgians could possess charm.

The Guard did win one point. The father of little Sam took alarm and withdrew the child from school. The master privately explained to Miss Sophia the wisdom of keeping him out "till this storm shall subside."

8.

The Georgia Guard had hardly bowed himself out of the presence of Miss Sophia when they both discovered that the Supreme Court had already passed on the case of Worcester versus the State of Georgia some two weeks earlier. The news had come late to the Nation.

It was at the time of the ritual of the new fire that the Cherokees heard the tremendous news. Symbolically, it was exactly at the time when Cherokees faithful to the old pieties were relighting their hearths at a brand from the sacred new fire kindled by the medicine men that they learned that the Supreme Court had at last decided for Worcester, for them. "The Cherokee Nation then is a distinct community, occupying its own territory . . . in which the laws of Georgia can have no force and which the citizens of Georgia have no right to enter but with the assent of the Cherokees. . . . The Act of the state of Georgia . . . is consequently null and void. . . . The Acts of Georgia are repugnant to the constitution, laws and treaties of the United States."

The news was so good that some Cherokees at first wouldn't let themselves believe it. The Cherokee winter, their own private winter of discontent, as one oppression succeeded another, worse threatening and nothing done about it by their sworn protectors, had lasted too long. Their hopes had been deceived too often; better not to hope at all, better just to endure.

These wouldn't accept the news until the *Phoenix* came out and they saw it with their own eyes in the precious syllabary of Sequoia. Then at last they believed, and with belief a great tide of rejoicing engulfed the Nation. For one blissful moment the Cherokees lived in the certainty that now had come an end to all doubting and fear; now oppression had been stopped forever by the just word of John Marshall.

It was as if a sun had risen. But the sun, alas, had risen in eclipse.

CHAPTER XII

In Eclipse

No Cherokee delegates to Washington had experienced a greater triumph than those who returned late in the spring of 1832. They had heard the Supreme Court vindicate the rights of their Nation on every point; there was no longer doubt as to where justice lay. As Boudinot had joyfully written home, it was not now a contest between Georgia and the poor Cherokees, but between Georgia and the United States of America.

Yet these delegates came home in a state of utter dejection. They shrank from the inquiries of those who waylaid them to learn what had gone on in Washington. State affairs were confidential, they said, and must keep for the called Council in July.

And hardly had they returned before Chief Ross, the steadfast, ever optimistic John Ross, appointed a day of fasting and solemn prayer.

To the naïve the ominous implications of Ross's proclamation came as a cruel blow. Out-of-the-way districts had hardly recovered from a round of celebrations in ball plays and all-night townhouse dances when the call came to fast and pray. The celebrants were shocked. But Cherokees closer to the center of events had been made aware during the spring of a mysterious malaise, a kind of spiritual confusion that was growing on the Nation.

In spite of the Supreme Court decision, the spring of 1832 had been an unhappy season for the Cherokees. Early in the spring Georgia had begun to carry out its threat to survey Cherokee land for distribution by lottery. This much the Cherokees had taken calmly; no one had expected the Georgians to surrender to the Supreme Court decision without pressure from above; and though the surveyors numbered some 550, they were harmlessly pre-occupied with their instruments, on the whole a welcome change from the whisky peddlers and pony clubs. Chero-kee farmers made little jokes for the *Phoenix* about the strange marks surveyors left on their shade trees, fences, and sheds; they went on planting and ploughing uncon-cerned.

The *Phoenix* editorialized the new violation of the Intercourse Act incurred by their uninvited presence. "Re-move not the old landmark," it quoted and, paraphrasing Scripture, continued, "and enter not the fields of the fa-therless, for their redeemer is mighty, and he shall plead cause for them."

Ann Worcester, vigilantly trying to carry on for her husband, spoke her mind to a former Baptist preacher to the Cherokees for accepting work as a surveyor. He was apologetic. He needed the money, he said, and if he hadn't taken it another would have.

More disturbing than the surveying (though the seri-ousness of that move was to become speedily plain) was the fact that Georgia was exerting pressure on Alabama and Tennessee to make the position of the Cherokees im-possible by extending their own laws over Cherokee terri-tory. Alabama had already complied. "When a man goes downhill everyone gives him a kick," commented the *Phoenix*. Davy Crockett's and Andrew Jackson's Tennes-see was so far only talking of following suit, but it was talking.

More distressing still were persistent rumors of the

defection of friends. It was becoming known that Ross had been approached by Worcester's lawyer, Chester. The latter had dismaying news. The missionaries were going to accept a pardon, with the approval of the American Board, before their case came to trial. The case of the Cherokees was hopeless, and Ross, as a responsible chief, must influence his people to accept removal while favorable terms could still be made.

In so approaching Ross and in circulating similar rumors among the Cherokees, Chester had no authority from Worcester, Butler, or the American Board. He was acting, as the missionaries discovered too late, as a confidential agent for Jackson; his statements were as of that date pure fabrication. But Ross had no immediate means of contradicting one who came straight from the missionaries and presumably spoke for them. He could and did coldly refuse to discuss Chester's proposition to treat for removal, but, as Mrs. Butler wrote the Board: "He deeply feels the change of sentiment among the friends of the Cherokees. To him it has been sudden and unexpected. It is much to be feared that there will be dissension should the matter be discussed in Council. . . . Oh I do indeed pity this people."

Lucy Butler was right about the dissension. That was the real cause of the spiritual malaise, the irascibility that was growing on the Nation. The Cherokees scented treachery; they believed that they had somehow been betrayed, and not by the perfidious Starr and Walker, but by their own lawfully appointed delegates—by such leaders as John Ridge and William S. Coodey.

2.

The first hint of betrayal came in the May 12 issue of the *Phoenix*, which was still being edited by Boudinot's brother, Stand Watie. Boudinot, however, though lingering in Washington to observe the progress of the delegates, could not disclaim responsibility; he had by mail kept in touch with his brother, directing him what to print, what to avoid.

The May 12 issue contained an article by one Colonel Newsome reprinted from the *Augusta Chronicle* of April 14. It stated that the Cherokee delegates in Washington had at last decided to induce their country to treat for removal; they would now either obtain authority from home to treat in Washington or return to make arrangements in New Echota.

Cherokee readers stared blankly at this announcement. They rubbed their eyes and read it again; then they searched the paper for an explanation. It was not uncommon for Boudinot to republish articles from the enemy press, often of a vituperative nature, but he always accompanied them with editorial comment. This time there was no comment; there was no explanation at all aside from an irrelevant masthead denying that Starr and Walker had power to make treaties—irrelevant because Colonel Newsome's statement could not possibly apply to any but the legitimate delegates.

Exactly what was going on among the Washington delegates? One of them, John Ridge, had been heard from just before Colonel Newsome published his letter. Young Ridge was all elation. The Supreme Court decision had made a new man of him, he wrote his father, had given the delegates the means to deal with traitors like Starr and Walker. "United we stand." Jackson, "the Chicken Snake," was resisting execution of the judgment, but the "Chicken Snake's" head would be cut off at the next election. There certainly was no suggestion of weakness in this letter. Yet now, in May, it had been written long ago. What had happened since? And to what purpose had Ridge's cousin printed such news without comment in the *Phoenix?*

Chief Ross was one who inquired. Hitherto he had let

Boudinot have a free hand. But the implication of the
Newsome article and the storm it stirred up were too serious to be ignored. He sent in for publication a formal
denial by one of the delegates, William S. Coodey, and
reproved the editor for publishing a statement so mislead-
ing to the public.

The resentment and suspicion enkindled by the report
did not die down. At the best the Colonel's letter was uneasy evidence of the prestige the discredited Starr and
Walker were enjoying in Washington. The *Phoenix* repudiated a rumor that these had made a deal with the
government to cede land in North Carolina and Tennessee
in exchange for Western territory. This repudiation was
not enough for the Aquohee District referred to. In July
the citizens of that community issued a formal statement
that they were unanimously opposed to any such cession
or to "making any treaty whatever until the stipulations
contained in those already in force" were complied with.
Sweetwater signed this, and Roman Nose, Spike Duck,
and Shawnee John, as well as many who concealed their
identity from the latter-day historian by signing in Sequoia's alphabet.

3.

Late in May, in the midst of this unrest, the authorized
delegates came back from Washington. And in the heavy,
exhausted look of them, their sensitive evasion of inquiry,
there was nothing to allay public misgivings.

There were those who could not be put off with evasion.
John Ross was one. He talked with them privately. Concerning the results of this conference he kept a tight lip,
but when he proclaimed the day of fast the Cherokees
knew without further announcements that evil was afoot.
They awaited the called-Council of July in a state of
ferment.

The steadfast John Ross had indeed been shaken by
events of the spring and by the information brought by

the delegates. One dismaying fact was already known to everyone. Faced with the Supreme Court decision, President Jackson had contemptuously remarked: "John Marshall made the decision; let him enforce it."

Such an attitude on Jackson's part was in character; few had expected anything better. They remembered that while their own Supreme Court case still impended they had obtained an injunction to restrain Georgia officials from hanging a Cherokee named Corn Tassel. Georgia, disregarding the injunction, had hanged him anyway, and Jackson had done nothing about it.

So there was nothing new about Jackson's attitude. What was new was the fact that friends in Washington, including the always sympathetic Justice McLean, had told the delegates that they were powerless to force the president's hand. This circumstance, if true, was a blow at the root of Ross's whole political philosophy. He had led the Cherokees in a policy based on faith in the inviolability of law and the sanctity of a word between nations. The word on which their national existence depended had been reaffirmed, but Jackson refused to honor it, and there was no way of making him do so.

No facile optimism sufficed in so grim a situation. Ross would not give way to the defeatism of the delegates, but he agreed that the public should not be kept in ignorance of the gravity of the situation. To this end he had recommended the fate of the Cherokees to the prayers of the believers.

He did not, however, relinquish his faith. Principle, regardless of Jackson, remained what it had been, was greater than hope. Let the Cherokees hold to it, and all would somehow yet be well.

4.

The Ridge received John at his home at the Head of Coosa, looked into the young man's haggard face, and read disaster there. Then he heard the story; friends in Washington had made it bleakly plain that the Cherokees were done for in the East. The delegates now considered it their duty to go before Council and insist on the necessity of treating for removal.

It was a courageous decision. The Cherokees were in no mood to respect an honest change of opinion on the part of their leaders; they would have only one word for it — betrayal.

Even to approach his own father with such a decision took courage on the part of young Ridge. No one, not even Ross, had a more consistent record of opposition to removal. It had begun in the days of Jefferson; when, in 1808, some of the chiefs were persuaded to accept territory within the Louisiana Purchase a youngish man, then little known, had risen and denounced the plan with passionate eloquence. His name had come out of that day, in Cherokee "One Who Walks on Ridges" and hence sees farther than most. And he had carried his point; since then the Cherokees had never as a nation seriously considered removal.

The Ridge had never wavered in his attitude. He had been second chief with John Ross in 1828 when the blood law, making it an offense punishable by death for Cherokees to do separately what the nation would not do collectively, was made part of the constitution. He had set his mark to its ratification.

Again and again in times of crisis he had lifted his magic voice in Council, always to one end, to hearten his people in their defense of their integrity. "A *great* speech," Worcester had written of one such occasion. There was indeed no greater speaker in the Nation; John Ross, always carefully factual, was a dry contrast to this great cherry opal of an Indian with his instinctive gift of phrasing, his rich sense of the living past, and his disciplined emotional power. To the Cherokees, when The

Ridge spoke it was as if a man out of myth were speaking. He gave voice to the folk spirit of his people, and there lay his power.

And now this man's son asked him to divorce himself from that folk spirit, to substitute for the Cherokees' profound emotional conviction of right the white man's logic of common sense and expediency.

A deep troubling of spirit came upon The Ridge. In these days when the Cherokees most needed him, his great voice fell silent. He went about with a mask drawn over his broad face, and as his was normally the most expressive of countenances, the mask was visible and recognizable as the mask of tragedy. There was a weary fixity about his eyes; he now seldom exchanged a frank look with his friends, but stared away from them into vacant horizons.

And since he could not bring himself to accept the testimony of even his son without judging for himself, he was seen in strange company. With incredulous eyes the Cherokees saw this man whom they had revered talking with the enrollment agents, consulting with the hated Chester.

One day what had hitherto been only an ugly rumor, furiously denied by his friends, became an undisputed fact. The Ridge agreed to back his son's effort to persuade the Cherokees to accept the inevitable, to treat for removal.

What had persuaded him? Apparently it was a kind of humility before his son, the humility that the most generous of an older generation sometimes feel before the young. Since The Ridge could neither read nor write, and had missed participation in the great upsurge of Cherokee folk spirit by failing to learn Sequoia's alphabet, he had an exaggerated, an almost superstitious respect for John's book learning. Only the literate were in The Ridge's eyes fit to rule the Nation. When John had returned from the

Cornwall school, the father had inducted him into the world of Cherokee state affairs, and had begun deliberately to efface himself. Although, in his upper fifties, he was still so vigorous that Ross could trust him with the lively responsibility of ousting a band of horse thieves, he no longer sought high office for himself. All his ambition was centered on John, who was rising fast. Already the young man was president of Council and had been delegate to Washington in two critical seasons; there was every prospect that he would presently become principal chief.

But John's present decision could not have been motivated by personal ambition. He could hardly have found a better method for ruining his prestige, at least for the time. No mere self-seeker would have undertaken to oppose the deepest will of his people. John's integrity was beyond question; it was only his judgment that his father must consider.

But how could he, a simple, unlettered Indian, put his judgment above his learned son's? How could he believe that even Chief Ross, with whom he had worked congenially and for whom he had respect and affection, knew more? The Chief had had no such education as that which John had received at Cornwall. No, there could be no doubt about it. All the faith in white man's civilization and Cherokee progress that had caused The Ridge to give his son a white man's schooling bore on his decision.

In July, while Council sat in stormy session, the *Phoenix* published an odd item, a prophecy that a chief was supposed to have made fifty years earlier:

"He will even teach you his language and learn you to read and write. But these are but the means to destroy you, and to eject you from your habitations. He will point you to the West, but you will find no resting place there. . . . Our feet are turned towards the West—they are never to turn round."

The Ridge did not speak at the called Council; at least, there is no record of his doing so. He sat in sad, consenting silence and left the speaking to his son, to his nephew Boudinot, to Ross's nephew William S. Coodey. In a sense he was never to speak again, at least not in the grand manner, not with the conviction that irresistibly stirred Cherokee hearts. His choice was hard, not lightly taken, but in making it virtue had departed from him. The Ridge was an old man now and very tired.

5.

Council now met in Red Clay, Tennessee, as easier of access than the Alabama council grounds. It convened in July, and though it had only three main items on its agenda, these were so productive of high feeling that it ran until mid-August. Its business concerned the report of the delegates, a fresh removal offer that Secretary Cass had entrusted for delivery to the despised Chester, and the question of national elections.

So intense was the bitterness provoked by the report of the Washington delegates that Ross refused to let a detailed account of it appear in the *Phoenix*. But the observant Chester wrote Edward Everett of the event. Rumors of the defection of the delegates had brought the councilors together in an ugly frame of mind; they were now convinced that their own delegates, not Starr and Walker, had inspired the *Augusta Chronicle* story, and such conduct was in their eyes treachery. When they heard with their own ears that these delegates did indeed advocate removal, their anger was such that they would neither hear the delegates out nor listen to their "distinguished friends," a category in which Chester seems to have included himself. In withholding from publication the proceedings of Council, Ross probably had several objects in mind, one of them the safety of the delegates themselves.

Presently Chester was allowed to bring forward the message of Cass. There was nothing in this calculated to restore faith in the integrity of the delegates or to assuage the exasperation of Council. It began: "Your great father, the president of the United States, has recently been informed that a change of heart has probably taken place in the sentiments you have hitherto entertained on the subject of removal, and that propositions will be favorable to you." So that was how the delegates had busied themselves in Washington!

It concluded: "Shut your ears, I entreat you, to bad counsels, if any should be offered you. Whatever may be told you, it is impossible you can remain here. . . . And if you persist in the effort the time of regret will come, I am afraid, after the most injury to yourself."

The Cherokees were in no mood for expression of filial loyalty to their "great father," who was Jackson, whose term was nearly over, and who would soon, they hoped, be replaced by Henry Clay. They disagreed with Cass as to what was bad counsel; they took their own and rejected the offer.

"It is with much astonishment," they replied, "we hear from the letter the president has been informed that a change of heart has taken place. . . . The basis of his proposition is objectionable." They reminded Cass that his government had given them no protection against the illegal acts of Georgia, and told him that such Cherokees as had recently enrolled for the West had been subjected to disagreeable methods of persuasion.

Finally they expressed themselves on Cass's bad taste in transmitting such an offer through so equivocal an emissary as Chester. Cherokee contempt of the latter, who had used his connection with Worcester and the American Board merely to cloak his full-time employment by Jackson interests, knew no bounds. Not that they said quite so much in their reply. They contented themselves with a cold comment on the irregularity of choosing just this agent and stated that propositions could be considered only when they came through authorized channels.

Chester sorrowfully commented that this reply would, he feared, only irritate.

The third item of business was the most troublesome of all. National elections were due, but Georgia had forbidden them on pain of wholesale arrest. Hotheads were in favor of holding them anyway and letting Georgia do its worst, but more cautious elements prevailed. There seemed to be nothing to do but swallow the bitter pill of suspending the new constitution, now barely four years old. Representatives of the several districts worked out a measure that Council reluctantly adopted: elections would be suspended until further notice, the principal chiefs and members of Council continued in office another term, and vacancies filled by appointment.

It was not a popular measure. With the Cherokees, free elections had been the custom decades before the constitution had been thought of. Why, asked some, make a pretense of holding out against Georgia if every Cherokee liberty was to be surrendered one by one? It was not Chester, but Butrick, who reported that people murmured against the measure and threatened to disregard the acts of sheriffs so appointed.

The Ridges were further alienated. It was as if the measure had been designed expressly to deny them a hearing just when they had matters of urgent importance to impart. Chief Ross would not countenance the printing of the minority position in the *Phoenix;* Council would not listen; and this Council and this Chief were now to be continued indefinitely in office without giving the public a chance to make itself heard. Any doubts that The Ridge had had of the wisdom of his son's choice were swept away by these developments. John's point had been that the Cherokees could not maintain their national integrity in the East. Already his warning had been substantiated. Under duress the sovereign and independent Cherokee nation had suspended the processes of representative government.

However, with the public at large the murmuring died a natural death. The dilemma was obvious, and though the solution was unsatisfactory, no one could think of a better.

6.

"I love my country," Boudinot was writing, "and I love my people as my own heart bears me witness, and for that reason I should think it my duty to tell them the whole truth or what I believe to be the truth. I cannot tell them we will be reinstated in our rights when I have no such hope."

The lean, long-faced young Indian paused and stared at his words. They were part of his valediction to the *Phoenix*. He had had enough of Chief Ross's snubs and refusals to let him air an honest opinion in the press; on August 1 in the midst of the stormy Council session he had tendered his resignation. But because another editor could not immediately be found, he was continuing his duties another month. In the meantime, whether Chief liked it or not, he was working off some of his pent-up feelings for publication in the August 11 issue.

Boudinot, though not one of the delegates, had been with them in Washington, had shared their discouragement, and presently their decision. He had had the courage to assist them in presenting their point of view to Council, and was outraged by Ross's refusal to permit publication thereof in the *Phoenix*. To his mind Ross was consenting not only to unconstitutional government, but to the suppression of free speech. Ross had written him: "The toleration of diversified views in the columns of such a paper would not fail to create fermentation and confusion among our citizens, and in the end prove injurious to the welfare of the Nation. The love of our country demands unity of sentiment and action for the good of all."

What then, Boudinot indignantly demanded, was the *Phoenix* for? Had it any function at all under present circumstances? Boudinot thought not, and in turning in his resignation he recommended that the *Phoenix* itself be discontinued. As he saw it, it had two purposes, to defend Cherokee rights and to arouse the American people to Cherokee grievances. The first purpose had been achieved in the Supreme Court decision; the second the weary platform speaker now pronounced futile. The public "knows our troubles and yet it was never more silent than at present." The situation was hopeless, and not to say so was in Boudinot's mind the real treachery. Only three alternatives were left: to fight and be annihilated; to submit to oppression and suffer "moral death"; to remove. Boudinot saw hope only in the last; in any case he had demanded open discussion of the full situation—"and if possible come to some definite and satisfactory conclusion while there is yet time."

In Council, Boudinot had delivered himself of these unpleasant truths. He had also pointed out the significance of the Georgia survey, which many Cherokees had taken lightly; the land was to be distributed by lottery and a population that considered itself superior to the red men and would enslave them was to be loosed among the Cherokees. As for the Supreme Court decision, Chester was right when he said that the Cherokees were hoping too much from it. Jackson had recently made his attitude plain when he said in regard to his veto on the recharter of the bank, "the executive is not bound by the decision of the Supreme Court." Wrote Boudinot: "However unpleasant the fact may be to us, yet it is a fact which our eyes see fully demonstrated every day that the President of the United States does not intend to take the first step to defend the Cherokees under the decision of the Supreme Court. But this is not all—he now officially tells us that he is not bound by that decision and intends to disregard it. . . . But supposing he obeys and executes the mandates of the Court; that will be no relief to the Cherokees, for the action, we take it, of the tribunal which issues the mandate, terminates in the person of the individuals incarcerated in the penitentiary."

To speak thus to a nation whose overwhelming majority was determined to fight to the end, no matter how bitter that end, had taken courage on the part of Boudinot as it had for the Ridges. He had not been honored for his plain speaking; prophets who speak their minds under such circumstances are not the sort who can hope for contemporary honor in their own country. In the eyes of the Cherokees, Boudinot and his kinsmen were giving aid and comfort to the enemy. Their motives, Boudinot complained, had been misunderstood and misrepresented. Sadly he added to the *Phoenix* statement: "I have done what I could. . . . I have served my country, I hope with fidelity."

The resignation was accepted and on September 8 Elijah Hicks took over the management of the *Phoenix*.

The *Phoenix* issue containing Boudinot's point of view went into the world and was read by the editor of the New York *Spectator*, who added his own voice to the controversy. "Mr. Boudinot should remember, however, that in Jackson Nature's copy is not eterne, that there is no intention on the part of a majority of the people to let him play any more fantastic tricks before high heaven after the fourth of March, 1833."

For the Cherokees still had a rational basis for hope quite aside from the energy of their own determination. Jackson was coming up for re-election, and opposing him, quite certain to win, was a good friend of the Indians, one Henry Clay.

7.

It fell to Miss Sawyer to gauge the temper of the Cherokee plain folk at this time.

It was summer. First the hills had bloomed like wild rose gardens with the masses of mountain laurel; then the stately rhododendrons had come. Miss Sophia let out her school at New Echota and permitted herself an outing. She went with a Baptist missionary named Jones on a circuit of the Valley Towns.

Miss Sophia in her turn discovered the splendor of the Great Smokies, beloved by Butrick. The mountain roads were barely passable in their buckboard; often they rode twenty rugged uphill miles without seeing a cabin. Sometimes their hard-breathing horse stumbled at the edge of a precipice, and Miss Sophia only just didn't scream. But they arrived safely at the Valley Towns.

The Reverend Mr. Jones had come to help two native preachers conduct the ritual of the day of fasting and prayer appointed by Chief Ross. The people were alive to the solemnity of the occasion. At sunrise of July 19 they began assembling at the meetinghouse. They listened in silence to an account of the Nation's sins for which God was punishing them; the greatest of these, said a native preacher, was slavery.

After meeting they crowded around to hear what news the visitors had brought. Their faces darkened when they heard, for now, even in advance of Council, it was well known that the delegates had returned from Washington with a counsel of despair: the Federal government would not protect the Cherokees; they must remove or die.

"Then we will die," the Cherokees told Miss Sophia. "They shall not remove us. We will not leave this."

They looked about them at their possessions, and Miss Sophia, following their glance, thought these little enough: a few casual cabins, hillside corn patches, pastures where a few cows grazed. But in the look of their eyes she perceived that they saw more than she. They would not leave, she wrote, "a land which to them seems flowing with milk and honey."

Miss Sophia was right: they would not; they did not; to this day they have not.

CHAPTER XIII

The Pardon

The fine Indian summer weather that the Cherokees could usually count on for fall Council failed them when they assembled again at Red Clay on October 8. Rain and swollen rivers delayed Chief Ross on his way up from Head of Coosa; they had to mark time and wait for him.

Ross presented his annual message. He summarized Federal relations with the Indians in the terms of Monroe and Adams and characterized Jackson's dealings as a "newfangled system of policy." He pointed out what was, apart from love of the land itself, the essential Cherokee objection to compliance with the terms of the Removal Law: they would thereby forfeit their national character, become mere wards of the War Department. Council could do little for the present but hold fast, adopt legislative measures to keep the public informed, and hope that the "virtue of the people of the United States will ultimately control the faithful execution of their treaty obligations."

Chester was present. In spite of the protest of the Cherokees, Cass had again given him a letter to deliver. Council found the letter "dry and unwelcome," while as for Chester, according to Elijah Hicks's *Phoenix*, "only Lumpkin could be less popular with the Cherokees."

By this time Chester's reputation for double-dealing was doing the prestige of his clients, the missionaries, little good. In spite of Ann Worcester's warnings, both Worcester and the American Board seemed oblivious of the danger of the situation; apparently they discounted her testimony as that of a woman little experienced in worldly affairs and carried away by her emotions. Besides, she voiced suspicions rather than specific charges. It was left to Butler to report that when Chester had gone to Washington to help William Wirt prepare the case for the Supreme Court, he had made a deal with the Jackson men; he would make use of his strategic position of trust to induce the Cherokees to remove, and when he succeeded they would pay him for his work.

But when Butler learned this situation it was already too late by at least a year to undo the ingenious work of Chester.

Chester had repeatedly lied to the Cherokees about the plans of the missionaries. His lies were the more difficult to discredit in that each contained a germ of half-truth, and were in general, thanks partly to his efforts, prophetic of what actually happened. Some few, notably the Ridges and Boudinot, he was instrumental in winning over. With the general public his only achievement was the gradual growth of a suspicion that the missionaries were not such good friends of the Cherokees as they had pretended to be.

Stricken by the defection of such a man as The Ridge, the Cherokees now asked whom they could trust. Was there some chance that Chester, who even the *Phoenix* admitted looked like an intelligent man, was after all telling the truth about the prisoners? What significance lay in the fact that Boudinot, before his change of heart, had visited Worcester in Milledgeville? What exactly was going on in the penitentiary that Worcester, at least, had entered with so heartening a show of courage?

2.

But Worcester's courage had not been unshaken when he entered prison in September 1831. He was a very tired and saddened young man, worried for his wife's health, grieved for the child who had died during the summer of indignity and frantic uncertainty, and distressed by the conviction of some of his fellow missionaries that his course of action was not only injudicious but unchristian. Butrick carried his disapproval to bitter lengths; piqued by Boston's support of Worcester's views rather than his own, he at one time, according to his diary, threatened to resign from the American Board.

The first effects of prison life had been to restore the serenity of both captives. Ann Worcester, faced with the ultimate worst, had made a remarkable recovery; her husband need have no further anxieties on her account. Butler wrote in October: "Whilst in confinement I have had happy hours, some of the happiest of my life."

In the penitentiary the prisoners were receiving many tokens of sympathy from the world outside. Slanders had largely ceased; no one could now accuse Worcester of writing the *Phoenix*, which was getting along very aggressively without him. In submitting to arrest, the missionaries had demonstrated their integrity of purpose; in the states directly involved in the Cherokee affair—Tennessee, Alabama, and Georgia—they now commanded real respect.

"Could the voice of a majority in Tennessee be heard," a spokesman for the Union Presbytery of East Tennessee wrote Ann in October, "I verily believe the Cherokees and their missionaries would receive the protection that they ask. . . . I am more than ever encouraged in the belief that there is a redeeming spirit in the Christian republic which will soon put a stop to such measures of oppression."

Governor Gilmer was learning how high the reputation of the missionaries was in the country at large. At this point he gave place to Lumpkin and went North for an outing. A North Carolina innkeeper denounced to him the tyranny of his state; a Congressman expressed frank surprise at finding him of likable personality in spite of his record. Gilmer was taken aback by such encounters. It had not occurred to him that so many in the United States cared to mind Georgia's business. Wherever he went he was put to it to point out that in reality Worcester and Butler deserved no sympathy; they were inconsequential little people who had made the most of a chance to get national notoriety.

3.

In most Southern expressions of sympathy, real admiration for the missionaries' self-sacrificing devotion to duty was combined with a suggestion that this devotion had been misguided and misdirected. The missionaries were urged to reconsider; the pleas were the more effective bcause the sympathy was sincere.

Distinguished Georgians visited the missionaries in prison to pay respects to their principles and to argue with their premises. In November 1831, Worcester had conversations with Dr. Alonzo Church, president of Athens University, which ended by troubling him deeply and setting him to re-examining his course.

Dr. Church was, like Worcester, a Vermonter by birth, and though he had long lived in Georgia, his point of view was not parochial. His approach was warmly friendly. He insisted on giving the prisoners ten dollars for buying comforts, and applauded the strength of character that had enabled them to take their stand. But had Worcester, he asked presently, given careful thought to a possible result of his action? Did he realize that, carried to their logical conclusion, his acts would result in civil war? Georgia would not be coerced; a Supreme Court decision such as he hoped for could be executed only "at the point of a bayonet." Was Worcester really convinced that the local, sectional Cherokee cause was worth a national disaster?

Stoutly Worcester replied that if such men as Church were fearless enough they could dissuade the state from violence, and the conversation ended thus. But Church returned, and on his second visit, as he reported to Governor Gilmer, and the governor to Dr. Reese, he found Worcester "less fiercely convinced." And Reese told the Cherokees that Worcester was changing his mind.

Was he? Not even Worcester could have given a categorical answer to that question. Dr. Church, in insisting with manifest sincerity that his course would lead to civil war, had made a deep impression. It was not, to be sure, that the possibility of such a conflict had been ignored by the missionaries. Evarts in particular had been publicly quoted as proclaiming that war for so just a cause was preferable to national dishonor. But Evarts was dead; he was not on hand to guide either Worcester or the American Board. And Evarts had been reasoning from abstractions, had not been exposed quite as Worcester was to the personalities of these sincere and honorable Georgians whom he had unhesitatingly consigned to destruction.

It was Worcester, and almost Worcester alone—for Butler was a practical man who took life as it came—who was faced with the reality of the situation. Butler would probably do what *he* did. Worcester alone must decide if the newly created union were to be shattered by a war of brother against brother.

At least, that is the way Worcester saw his situation in the sleepless nights when he lay pondering the frightening issue; he had unwittingly, unhappily become a man of destiny. He described his conversation with Dr. Church, and agitatedly, almost incoherently urged the question raised by the latter on the Board for serious deliberation "if the probability be considerable if we may recede—I had almost said, perhaps I should say, we *must*."

Thus early had Worcester been shaken.

Now his letters to the Board were concerned with analyses of the psychology of Georgia. He asked Boston to deal warily with Georgians in the *Missionary Herald* so as "to diminish at least some of their unhappy prejudice. They are exceedingly sensitive and great care must be taken not to touch roughly any sensitive strings. The jealousy of the South towards the North stands greatly in the way of producing a happy effect. The asperity of the Northern prints must be carefully avoided. . . . There may be much piety and fear of the Lord even with those who support measures which to those at a distance it would seem as if piety and fear of the Lord would utterly preclude."

By January 1832 the mood of discouragement occasioned by all this self-questioning had advanced to such a point that Worcester asked for instructions if the Supreme Court case was lost. Should the prisoners then petition the governor for clemency?

It was only a request for guidance, but the very fact that he had raised such a question gave the watchful opposition substance for rumor. It was probably this knowledge that Worcester had so inquired that gave Chester the effrontery to approach John Ross with the statement that the missionaries were to seek pardon before their case could be tried.

4.

Chester to the contrary notwithstanding, neither the prisoners nor the American Board applied for such a pardon. On March 3, 1832, the case was decided, and no decision could have been more gratifying. It accomplished —on paper—everything that the missionaries had hoped to achieve for the Cherokees or for themselves. The private consciences of Worcester and Butler had been pub-

licly justified by the Supreme Court. No saint of legend
had ever been more spectacularly vindicated by sundry
miracles such as the turning of bread into roses. This was
the best kind of miracle, evidence that man would render
justice to man, that the ideals of the republic had not
been empty words.

But no such heady exultation (indeed, no exultation at
all) appears in the letters of the missionaries. They
seemed curiously indifferent to the moral aspects of their
victory. A letter by Worcester on March 29 was taken up
with the purely practical question of whether the Supreme
Court mandate would be honored in Georgia. Chester, always more interested in his contacts with officialdom than
with the missionaries, was taking his time about inform-
ing them. However, the prisoners knew Georgia too well
to expect anything but defiance. No matter what verbal
miracles had been worked in their behalf, they were exactly where they had been, in the penitentiary. They had
adapted themselves cheerfully to their confinement. No
trace of self-pity appears in their letters, but confinement
bravely endured is none the less wearisome, and there
were now no prospects that it would end within the appointed four years.

What, however, of Jackson? Could he connive with
Georgia in an act of nullification at the very moment
when he was attacking South Carolina's proposed nullification of the tariff issue? Logically, no. But Jackson rose
majestically above the petty syllogisms of Aristotelian
logic. Northerners might call it nullification in Georgia
too; Jackson need not; and even if he did, it was simpler
to crack nullification in South Carolina alone than to let
the state form a dangerous alliance with Georgia. For,
whatever Jackson's faults, he did clearly visualize his
responsibility of preserving the precarious federal union.
This might be not the most idealistic way to do it, not in
accord with the fine words of Thomas Jefferson and

George Washington; but the founding fathers were dead, and it was left to him, Jackson, to carry on the grimy business of administration in the best way that came to hand.

Not that Jackson necessarily went through any such mental processes in connection with the Cherokee affair. The simple fact was that he had no sympathy for Cherokee claims, was annoyed that the Indian question was still hanging fire two years after the passage of the Removal Bill, and desired to dispose of it with no further nonsense.

Also he had no affection for meddling missionaries. This the American Board discovered when they appealed to him to enforce the mandate. His correspondence with them contained a paragraph that discouraged further approaches: "I do not wish to comment on the causes of the imprisonment of the missionaries alluded to in the memorial, but I cannot refrain from observing that here, as in most other countries, they are by their injudicious zeal (to give it no harsher name) too apt to make themselves obnoxious to those among whom they are located."

5.

The Board nevertheless instructed Wirt to push the case further to see if anything could be done to force the hand of Jackson. And Worcester continued to debate the agonizing question, Could his end be achieved without provoking civil war, and was war in behalf of the Cherokees God's will?

Georgians assisted him in these reflections; they showered attentions on the prisoners in an effort to persuade them to seek pardon. For in spite of the demonstrated impotence of the Supreme Court, the presence of the prisoners in the penitentiary remained a reproach to the good name of Georgia and a potential threat to its sovereignty.

One typical appeal Worcester copied for the Board in

April 1832. Now that he had won his case, wrote "a lover of my God and country" from Washington, he could honorably ask for pardon. Not to do so could only have one of two results, both injurious: impairment of the authority of the Supreme Court, or civil war. The time had come to think of expediency rather than of abstract principles. The letter closed with an insinuation that Worcester had not heard for some time, a statement that there was "a growing inclination to believe that you are agents for the purpose of producing political effects. . . . You may not be so generally considered martyrs if things come to the worst."

Occasionally there was a note of different tenor, like one from a church in Tuscumbria, Alabama, which promised to direct its prayers to the enforcement of the Supreme Court decision and hoped that if this did not happen, strength would be given the prisoners to endure persecution.

And back in the Nation, Ann Worcester had only one prayer, that the prisoners would endure to the end. No consideration of expediency impressed the single-hearted, steadfast Ann; to her, right was right, and surrender wrong.

Not even Governor Lumpkin could persuade her. He made a personal attempt to do so. Some months after the Supreme Court decision, Ann Worcester and Lucy Butler came to Georgia to visit their husbands, and were invited to dinner by the governor, no less. For a governor to receive in his home the wives of two felons was hospitality indeed; they did not refuse, and the governor put himself out to be gracious. He had no animosity against their husbands, he told them across the candlelit table; it was all principle with him. But Ann too had her principles. To a suggestion that the prisoners could get their freedom by the simple act of petitioning for it she firmly shook her head. Such action would be wrong.

But Ann was none the less afraid. Well aware of the pressures to which her husband was being subjected, she dreaded their effect. He must not give in; God give him strength.

6.

Worcester, however, did not after all have the holy fire and endurance of the prophets and martyrs of old. Neither did Butler. They gave in; they asked for pardon and got it. On December 7, 1832, Worcester wrote for both asking the Board to come to a specific decision. His letter, a long one, summarized arguments presented to him by Georgian callers. Particularly impressive had been a representative of the Georgia Legislature who claimed that his whole sympathy was with the Cherokees, but that the situation was hopeless and that he could only urge the missionaries to remove a threat to national security by giving up. On December 19, Worcester added further political intelligence. He had discovered that those who urged him to surrender were friends of the Union; nullifiers hoped he would persist, for the effect was to swing the state to the support of South Carolina.

On Christmas Day of 1832 the members of the Prudential Committee of the American Board assembled in their rooms on Pemberton Square, Boston. They had a heavy decision to make. They read Worcester's letter and reviewed the whole history of the Cherokees versus the state of Georgia; then each gave his opinion. When these were tabulated they found that they were in agreement on two points: Worcester and Butler might now honorably seek pardon; the Cherokees must be advised that hope had ended; they must remove.

This decision went out from Boston on December 26; on January 7, 1833, it arrived in Milledgeville. Worcester and Butler at once instructed Wirt to prosecute their case no further, and applied to Governor Lumpkin for pardon.

They did not at once receive it. The tone of their petition, which explained that their application was not based on any change of principle but only on a fear of harming their country, displeased Lumpkin. He did not, he austerely told them, expect supplication, but he must insist on a respectful application "to the justice and magnanimity of the state." It took the missionaries several days to bring themselves to the required revision; in particular they balked at the word "justice." Finally they evolved a compromise phrasing: "to leave the question of the continuance of our confinement to the magnanimity of the state." Lumpkin examined this document and decided it would do. On January 14 the prisoners were informed by their good friend Mills that they were free; next morning they set out for home.

7.

It was now sixteen months since they had been imprisoned, and it was delicious to be free again. For nearly a year and a half their eyes had been wearied by looking on horizons no higher than those afforded by the narrow quarters of the penitentiary. Now at last they lifted their eyes again to the hills, the lordly, incomparably lovely Cherokee hills, and they breathed again the bright air that came down from the forested mountain tops.

But this sense of happy release, concerning which they naturally made no reports, being serious men and not enthusiasts like Miss Sophia or Dan Butrick, quickly ran its course. They examined the human details of the country to which they had returned, and Worcester, at least, was appalled by what he saw. What had been a generally sober, industrious, progressive people had, during his absence, suffered a tragic deterioration.

It must be remembered that Georgia's law of 1828 had suspended every Cherokee law within Georgia's limits. When it went into effect in June 1830, Ross, his assistant

Lowry, and The Ridge had made a circuit of the Nation, instructing local Cherokee courts and sheriffs to go ahead with business as usual, enforcing their own laws as they always had. It had been impossible for the Cherokees to obey that directive. Georgia had retaliated by making such enforcement a penal offense, and the Cherokees, while awaiting action on the two Supreme Court suits and their protests to Congress and the American people, could not take direct action against Georgia. In effect, through no fault of their own, they had become a lawless nation.

The newly liberated prisoners were appalled to see how general drunkenness had become, even among small children. Miss Sophia, a lady who did not spare the rod when occasion demanded, was hard put to it to keep her children away from a grogshop newly opened in New Echota. Its proprietor, pretending tender sympathy for the Cherokees and loathing for the brutal Georgians, pressed his wares on passers-by of any age; then, when he got them drunk, he suddenly became all Georgian, invoked unsuspected Georgia laws upon them.

Sober, the Cherokees were a friendly, quiet folk; drunk, they were quarrelsome. So there was disorder, violence, even murder. Every few days, Worcester reported in April, there was a new murder in the Nation and nothing done about it.

Worcester beheld this degradation with grief; and yet it curiously comforted him. His spiritual struggle in the penitentiary to discover where true wisdom lay had been long and severe; in asking the Board to decide for him he had recognized that he himself lacked the grace to decide the issue to the unequivocal satisfaction of his tender conscience. Even after his resolution had been taken and acted upon he was still haunted by the question whether it had been right.

Now, looking at the condition of the Nation, he was certain, or thought he was. The Cherokee situation was

intolerable. His tragically misunderstood friend Boudinot
was right: for the Cherokees to cling to their land under
such circumstances could only result in moral death. And
there was no persuading the Cherokees to give up while
one faint hope was left them. Worcester in prison had
represented such a hope. Kinder to them to force them to
face the realities of their situation by destroying the last
illusion. Yes, there was no doubt about it; the surrender
had been right.

Or was it? Again and again Worcester settled the issue
only to find himself doubting again. In spite of himself
these doubts intruded into his letters to the Board, letters
that should have been devoted wholly to practical affairs.
Should he have surrendered?

No one in so many words and to his face had quarreled
with his decision. To be sure, Chief Ross, now in Washington with the latest delegation, had been distressed by
the Prudential Committee's Christmas Day resolution. "I
can but feel that the expression of this opinion was in
some ways premature." But Ross in no way blamed
Worcester and Butler; they could hardly have acted otherwise, he told the former in a cordial letter of congratula-
tion.

But even this generous letter gave Worcester cause for
uneasiness. Ross had mentioned steps he had taken to
suppress a slander that the missionaries had got their
freedom by taking an oath of allegiance to Georgia. People then were behind his back imputing to him dishonorable acts. Good that the Chief was giving the lie to such
talk; still, talk there was.

Once aware of this fact, Worcester discovered a subtle
difference in his relations with the Cherokees. He who
had dared so much for this people was now perceptibly
less popular than before he had done anything at all. No
one said anything to him directly; but his flock, silent,

unreproaching, turned inscrutable eyes away from him, as from a leader whose courage had not been equal to the final test, a shepherd who had strayed from his sheep. Sometimes when he held meeting only strangers came to hear him; people who knew him kept away.

Worse still was evidence that the whole Mission Board had lost face with the Cherokees. An itinerant preacher named Adams had been pressed into the service during the absence of the prisoners. After their release Adams began to meet with hostility. In April 1833 some drunks near Hightower threatened to kill his interpreter "because he followed the missionaries about persuading the people to go to Arkansas." At Six Towns next day he found people "bitterly prejudiced against the missionaries and religious people thinking that they are friendly to emigration. I told them that there was nothing about Arkansas in the Bible and that I came to deal with their souls." But the Cherokees said that they could not longer listen to him without hypocrisy. "Some said they would believe the Gospel if Mr. Ross would tell them to do it."

Adams persevered nevertheless in his adventurous labors, sleeping sometimes in the woods, preaching sometimes "under the imperfect shade of a few peach trees."

Were the discourtesies offered the innocent Adams by the once courteous Cherokees the fault of Worcester? Had the whole work of the missionaries been imperiled by the unpopularity of his decision? Was it possible that the decision had been wrong?

Presently Worcester discovered that it was not entirely the pardon that had antagonized the Cherokees. It had indeed disappointed them, and a few had muttered about the conditions under which it had been secured, but it was not the real point. The special grievance against Worcester was that since his release he had become the inseparable companion of Boudinot.

8.

The friendship between Worcester and the former editor of the *Phoenix* was nothing new. From the moment that Worcester had discovered the young man's qualities he had refused to be parted from him. Their association had long ago attracted the attention of the Georgia Guard, who refused to believe that the Cherokees could publish the *Phoenix* without Worcester's supervision. Actually the dependence was the other way around. It was Worcester who had been unable to make headway in translating the Scriptures until he enlisted the services of the well-educated and intelligent young editor.

Released from prison, Worcester went back to this collaboration, only now with a difference. Hitherto he had had only the part-time services of the Cherokee. Now Boudinot was a full-time employee of the American Board.

Boudinot's stand for removal had cost him dear. Not only was he generally regarded as a turncoat, but he had lost the work on which he was largely dependent. He had, to be sure, twenty-five acres in cultivation, but these were just now yielding chiefly debts. Part of the crops that he had planted with the help of his father's slave and a hired servant had been ruined by drought, the rest by the wild hogs of a neighbor. Boudinot, now jobless except for his $100 a year from the Board, found himself after so unprofitable a season with a servant to pay, an ailing wife and five children to support, and the duty of providing proper Cherokee hospitality in a centrally located community where it was much sought.

Worcester heard of these difficulties in prison. At once he asked the Board to employ Boudinot full time at a salary of $300; later it was raised to $400.

During Worcester's imprisonment, the translation of St. Matthew and a Cherokee hymnal on which they had collaborated had come off the press at New Echota; Ann herself had helped Wheeler fold the paper for the binding. Both volumes had great success. The Baptists and the Moravians also made use of them, and disposed of so many hymnals that a second and even a third printing were demanded. Cherokees who would have no part in religious meetings put on their spectacles and sat down to pore over St. Matthew as revealed in Sequoia's alphabet.

It was time such as these were given more food for thought. Worcester and Boudinot set to work with a will on a translation of St. John and the Acts of the Apostles. Absorption in creation began to relieve the unhappy introspection of the former; and his dismay at the conditions in the Nation gave way to the projection of plans for a happier future. Sequoia's alphabet, for instance: had not the time come to teach it systematically? Half the Nation knew it already, but some, he suspected, had contented themselves when they knew a few words and made no really practical use of it. Besides, punctuation was something Sequoia hadn't thought of. Perhaps it would be wise to send a qualified native teacher on circuits through the Nation to give further instructions. Also it was time to introduce the syllabary into the mission schools, for children who learned to write English seldom learned to write in their own language.

Worcester never carried out the latter project; the fact that mission teachers had not learned Cherokee was too serious a stumbling block. But a native teacher, one Jesse, did presently ride circuit to offer classes in the syllabary, and in spite of the misery of the Cherokees at that time he had much success. Perhaps the very misery contributed to that success. There had always been something spiritual about their feeling for their alphabet; it was their own, something that could not be taken from them; in the days of their distress they still clung to it.

In spite of these plans, Worcester's doubts still lingered. Once a word from Boudinot, who appeared to have no doubts at all, set him to self-questioning again. Boudinot had just shown him, in March 1833, a paper from the world outside, reporting that the South Carolina issue had been settled at last. "Without war?" Worcester had asked.

Boudinot smiled. "Oh," he said, "they aren't going to war, much less for the Indians."

Boudinot's assurance that, whatever white men might fight about, it wouldn't be Indians, stirred up again the sediments of doubt. It had been fear of civil war that had induced Worcester to yield. Had the fear been groundless? Had he surrendered to no end more noble than that of getting out of jail?

Worcester had acted, however, in good faith, to the best of his understanding, and what he had done could in no case be undone. The introspection in his letters gradually gave way to pragmatic consideration of how soon he had better remove to the West. The Georgians had served him notice that his mission would be seized under the lottery system; such action was illegal, but he knew now how little could be done about Georgia's illegalities. His work in the East was done. Best now to go West and prepare for the coming of his flock, who would one day be glad that he had in the end acted, if not heroically, at least realistically, and by so doing had demonstrated the insubstantial nature of their hopes.

What in the meantime of Ann? Her husband had done what she had prayed he need never do. But when he came home he took over the duty of reporting to the American Board; her feelings are not on record. The rest of her life, which was to be a short one, was silence.

As for the Cherokees, they were a stubborn people. Without possible basis for hope, they nevertheless endured.

CHAPTER XIV

Indian Chief

Dean of all the missionaries to the Cherokees was the Moravian Gottlieb Bynham, who with Steiner had begun work in 1801, sixteen years before the founding of Brainerd. Now, in November 1832, Brother Gottlieb, grown too old to play his part further in the increasingly intense Cherokee drama, retired and left the care of his mission to a younger man, the Reverend H. G. Clauder.

Spring Place, near the present Dalton, Georgia, was one of the most gracious spots in the Nation. It was dignified by the finest of old Cherokee homesteads, built by James Vann about 1799, a two-story brick house, high-ceiled, built on simple classic plan with a "floating" stairway in the front hall. The mission, where Boudinot had received his early schooling, stood near by in its famous garden of herbs collected through the years from Europe and America and cultivated with loving care. Even medicine men and old wives, who in other respects hardened their hearts against the missionaries, took a fascinated professional interest in the aromatic details of that herb garden.

On the eve of that Christmas Day of 1832 when the Prudential Committee was to go into dismal conclave on the fate of the Cherokees, the last of the fall had smoldered out in the sweet gums and hickories about Spring

Place, but hardy roses still bloomed in the garden. Brother Clauder, peacefully at work on a sermon, was interrupted by a knock. Several strangers stood at the door, white men.

"I represent," said their spokesman ingratiatingly, "the fortunate drawer of this place. He has given me power of attorney. You will pay your rent to me."

Fortunate drawer of what, demanded the astonished Clauder, and rent for what purpose? The gentleman had made a mistake; this was the Spring Place mission, for thirty-one years the property of the Moravian Brethren.

The stranger smilingly shook his head. The place had never been Moravian property: not even Indian law granted property rights to the missionaries; it had been held as a kind of loan, and now that arrangement had been annulled. The house and lot had been put up for distribution in the Georgia lottery of October; it had fallen to a fortunate drawer, who was now permitting Clauder to rent it for $150 a year.

Bewildered as Clauder was by these strange tidings, he could not have been entirely ignorant of their background. He too read his *Phoenix*, and had seen an editorial on the Georgia lottery set for October 22. Georgia's honor, Hicks had written, was "to be run through a sporting wheel to seize our lands. . . . The drawing of the lottery and the settling of our lands can never convey to Georgia a title; it can only be a forcible entry and illegal possession . . . will endanger further American institutions and plunge the general government into deeper and darker chaos." But Clauder, in common with most Cherokees, had not clearly visualized the lottery in practice, at least not as applying personally and to him.

But now a stranger stood at his door to claim possession.

Up to then there had been nothing belligerent about the Moravian Brethren. In 1831 they had compromised with Georgia law by retiring over the border until the excitement should have died down. But there was not in Brother Clauder sufficient meekness to comply with a demand that he pay rent to a stranger for use of a property that the Brethren had occupied with the blessing of the Cherokees and had developed at their own expense. It had never been his custom to deny hospitality to strangers, but he did so now. He closed his door in the faces of these men and bolted it; then he went back to his table, thrust his sermon aside, and wrote the government an appeal for help.

The government still had not been heard from when, on New Year's Eve, a covered wagon heaped with household effects drove up to the mission. This time the driver was the fortunate drawer himself, or so he said. The furniture he proposed to move into the house for the use of a company scheduled to arrive next day.

But neither the furniture nor the fortunate drawer got into the house that night. The furniture remained in the wagon, and the baffled drawer slept under the cold stars with his horses. The gentle Moravian Brother, who had never denied hospitality to the meanest of Cherokees, had bolted his door again.

Next morning the bolt was drawn, but not by Clauder. The interloper had told the truth; a company followed him on New Year's day. There were eighteen of them; they forced the door and tramped noisily about the house moving the possessions of Clauder and his family into two rooms designated for their temporary use. The house they converted into a tavern, the chapel into a courthouse, for Spring Place was now to be a Georgia settlement.

Thus began the New Year of 1833 for the Moravians and for the Cherokees.

2.

Clauder was one of the first to experience the effects of the Georgia invasion; he was not the last. In 1833 a trek of pioneers called into being by the lottery began moving their covered wagons down the red roads from Georgia to settle their families among the Cherokees. They were homesteaders, and as such more respectable than the gold miners and pony thieves; observers testified that they were prevailingly honest—except with the Indians.

In these early days the possessions awarded them appear to have been chiefly property abandoned by the Arkansas emigrants or the possessions of white men who had not taken the oath. This category naturally included the missionaries; Worcester and Butler had not been long home when they were notified that they were to be dispossessed. The lottery had given Georgia authority an excellent excuse to get rid of the troublemakers without re-arresting them and thus stirring up more inconvenient clamor. Much simpler to hand over all mission property to honest homesteaders; then the missionaries would have no choice but to get out.

Butler showed fight, his moral indignation reawakened by the heartbreak of a Cherokee member of his congregation who had been duped by white men into signing some vital papers. On the advice of Ross he carried the case to court, but while it was pending the family and followers of the white claimant moved into his meetinghouse, turned his horses out of the stable, and took such interest in peering through windows to spy on the doings of the mission family that Butler too gave up and moved to Brainerd. His parishioners wept when he left.

Later the Georgians were to find the "fortunate drawer" technique useful in applying pressure to the ringleader of Cherokee resistance. Real plums began to fall from the lottery wheel—the pick of Cherokee property, the estates of the chiefs. In 1828, when Ross had become principal chief, he had left his father's house at Rossville and had settled nearer the capital, not far from The Ridge, at the Head of Coosa. This home, according to a visitor, resembled the house of a "well-to-do farmer in the North," was distinguished within by a "small but well organized library" and without by peacocks, which the delighted Cherokees called "star feathers" and incorporated into legend.

In early April 1834 the estate was seized, peacocks and all, to say nothing of the ferry. Late one night Chief Ross rode home and found a stranger waiting to take his horse from him. His sick wife Quatie and her children had been crowded into two rooms while awaiting his return. Ross in turn followed the missionaries over the Tennessee line. He did not return to Rossville, probably because members of his family, including his brother Andrew, had joined the opposition, but roughed it in a cabin near Red Clay. Other chiefs followed suit. A member of the Hicks family was evicted in the dead of winter when snow lay on the ground.

The invasion disorganized Cherokee life more than anything that had happened before. To be sure, the rank and file of the people remained relatively undisturbed while the Federal government exhausted its efforts to make them listen to reason. But now while they plowed and planted, they could not rid themselves of the agonizing thought that fortunate drawers were already moving up from Georgia to reap what they had sown. Besides, nearly everyone in the south and east of the Nation had neighbors who, while peaceable and industrious, made no secret of the fact that they regarded the Indians as a species of vermin.

If these conditions were not pleasant for the Cherokees, they had, in the opinion of the invaders, only themselves to thank. At their October Council in 1832 they had been fairly warned. Chester, speaking for Secretary Cass, had explained exactly how the lottery system would work. John Ridge had urged them to listen to reason and remove before conditions became unbearable.

But the Cherokees had turned from the counsel of such friends with aversion. They still clung to hope, this time the hope that in the impending presidential elections Jackson would be replaced by Clay. And even when the elections resulted in the defeat of Clay they persisted. They sent yet another delegation to Washington to present their grievances. This time they sent Richard Taylor, John F. Baldridge, and Joseph Vann; and Chief Ross went with them to make sure that these delegates were not seduced by the wiles of Washington.

3.

Without John Ross it is possible that Cherokee history might have taken a different course.

Strangely enough, though Ross was the trusted leader of his people for nearly forty years, nearly all Cherokee tradition is unflattering to him. Many of the North Carolina Cherokees have an ancestral impression that he was Jackson's man, and as such guilty of the horrors of removal. Such a tradition, fantastically in contradiction of the facts, offers a sobering commentary on the authenticity of oral tradition; it is, however, psychologically explainable by events that were to take place in 1838. In Oklahoma, where the descendants of the Ridge faction have been more articulate, have written more books than the Ross descendants, a common view is that Ross was an unscrupulous politician who deliberately misled his people in order to gratify his own ambition, and thus prevented their profiting by the kindly overtures of Jackson.

There is also a third point of view, also current in Oklahoma, that Ross was a hero without blemish and his opponents altogether outrageous. But there is a certain pallor to this legend, an insubstantiality, as there often is in traditions of the unco guid. The fact seems to be that, though Ross led his people ably for so many years, he did so by virtue of a prosaic dependability that does not lend itself well to legend. He seems to have lacked the magnetism of such a character as The Ridge, and since it was his fate to die of natural causes and in bed, tragedy did not endow him with the glamour with which it was to endow the Ridges and Boudinot.

Ross was no such speaker as The Ridge. To be sure, there is no historical basis for a fair comparison; only fragments of The Ridge's oratory are available, and those in pale translation; its power one can deduce only from its reported effect on contemporaries. Ross's talks, on the other hand, are preserved in the files of the *Phoenix*. They are common-sensible and pedestrian. Not for him the Shakespearian turn of phrase accredited to The Ridge, though once in a while, as in his words "in the appearance of impossibilities there is still hope," he said something that sticks in the mind. Like John Ridge, Ross's English style had been formed by an educational philosophy that put correctness and pedantic rules of rhetoric above sincerity and simplicity. So when Ross wrote a speech or a letter he used the copybook phrases of neoclassicism.

There is sometimes something touching in the use of such phrases. Cherokees, unlike white folks, dared take no liberties with what they had been told was proper. They were parvenus in the civilized world. Always there lay upon them the onus of proving by meticulously correct conduct that they were no longer savages. For the Cherokees the virtue of Ross's speeches lay not in his style, but in that they were all of a piece and contained good sense. That in the long run the dry reasonableness of Ross counted more with them than the emotional effects of The Ridge's oratory is a commentary on their advancement. It must also be added that Ross told them what they wanted to hear, and The Ridge presently did not.

There was nothing of the untutored savage about Ross. He had so little Cherokee blood that it is surprising that his enemies did not assail him on this ground. Eventually it did occur to Georgia to do so, but belatedly, and with unfortunate results for the state's reputation. Ross's nearest Cherokee relative was his grandmother, Anne Shorey, who was herself only a half blood. But though Ross's ancestors were with this one exception pure Scotch, though he had a white man's education from a tutor, John Barber Davis, and brief attendance at an academy in Kingsport, Tennessee, and much reading in his father's library, though he looked white, no one, either friend or foe, ever thought of him in these years as other than a Cherokee.

If John Ridge was a red man who learned to think white, Ross was a white man who thought red. Growing up in the heart of Cherokee country, under the shadow of Lookout Mountain, where his name is still preserved by the city of Rossville, Georgia, he ran around with Cherokee playmates, learned with them the uses of blowgun and bow, dressed like them in hunting shirt and leggings, fought them if they dared call him "Unaka" or white, and attended as seriously as they the Green Corn Festival. His brief attendance at the Kingsport school was no more interruption in this agreeable forest life than the attendance of his full blood companions at the school of the Moravian Brethren.

True, he and his brother Lewis were set to work as apprentices in a white man's store, and lived awhile with a white family. But presently John was back at Ross's Landing (Chattanooga) to set up a trading post of his own in partnership with J. Meigs, kinsman of Return Meigs, the Indian agent. At the plantation he later established near what is now Rome, Georgia, he was so successful that the missionaries say that in 1839 he refused, on principle, an indemnity of $20,000 for his property. But all of these activities and the business trips to the North which they periodically entailed were characteristic not only of Southern planters, but of the more prosperous Cherokees. In many ways Ross's business life ran parallel to that of his friend The Ridge, some twenty years his senior.

Any temptation that Ross may have felt to become a white man was arrested by his marriage to Quatie, who, though apparently not a full blood, was nearly so. She cooked Cherokee (her recipe for roasting corn ears is on record) and thought Cherokee and attended the oldest of the Cherokee missions, that of the Moravians, though Ross himself became a Methodist. Furthermore she bore him a brood of children (one of whom Ross sent to Princeton) whose tawniness would have determined his future for him even if his own inclinations had not. (Ross in his late years, Quatie having died on the Trail of Tears, was to remarry; this time his choice was a seventeen-year-old white girl, a Quaker, to whom he was devoted. Hence there are two sets of Ross descendants in Oklahoma, one white, one red, the red being by far the more numerous.)

Ross's earlier proclivities were all Cherokee. He, too, was a veteran of the Creek campaign, that ironic victory in which the Cherokees had established the reputation of their archenemy Jackson instead of shooting him down as some veterans now wished they had done.

After this campaign he took an active part in Cherokee politics. It seems to have been Ross who first saw that Cherokee opposition to the aggressions of Georgia must be conducted on legal grounds; he who more than any other was responsible for remodeling the tribal government into a miniature republic with a written constitution; and his knowledge of the writings of Jefferson that enabled the Cherokees to present memorials of dignity and moving appeal to Congress. For though Ross himself was no memorable writer, he did know how to make effective selection from the works of one whom even the most reactionary of Congressmen were bound to respect. There was real originality in this device; for an erstwhile "savage" people to plead their cause by quoting the Declaration of Independence to a country dedicated to that doctrine was an inspiration, almost a stroke of genius. Ross himself was no such statesman as Sequoia was philosopher, but he had qualities worthy of honor.

The ability of young Ross, his integrity as evinced in 1823 when he exposed Chief McIntosh's attempt to bribe him, had impressed his countrymen. In 1827 he, with The Ridge, succeeded Pathkiller and Charles Hicks, and in 1828 he was elected principal chief. It is unfortunate for his reputation that elections were impracticable in 1832, for the fact that he was thus unconstitutionally retained in office gave the opposition a chance to call him a schemer who maintained himself by illegal means. In doing so, however, Ross had not acted by fiat but by vote of Council; also, contemporary observers were all of the opinion that had the elections been held, Ross would have won almost unanimously. Later, when constitutional government was resumed in Oklahoma, he was to be not only a third-, fourth-, but almost a tenth-termer, was to remain principal chief until the outbreak of the Civil War threw the Cherokees into a state of confusion that not even Ross could cope with. The Ridges and Boudinot were never to command more than a handful of followers. Their decision to work for removal created such antagonism that Ross may have averted or at least postponed bloodshed by refusing to allow them to express themselves in the *Phoenix*.

For the sake of the record, however, let two charges of the Ridge faction be admitted: in 1832 Ross did countenance violation of the constitution; and he did restrict freedom of speech.

4.

One thing stands out in the mission letters. Barring the small minority factions, the people trusted John Ross, sometimes almost blindly. The statement of the Cherokee who told Adams that he would believe the Gospel if the Chief told him to believe sounds like cynicism, but may have been a simple statement of fact. Faith in the unassuming Ross could go to such lengths. Chester, commenting on the Council of 1832, had indignantly reported that the full bloods let the Chief do their thinking for them. The bitterest charge of the Ridge faction was not that Ross remained illegally in office, but that he used his great prestige to delude his people.

If Ross deluded anyone, however, it was for the honest reason that he himself was deluded. Perhaps he was somewhat naïve. That certain Congressmen were sympathetic encouraged him too readily in the optimistic belief that the rest of Congress would eventually follow their lead. Himself intent on the rights of the Cherokee case, he was too often blind to the compulsions of expediency that also motivate Congressmen and presidents. Yes, he was naïve, and yet in justice to him it must be pointed out that the contest for Cherokee rights was always close. The opposition to the Removal Bill had been powerful: John Marshall lent the weight of his authority to the contentions of the Cherokees; and when the Senate finally condemned them, it did so by the margin of one vote. Ross had well said that in the appearance of impossibilities there was still hope; there was always hope, to the very last, and Ross and the Cherokees clung to it.

It must also be observed of Ross as of the earlier Ridge that his power lay in his identification with the spirit of his people. Had Ross in 1832 swung over to the Ridge faction he might have fared as ill as they. In the final days of Cherokee resistance, government agents were to testify that it was not so much Ross who led the people as the people who led Ross. Had he, they said, dared abandon his policy, they would instantly have repudiated him.

For all his pleasant estate in Georgia, for all his impressive contacts in Washington, Ross was a man of simple and friendly habit, his house open to visitors of whatever degree. John Howard Payne has described his later home in Oklahoma. Wayfaring Cherokees crowded in after a Council as a cheery matter of course to seek hospitality for the night. They stretched out on the floor and gossiped the night through; whenever it seemed that sleep had come, someone would think of a new joke, and the chatter and chuckling would begin anew. There was nothing remote or austere about a celebrity who adapted himself to such customs.

Most of the missionaries liked him. Butler reported an 1830 incident that he said was characteristic of the chief. In the midst of the turmoil occasioned by the eviction of the pony thieves, while the Cherokees were gathered at Ross's home to discuss how to counter retaliatory measures taken by the Georgians, a white man stopped his shabby wagon outside and came to ask the way. He was a stranger, and white strangers at the moment were a cause for alarm. Nevertheless, none cast the forlorn nobody so much as a hostile glance, and the chief himself interrupted his conference to point out the way and sketch a rough map in the dirt of the road.

Butler later reported that Ross had, without seeking it, the popularity that young Ridge sought diligently and in vain. Butrick so admired the chief that Boston warned him against partisanship—this to the latter-day apostle who had steadfastly refused to let Ross persuade him to exert his influence in political affairs. The chief had endeared himself to Butrick by taking time out, in the midst of preoccupations with more urgent matters, to introduce him to "wise and ancient chiefs of the Nation" so that

Butrick might pursue further his researches into Cherokee lore. "He is the same lovely man as ever," Butrick wrote fondly of Ross, "supported by all those sentiments of virtue, dignity and honor which ever characterized him as a friend, a gentleman and a patriot."

5.

At the close of 1832 the new Cherokee delegation, Ross included, left for Washington. Ross had undertaken the journey for the same reason that latter-day plenipotentiaries fly oceans and continents to confer. The situation had become too grave to entrust to delegated authority alone. Besides, the last time a delegation had been sent unchaperoned to Washington the result had been the demoralization of the delegates and dissension in the Nation. It was time for Ross, who knew all the right people and enjoyed considerable prestige among them, to intervene personally.

The delegates arrived January 8, 1833, and settled themselves at the Indian Queen Hotel. This was a distinguished address, worthy of the dignity of the Cherokee Nation. Here Jackson had recently snubbed the South Carolinian Calhoun by his toast to the Union at the Jefferson Day dinner. Later, when their stay lengthened interminably, the delegates moved to Brown's Hotel, a more modest hostelry. But in the meantime Ross had busied himself to see that they made the right contacts.

They had at least two interviews with Jackson, several conferences with Secretary of War Cass, and were much in the society of the sympathetic Frelinghuysen; but the results of all these parleys, as Ross freely admitted to a May session of the Council and in a long report printed in an August issue of the *Phoenix*, were negligible.

They had hardly arrived before Frelinghuysen gave them shocking news from Boston: the American Board had asked Frelinghuysen to tell the Cherokees of their decision to accept a pardon for the missionaries and to urge the Indians to remove. It was an unhappy task for the Senator; he himself refused to take the responsibility of advising them to the step recommended by Boston. But he did not desert them, generously gave them his time, watched their progress, and now and then cautiously sounded them on possible solutions to their dilemma— citizenship for instance, or even removal. He found them, as he wrote Dr. Wisener of the Board, inflexibly determined to stand their ground. "They resent all suggestions but the faithful fulfillment of our treaty obligations."

Their conversations with Cass opened auspiciously. He led them in person to the president's office and gave them a dinner. Then, in answer to a long memorandum of their grievances and an appeal that the government satisfy the claims of the "fortunate drawers" by allotting them land elsewhere, he replied with an invitation to talk it over as simpler than so much correspondence. But when he saw them it was only to urge on them the benefits of removal. Only a few would suffer from such transplanting, he said —the well-to-do people like themselves. "I may appeal to their better feelings whether a transfer of their residence, essential as it is to the existence of this people, ought not to be cheerfully made."

Ross in his report to May Council was reticent as to what went on in the two talks with Jackson. It was Frelinghuysen who said that the president brought up the Supreme Court issue and that "other unwarranted things were spoken." It is known, however, that Jackson made Ross an offer of $2,500,000, which he later raised to $3,000,000, for all the land except that in North Carolina, and that Ross refused. The gold mines alone were worth more, he pointed out, and how could the President guarantee the Indians protection in the West when he could not give it in Georgia?

Congress was then in short session, and so preoccupied with the South Carolina nullification issue that Ross dared not memorialize the body lest the Cherokee claims be confused to their detriment with nullification. Yet, as he pointed out to May Council, Georgia was putting into practice a principle that South Carolina had asserted only in theory. Congress had now given the president power to suppress nullification. "Whether this Nation will be benefited by the decisive acts of Congress . . . is a fact which will depend as much on the unity of the Cherokee people themselves as on the wisdom and integrity of their representatives."

Unity. Even in Washington the delegates had been bedeviled by the activities of the unauthorized delegation which was willing to discuss removal. The egregious Jack Walker had appointed it. And at May Council, as Ross well knew, The Ridge himself was preparing to attempt to sway the people to removal.

6.

But before May Council, Ross received a wonderful piece of news. For a moment it looked as if in spite of all the disheartening events in Washington a new day had come for the Cherokees.

Returning in March to find the Nation beset with "fortunate drawers," Ross had written Elbert Henning of the Department of Indian Affairs for help. The reply had been gratifying beyond hope. Henning wrote back that he had given prompt orders for the expulsion of the intruders, that a military force "will forthwith be sent to the assailed parts of your country for the purpose of expelling and keeping out the intruders. . . . You cannot consider it a misplaced assurance and it is made with the utmost sincerity that the Department cherishes deep solicitude for the welfare of your people and will to the extent of its power endeavor to promote it."

Such glad tidings Ross did not keep to himself. Why should he? He passed the letter about.

But some Cherokees hesitated to take the letter at face value. One was John Ridge. He took it on himself to write Cass to inquire if Ross's optimistic interpretation was correct; William S. Coodey, Major Ridge, and John Fields added their names to his inquiry. Enemies claimed that Ridge sent a similar inquiry and a copy of Henning's letter to Governor Lumpkin.

In any case Lumpkin saw Henning's warm promise of help, and at once took action. He wrote Cass that Henning's letter had been indiscreet and charged the Secretary to remove at once the basis of the Cherokees' "idle delusion." Cass's reply went to the governor, who, receiving it on the eve of May Council, posted it by courier some 220 miles to young Ridge at Red Clay. At least such was the contention of the *Phoenix*, which said that Ridge didn't dare present it personally to Council lest his correspondence with Lumpkin bring him into further disrepute with the Cherokees.

The Cherokees, however, were not kept in ignorance of the nature of the reply. Again their brief joy was dampened. For Henning's promise, it was now explained, did not apply to citizens of Georgia or Alabama, but only to intruders from Tennessee and Carolina. His promise, therefore, was no help at all.

Worcester, watching the development of this affair, wrote the Board that Ross's prestige was bound to suffer from his misinterpretation of Henning's letter. Nothing of the sort happened. As a matter of fact, the misunderstanding seems to have originated, not with Ross, but with crossed wires in the War Department. It was John Ridge, the skeptic, who further lost face by going over Ross's head to insist that the Secretary of War straighten out a departmental inconsistency. "A consummate act of treachery," the *Phoenix* called it, and accused Ridge and his associates of influencing Cass to change an originally benevolent policy.

There began to be talk of impeaching the Ridges.

7.

There were two councils in 1833, the called-Council in May and the regular session in October. Both met in Red Clay, now recognized as the emergency capital of the Cherokees. Some Tennesseeans were disturbed by this distinction, and also by the number of refugees from Georgia persecution who were now finding asylum within the state. But in spite of the fact that Georgia had not relaxed its pressure to induce Tennessee to extend its jurisdiction over the Indians, sympathy for the Cherokees was in Jackson's state still strong enough to postpone such action.

The May Council, called to hear Ross's report from Washington, listened also to a plea from The Ridge to accept the inevitable. His eloquence did not stir them; they heard him through, but according to Enrolling Agent Curry, who also attended, would not admit his speech to the records.

In the memorial to Cass drawn up in this meeting there was, however, a first recognition of the possibility that removal might be forced upon them. If they were so forced, they now announced, they would not accept land in the Arkansas country, but would go beyond the limits of the United States. This form of removal was to receive some consideration by Ross and his friends. If the United States would not live up to its obligations, they would put themselves forever beyond the reach of such a government. Texas was spoken of in this connection, and the Oregon country. This solution, however, was never very seriously entertained: the one desire of the Cherokees was to remain where they were.

At the October session, Ross had only one piece of good

news to offer his anxious people. All else was unfavorable. The resolutions sent to Cass in May had brought only a reply from Acting Secretary John Robb that the president "considers it useless to continue any further correspondence on the subject of Cherokee difficulties." Intemperance was causing much disorder. Cherokee laws against whisky peddling could not be enforced and the Federal government would not enforce its own. The only hope for controlling the situation lay in example and persuasion. Let the Council, said Ross, "resist the monster and persuade others to do likewise."

But there was good news from Alabama. This state had extended its laws over the Cherokees, but more from a desire to please Georgia than from any craving to regulate Cherokee destinies. In September an Indian charged with murder had been brought before Judge Adair of Alabama. The latter, yielding to the plea of counsel that the jurisdiction of Alabama over the Cherokees was repugnant to the treaties, had declared the Alabama law null and void and had returned the accused to the authorities of his own country. Ross expressed his gratification over this decision.

The heart of his speech was an urgent appeal for national unity. Division was being created by the fact that individuals continued to enroll for removal in spite of a unanimous resolution of the May Council condemning such practice. The danger lay not only in the enrollments themselves, but in the disrupting spirit of party strife that accompanied such action. Ross was too cautious a politician to name names, but none could mistake the direction of his thought when he said that whenever differences arose "the sentiments of the majority should prevail, and whatever measure is adopted by the majority for the public good [it] should be the duty of the minority to yield and unite in support of the measure; this is the rule of order sanctioned by patriotism and virtue."

CHAPTER XV

Arkansas Travelers

At the Indian agency, a mile outside the town of
Hiwassee, government contractors were busy late in 1833
throwing together a series of barracks constructed of
roughhewn logs. These were to serve as a reception center
for Cherokees enrolled for emigration while they awaited
transportation to the Arkansas. For in spite of the expressed displeasure of John Ross and the condemnation
of Council, the activities of the Federal enrolling agents
and the pleas of members of The Ridge's party had produced some effect. Federal agents claimed that for this
particular exodus, scheduled for early 1834, they had
1200 emigrants. To receive them they were construct-
ing a small metropolis of log shelters, twenty-eight in
all.

Other preparations, probably not entirely authorized,
were made to relieve the tedium of the emigrants while
they awaited the flatboats. The travelers were known to
be in possession of ready cash, annuity money; white
traders arranged to possess themselves thereof; they came
drifting down the Hiwassee in "floating doggeries," boats
stocked with pies, cakes, fruits, and, best of all, cider,
applejack, and whisky. These were available to the Cherokees at a price.

In early February emigrant families began to straggle

down from their hills, all sorts of keepsakes crammed into their packs and blanket rolls, and settled themselves to wait in camp. They investigated the possibilities of entertainment, and in many cases preferred the fare provided by the doggeries to what the government offered. Those who frugally stuck to the government ration of salt pork and flour developed queasy stomachs. But those who frequented the doggeries could not always limit themselves to fruit and cakes when more enlivening refreshment was offered. Hiwassee, a quiet settlement not hitherto noted for its night life, began to be overrun by loud, drunken carousers, male and female.

Even when the Cherokees were sober, the camp, as it filled up, was not an appetizing place. Decent enough in their widely spaced forest homes, where they could observe their own taboos against filth, the Cherokees had no acquaintance with the military discipline that can maintain sanitary conditions in crowded quarters. The latter, to be sure, were by no means as crowded as had been anticipated. Of the 1200 expected, only 457 were finally mustered in. The rest had changed their minds about emigration. It happened that the *Phoenix* columns were just then full of stories of cholera epidemics, in the West among other places. Many a Cherokee about to leave his home read his paper and decided to elude the government agents and stay where he was. The conditions created by the Georgians were pestilential enough, heaven knows; but cholera sounded even worse.

So the Cherokees encamped on the Hiwassee were only about a dozen to the cabin. But even at this rate, as a housing project their camp left much to be desired. They couldn't maintain personal cleanliness; they were further crowded by having brought some of their livestock with them, particularly their ponies; their stomachs were in rebellion against the monotony of the salt pork diet, and some of them were often drunk.

They began to sicken, particularly the children. Measles broke out. Long exposed to white men's diseases, the Cherokees under normal living conditions possessed a racial immunity to the more dangerous effects of measles. But here on the Hiwassee the disease regained its primitive strength; the children began to die while they awaited the flatboats.

2.

The party was in charge of an army officer, one Lieutenant Joseph W. Harris, and his assistant John Mills, white spouse of a Cherokee wife. Harris was an exceptionally sympathetic young man who found time out during his labors to keep a diary; far from looking down on the Cherokees, by the end of the journey he looked up to them. Even the "poisonous" squalor, as he called it, of their personal habits did not make him despise them, for he understood that the cause was not natural depravity, but circumstances beyond their control.

The dangers, however, he recognized at once. When the expedition finally started in two installments on March 14 and 15, he engaged a doctor to attend the party to Tuscumbria. All the way down from Hiwassee to Tuscumbria on the Hiwassee and the Tennessee, the six little steamers that maneuvered their way through the rapids and shoals of the Suck, the Boiling Pan, the Frying Pan, and the Skillet had to make periodic stops to bury children. Measles was still rampant, and a physician still a necessity. In Alabama, Harris took on a substitute, a Dr. Roberts. Roberts was not to see Alabama again.

There were other adventures of the voyage besides measles. A keelboat went down in the Tennessee, and although all sixty-seven Cherokees aboard were rescued, they grieved over the loss of their belongings. And the crowding was then worse than before.

Presently the boats swung around the bend into the Mississippi. Here there was another incident. One Anne

Reynolds was working on the afterdeck of a keelboat, cooking her salt pork over a fire, when she tripped and fell overboard. It was after sunset, and there was no finding her in the darkness. Thenceforth Harris ordered that all the fires, over which Cherokee housewives struggled to make the rations palatable, be extinguished at sundown.

By April they had entered the Arkansas, and there they stuck. The river was low, and after Little Rock they hit so many snags and shoals that towing became impossible.

Previously the journey, though no pleasure excursion, had at least been continuous. There had been the shifting scenes of the riverbanks to watch, and Cherokee children could make much of hailing each other from boat to boat. Now the journey came to a dead standstill. Even a party of 102 sent overland got discouraged and returned to Cadron's Creek, where the entire party camped and waited.

What they were waiting for was rain to swell the rivers or local residents to bring teams to sell. What they got was cholera. On April 15 the mysterious pestilence of which they had read in the *Phoenix* struck them down in camp.

There was no help for the Indians in this horror. Good Dr. Roberts was dead within a week; a doctor summoned by Harris from Little Rock would not remain. The whites of the countryside turned deaf ears to all appeals for help, and kept carefully out of the way of the Indians—all but a few horse thieves, who sometimes ventured near enough to make way with an Indian pony. Harris himself fell ill, though apparently not of cholera, for he managed to keep to his feet and attend to his responsibilities as best he could.

The conduct of the Cherokees in this crisis made Harris wonder if Indians might not be superior to whites. They had, indeed, at the outbreak of the pestilence, scattered in terror to the woods, where they built camps over wide areas. But this device was common sense and may have saved them; to have remained in their "poisonous" quarters on the river might have meant complete disaster. In the woods also, as the sickness worsened, the Indians took to burning the underbrush. Whether this maneuver improved the medical situation or not, at least it did not worsen it.

In spite of precautions, fifty Cherokees died of cholera, swelling the death roll of the emigration to eighty-one. And when death came, the Indians bore themselves with a silent dignity that wakened the admiration of Harris. It was the whites and half-breeds who in this crisis fell prey to a thousand superstitions, who shuddered away from the necessity of tending the victims of the plague, and who, when the worst came, gave way to noisy lamentation. The full bloods, on the contrary, cared for their sick, buried their dead, performing the last office with a self-control that Harris called sublime. "The grief of the whites in my party is louder and more distressing," he wrote in his diary, "yet less touching than the untold sorrow of the poor Indians."

By April 27 the crisis had sufficiently abated for Harris to reorganize the expedition. Fourteen wagons had been found to carry the sick. All who could stand upright walked beside them, some of them barefoot. Their property they had to abandon for a time, all but blankets, cooking utensils, and what else they could load on their backs. By May 8 they had reached the new Cherokee country and were preparing to disband. But half of these survivors, according to Harris, died during the first year of settlement. He himself returned to his task of overseeing removal, but died in 1837 without living to see the climax of the Cherokee story.

3.

News of the tragic pilgrimage, filtering back to the Nation, was not such as to convince the general public that removal was a solution to its problems. To be sure, accounts varied. John Ridge evidently had an optimistic correspondent, for he wrote the American Board in July that he had heard fine things of the new land, and of the cordial welcome extended the newcomers by the old settlers. There had been certain discomforts on the way, including cholera, but these facts Ridge dismissed lightly.

A letter in a gloomier vein, though perhaps not written of this specific migration, came from William Bolling, who wrote home to urge his friends to stay where they were. The country was infected with fevers and agues in the summer and "cold plague" in the winter, and "you can go to no place hardly but what you see tolerably large graveyards. . . . If the government keeps payment back much longer we shall have no use for it, for the people generally are dying up very fast." He cautioned further about trusting enrolling agents, on whom "there is as much dependence as on a wolf."

The Cherokees at large were bitter about the means used by agents to enroll citizens for emigration. The "voluntary emigration" was, according to them, anything but that: Cherokees were threatened with confiscation of their property if they would not consent to go; firewater was used by some agents as a method of persuasion. Indians made drunk discovered when they sobered up that they had committed themselves and their families to emigration. The letters of the missionaries corroborated these details and added others. They told of a Cherokee woman who was induced to enroll by the story that her relatives had already done so; when she discovered the falsehood, her home had been possessed, and she was not allowed to return.

Elijah Hicks, undeterred by being arrested by Georgia officials and made to post a bond of $1000 for his release, returned to write a blistering attack on the wiles employed by the agents in the March 29 issue of the *Phoenix*. His piece, "The Tyrant's Masterpiece," compared them to swine rooting from place to place in search of food and described the bewilderment of a lone Cherokee woman as "the white and tawny faces" bore down on her and promises were alternated with threats. "It is our desire that these *pests* shall be withdrawn for the present to give the *oppressed* Cherokees a few days for the planting of crops."

It must be added for the sake of the record, however, that not all volunteer emigrants had been coerced. There had been a small but steady movement westward ever since the Louisiana Purchase. The Cherokee Nation West had long been a kind of colony, an outlet for excess population and enterprising energies. This movement had existed independently of pressure from Georgia; now it was somewhat accelerated by the addition of people who agreed with the Ridges that the situation in the East was intolerable and incurable.

The Cherokees found an unexpected champion in their opposition to such emigration in the ubiquitous Chester, who was now remarking that this piecemeal form of removal defeated its own purpose. It took away from the Nation those very Cherokees who were favorable to removal; their voices were no longer heard in Council or in the townhouses; relieved of their influence, the general public was reinforced in its resolution to stay where it was.

Georgians, well aware that voluntary emigration would never answer their purposes, were not only doing their best through the lottery system to make the life of the Cherokees unbearable, but were also pressing Washington to carry out the provisions of the Removal Bill by achieving one general compulsory act of removal.

All these pressures told on the Cherokees. In that April when the emigrants were scattering in panic before the cholera, a note of desperation crept into the columns of the defiant *Phoenix*. "Human nature," wrote the editor in one of his last editorials (for the paper was to suspend publication late in May), "being absolutely incapable of bearing the present state of things in our country, we have to express our deep conviction that the crisis has arrived, that something must be done for the Cherokees."

And Butler wrote the Board that not for the whole state of Georgia would he be answerable for the tears that its politicians had wrung from the Cherokees.

4.

Until now the activities of the Ridges and Boudinot had been constitutionally correct. Cherokee law gave them the right to express their point of view, however unpopular, to the Council, of which they were members; they had by no means deserved to be called traitors. But in the spring of 1834 they took highly questionable action: they followed the precedent set by Starr and Walker in going to Washington to conduct negotiations for which they had no authority.

This act was impulsive rather than premeditated, and was not originally designed as defiance of the authorized delegation headed by Chief Ross. It had the effect, however, of impairing the unity for which Ross had appealed: it confirmed the impression of Jackson's representatives that the only way to handle the Cherokees was to follow the rule of "divide and conquer."

Ross's delegation was the first to reach Washington, in winter. It was closely followed by the Chief's brother, Andrew, and some representatives of prospective emigrants from North Carolina and Tennessee. These, according to the *Phoenix*, had originally set out with no more subversive design than to urge a compromise on their

chief and to arrange favorable terms for their own emigration. It was not entirely their fault that Jackson was
more interested in meeting Cherokees favorable to emigration than known intransigents such as the official delegates. He received them, and it was he who sent Andrew
back to the Nation to get additional information. On this
trip Andrew conferred with the Ridges and Boudinot, and
when he returned in April they came with him. Their
avowed objective was modest: they would try to persuade
the authorized delegates to negotiate a removal treaty.

Their act, however, provoked fury in the Nation.
"Kitchen chiefs," the *Phoenix* called them, and said they
would have been arrested before they set out had they not
kept their intentions quiet. Ugly threats were muttered
against them. If they dared go so far as to discuss cessions
of Cherokee land with the government, they had better
not come back.

But threats in the Nation could have no immediate
effect on men in Washington; the Cherokees were afraid.
A rumor went the rounds that Jackson was planning to
profit by this factionalism, that he would compromise the
fate of the whole Nation by coming to terms with a
minority. It was reported in April that he had promised
Georgia such a treaty within four weeks.

Indeed, one treaty was made. But it was made by
Andrew Ross's group, which signed away all the Eastern
lands for Western territory and other considerations.
The Ridge's group denounced this treaty, which, according to John Ridge, was "made at loose ends and containing no national privileges" and was nearly as objectionable as the line pursued by Chief Ross. The treaty
came to nothing; Council angrily disavowed it, and the
Senate rejected it.

After the called Council held in late summer, unidentified patriots demonstrated to the makers of such illicit
documents what they might expect. Walker, the first

Cherokee to undertake an unsanctioned embassy to Washington, was shot from ambush and killed.

5.

In spite of the failure of Andrew Ross's treaty, the dogging of the official delegates by the minority faction did have some effect. Hitherto no accredited representatives had been willing to discuss a new treaty at all; their point was that they saw no safety in doing so while the government disregarded all the obligations it had incurred under the old compacts.

But in March 1834 the Cherokee delegation, which besides Chief Ross included Richard Taylor, Daniel McCoy, Hare Conrad, and Johnson Tinson, did discuss the possibility with Secretary Cass. To be sure, they only raised a question. If the Cherokees ceded part of their land, would they receive protection in the rest? No, said the secretary; the president had no power to control their treatment by a state. Nevertheless they persisted in this line of approach; if they surrendered some territory would they be protected in the rest on the understanding that they would eventually accept citizenship in the several states? No, said Cass again. Removal to the West was the one acceptable basis of negotiation.

In spite of this setback the delegates believed, if the testimony of their opponents can be trusted, that they had hit upon a formula that might eventually solve their difficulties. Chief Ross had once in Council prophesied that the Cherokee Nation would one day be admitted to the Union as an Indian state. The notion of citizenship in the Republic was not repugnant to him, and probably not to his listeners, since they did not protest his prediction. The citizenship now projected, however—citizenship in the several states claiming Cherokee land, among them Georgia, with Cherokees installed in local office—was a very different thing. What the Cherokees would have said to such a proposition cannot be known, for Ross never discussed it with them. Boudinot said that the delegates avoided revealing this plan to Council lest it be summarily rejected, and John Ridge charged that they had no more authority to discuss such proposals in Washington than Andrew Ross had to make a treaty. Worcester added his own testimony. All three wrote the American Board that Ross had now adopted a policy that could result only in racial amalgamation and national extinction.

The issue between the two factions now took a new turn. Hitherto there had merely been disagreement about whether it was possible for the Cherokees to remain in the East at all, the Ross majority insisting that hope remained if only the Nation would present a united front to the aggressor, the Ridge minority claiming that the last basis of hope had been destroyed. Now the Ridges conceded that the Cherokees might stay where they were, but denied that they could preserve their national integrity thus. The only hope of independence lay in removal.

Worcester, who talked with a member of the authorized delegation in September shortly after it had returned from months of fruitless negotiations in Washington, expressed in a letter to the Board the conviction of the Ridges. Ross's delegation, he said, had decided on eventual submission to the states, but were not yet ready to make their decision public. A removal treaty would probably never be made; only a minority of the Cherokees would go, and yet soon the only Cherokee Nation would be in the Arkansas. In the East the more civilized Indians would hold their own and amalgamate with the whites. "But the body of the lower class, according to my forebodings, will be perpetually made drunk by the whites, cheated, oppressed, reduced to beggary, become miserable outcasts, and as a body dwindle to nothing."

This gloomy prediction was the moral basis of the

subsequent conduct of the Treaty Party. In Red Clay in November their representatives made another attempt to convince the Council of the futility of further resistance. Reinstatement in the present locality was impossible, they argued; the Cherokees should not be encouraged in impossible hopes. Exile was preferable to submission, and the majority of the Cherokees would choose it if they knew the whole truth.

Their warning was sincere, but Council, already incensed by their unsanctioned visit to Washington, would not entertain their resolution. There was again murmuring about impeachment, though Chief Ross, always intent on peacemaking, still hoping to convert the dissidents, managed to avert such action.

Chief Ross was not so forthright in presenting his own delegation's latest plan. That it was not in any case a mature plan of action so much as a device for gaining time is suggested by a conversation that he had with a missionary in September 1834. He had told J. E. Ellsworth that the Georgian, Judge Underwood, who had acted as counsel for the Cherokees, held that it would yet be possible to "law the intruders off." Ellsworth shook his head over such optimism. "I hope," he wrote the Board, "that Mr. Ross and the poor Cherokees will not at last find themselves overwhelmed with disappointment and the people curse the hand that has led them. Mr. Ross's position is one of great responsibility. The blessings or the curses of the Nation will be his. It seems to me that he is completely infatuate."

6.

So vivid were the emotions engendered by the division among the Cherokees that few could work among them without becoming a partisan of one side or the other. There was indeed a very serious split among the missionaries of the American Board, with an important difference. Among the Cherokees only a slim minority favored removal in spite of the fact that they were led by three of the most distinguished figures in the Nation. Among the missionaries the majority now favored it. Even Chamberlin, who had not only been opposed to the pardon of the missionaries but had the temerity to reply to Georgia's warning of blood-letting that "a moderate degree of blood-letting might be wholesome, as any physician could testify," had now been won over to The Ridge's side. The American Board itself had let its policy be shaped by Worcester, its most famous representative, a man whose name was going down in the schoolbooks.

Worcester was now committed to Boudinot's views, though he had some skepticism as to the wisdom of his tactics. Also he was troubled by the violence of feeling expressed by the Cherokees. One of his parishioners slyly commented on Worcester's own intentions by denouncing a Methodist preacher. "He was at my house . . . and he kneeled down and prayed at night, and kneeled down and prayed in the morning, and now he is going to Arkansas." "As if," said Worcester, "going to Arkansas nullified all pretensions to religion." He was sorry that they felt that way; but it was not only true that he himself was going to Arkansas, but also he was praying that the stiff-necked people would see the light and consent to follow.

Between Worcester and his late prison mate had come a parting of the ways. To be sure, Butler said little, but the fact was that in attempting to fight dispossession of the mission property at Haweis he had accepted the advice of Ross against that of Worcester, and had thereby incurred the opposition of the Ridges and Boudinot. Also Butler was not going to Arkansas; he was going to build anew near the council grounds at Red Clay.

So intense was Butrick's bitterness at the harm the futile outcome of Worcester's gesture of defiance had done the Cherokees that he was in danger of forgetting the original premises of his own opposition. He himself was showing symptoms of developing political leanings. Whether or not he was pro-Ross, he was well on his way to becoming passionately anti-Ridge, anti-Boudinot, and above all anti-Worcester.

7.

In spite of such dissension, in spite of the infiltration of the Georgians and the evils they brought with them, life in the Nation was still not wholly tragic. Many Cherokees had the character to keep to business as usual and to avoid putting in their full time worrying about the Georgians.

Miss Sophia was going ahead happily with her school in New Echota. To be sure, there had been one contretemps: she was now involved in a lawsuit. A "fortunate drawer," one Burke, had rudely ordered her Sabbath school out of the courthouse, to which he had lately fallen heir. When a local lawyer chivalrously came to her rescue there was a free-for-all fight in which, Miss Sophia carefully assured the Board, she personally did not participate.

Aside from this incident Miss Sophia had only happy things to report of the school. The parents had shown an unexpected degree of co-operation in helping her keep the children out of the grogshop. She now had, in spite of the Georgia Guard, several "black boys" in class, among them Peter of the late controversy. Her good friend Harriet Boudinot came regularly to teach singing. On a festal Friday when swarthy parents sat against the walls to watch their young go through their paces, the children had sung so beautifully that tears came to the eyes of the fathers. (Miss Sophia underscored the word "fathers.")

She herself was full of plans for the future. She longed for self-improvement, to attend a Miss Beecher's school in Huntsville, Alabama, during her vacation. She had no money, but perhaps some charitable family would take her in. "I am willing to become a beggar if I can be better qualified to teach."

One of Worcester's recent plans had materialized. Schools had now been set up to give systematic instruction in Sequoia's alphabet. These were managed on a circuit-riding basis by two Cherokees, a newly ordained preacher, John Huss, and Jesse, erstwhile ball player and all-night dancer, who had recently got "a seriousness." The Cherokees were responding to this opportunity with enthusiasm; to be sure, here and there the teachers encountered a class of only half a dozen; but more characteristically their classes ran to seventy or eighty, and these, in spite of their numbers and the fact that ages ranged from six to eighty, met in dignity and order.

Butrick wrote happily from Carmel of a communion service that Indians had ridden twenty to fifty miles to attend. He had preached in English, Brother Foreman in Cherokee, and both had officiated in administering the Lord's Supper, a rite rendered doubly impressive by the eclipse of the sun that was nearly total at this exact moment. The two preachers had made use of the solemnity of the occasion to discuss a sensitive point, polygamy. Foreman expounded Bible passages on the subject and recommended that polygamous Cherokees retain only the wife they had lived with longest. "Consult your wives and regulate your domestic concerns," Foreman had charged, and the Indians promised to do so.

Butrick preached with somewhat less conviction. Unlike the native preacher, he had qualms. How could a pious Cherokee choose between two wives whom he had married native fashion in one ceremony? And even if

Foreman's advice could be taken literally, was it not like ordering Jacob to renounce Rachel because he had married Leah first?

He wrestled with his conscience on the subject, searched the Acts, and catechized the Board, but what remained uppermost in his mind was the dreadful beauty of the Lord's Supper served in eclipse, and the hush of awe that prevailed over his congregation at that moment.

The Worcester-Boudinot translation of St. Matthew was reaching Cherokees whom the missionaries themselves would hardly have ventured to proselyte. One copy had fallen into the hands of a "wicked and dissipated" Cherokee at Long Savannah, the last sort of person expected to respond to such literature. But the profligate had pored over this volume with consuming interest, and had been so struck by one passage that he had made a special trip to Rolling Waters to have it expounded by a Christian Cherokee. Butrick, to be sure, had no report on the spiritual results of that expounding; he knew only that a leaven was at work.

So in spite of many anxieties the missionaries persevered at their apostolic labors, and they and their flocks could still find moments of contentment together. Not that the uncertainties diminished; anxiety was like a chain whose pull one felt more heavily after a chance moment of lighthearted forgetfulness. "Should we," wrote Butrick sadly, "be moved from this place in a week it would not be surprising."

CHAPTER XVI

The Treaty

The Cherokees who partook of the Lord's Supper with Butrick and their own Reverend Foreman were not too alarmed at the solar eclipse of December 1834, because they had been told what to expect.

Nevertheless, the experience was awesome and disturbing. The sun withdrew its light in full day, not because of a cloud, but in a stainless sky by reason of the interposition of an invisible opacity. Even the animals noticed it. The horses at the hitching posts stamped, flicked their tails, and whinnied; a dog howled and sought comfort from his master inside the chapel. Animals were people too; they knew when something dark and evil had wrenched apart the normal courses of nature.

Butrick had explained the event by modern science with theological embellishments. It sounded reasonable, but some of his parishioners saw no harm in getting an opinion on possible deeper meanings of the event from a more ancient source. In Cherokee lore Sun was closely related to Ancient Red, the Grandparent Fire. Sun-Fire, always invoked before the severe discipline of a ball play, was the only proper recipient of prayer according to the oldtime religion; for this reason some converts had the confused impression that Sun-Fire was what Butrick meant by God. Now they had seen that God sicken nearly to death before their eyes while they broke the bread and drank the wine which were God's own body and blood. There might be a sign for the Cherokees in this; no harm in calling on a reputable medicine man, and the good Butrick need never know.

Since Sequoia's day, medicine men too had become literate. Inasmuch as the whole virtue of their formulas could be lost by the omission or transposition of one syllable, they appreciated the convenience of recording the ritual on bits of paper in ink, in pencil, in colored crayon; these papers, mislabeled on purpose to throw prying busybodies off the scent, were their most sacred and jealously guarded stock-in-trade. (Long years later some of them were to fall into the hands of the Smithsonian Institution and become the basis of learned treatises.)

The formulas of the medicine men were on the whole only a kind of materia medica, however. They were strictly practical measures for dealing with the more usual manifestations and aberrations of nature. A skilled medicine man could by chanting alleviate the effects of "the yellow," frostbite, snakebite, toothache; he could induce the "jumping down" of a babe from its mother, stimulate love and potency.

But the eclipse was so rare a phenomenon that they had no formula for dealing with it, though by way of explanation they had a frivolous tale about the sun's being swallowed and then regurgitated by the prototype Frog. Some Cherokees decided that, after all, Butrick's matter-of-fact explanation would do. Others went on wondering. The sick fading of the sun in full day had a special meaning for a nation that in the full day of its pride and property had entered into a sick period of eclipse. Occult forces had nearly put out the sun; treachery, the eclipse of the honor of one of their great ones, was threatening to extinguish their nation.

2.

The new year of 1835 had begun dismally with a cold beyond all precedent—a "Lapland winter," the missionaries called it. Often in the pleasant latitude of the Cherokees winter is easygoing, intermittent, and brief; sometimes it is hardly a distinct season at all, but rather an indeterminate halfway point between the last smoldering of autumn and the first budding of spring.

But Grandparent Sun, recovering slowly from the wound inflicted in December, had no power over snows that in other seasons he hàd cleared away in a day, except from the mountaintops.

February was the worst. In February came cold so intense that water froze in pots placed close to the fire. No one knew what to do with such weather. The Cherokees, crushed by it, forgot to hunt, kept their children from school, and crouched all day in their chimney corners.

Late in February came a thaw. Fruit buds incautiously expanded. But the cold returned to destroy them, and with it came snow that lay deep on the ground through March. Not until nearly April did another bud unfold. Then the peaches bloomed, but their blossoms were scattered, promising a lean crop, and even then the Cherokees were reluctant to pick up their hoes and set out for the corn and squash patch.

More than distrust of a season turned all awry restrained them. Huddled in their frosty cabins during most of the winter, they had had too much time to brood. The cold had not nipped off the supply of bad news. Georgia was going ahead with its tactics of hounding the Cherokees off the land, and what Georgia did was not the worst, for Georgia alone could never break the spirit of the Cherokees. But in Washington there were Cherokees once honored and trusted who were bargaining to sell their country to Andrew Jackson. The Cherokees looked listlessly at their fields as the snows receded at last. Of what use to plough and plant if treachery was to reap the planting, if the Nation was to be dispossessed before the corn could ripen?

Nevertheless, as the season advanced, as spring became a certainty, the spirit of the Cherokees reasserted itself, and most of them went out to drop kernels in the ground and hoe their rows. The planting was an act of faith in the Cherokee future and an act of defiance to Georgia and their own false prophets. But some had grown too sick at heart for faith and for defiance. There were gardens that were not planted that year.

3.

When Miss Sophia released her children for recess, they darted out into the woods and came running back with fistfuls of flowers. The classroom was filled with spring. Even when they sat at their books, the children could not keep from cocking an ear to the fireplace; swallows had nested in the big chimney; through the fireplace one could catch a subdued flutter and chirp as the mother came and went, feeding her young. And all around and overhead in the trees outside, the birds sang in a joyous jangle.

Miss Sophia had a new schoolroom now. The Council House had become a grogshop; the courthouse had fallen to the jealously possessive Mr. Burke. The school had finished the last session in New Echota in Candy's house. Now Miss Sophia and her brood had moved into the country, out of reach of the temptations of the forlorn capital. They were at Running Waters, John Ridge's plantation, and their classroom was a front room of the homestead. Children from far away boarded there with the lively little Ridges, and so, to her happiness, did Miss Sophia.

The children took pride in their new classroom. Nancy

Fields, an older girl who not long before had come to Miss Sophia without a word of English and now had progressed so rapidly that she sometimes took charge as a Lancastrian "monitor" when Miss Sophia was preoccupied with the illness of one of the pupils, bragged to the Board that the planks of the floors were planed smooth and that the five windows were all of glass.

Miss Sophia's present situation was the result of complicated correspondence during the previous summer when the question of her future had come before the American Board. Was she to remain with the Cherokees and, if it came to that, remove with them to the Arkansas? Worcester, whose opinion was asked, thought not. To him Miss Sophia's character presented "a strange compound of inconsistencies"; he doubted her ability to live in peace with her Cherokee friends. "I am confident that no Cherokee would bear what we have borne."

But the Cherokees disagreed. Ridge and Boudinot took issue with their good friend and tried to counteract the impression he had given by writing their own estimate of Miss Sophia. Boudinot said she was popular, had won influential Cherokees to the mission idea, and that the whole reputation of the missions would suffer if it became known that missionaries had caused her to leave. John Ridge called her "a lady of fine feelings and susceptibility of mind." Mrs. Boudinot also wrote, and warmly. In spite of the trying circumstances of present existence, Cherokees would always be glad to provide a schoolhouse for such a teacher and would count it a privilege to have her in their families. In view of Miss Sophia's delicacy of feelings, continued Mrs. Boudinot, née Harriet Gold of Cornwall, Connecticut, it was best that she continue "under the patronage of the Board, and individuals . . . give as they should feel able."

By August 1834 the issue had been settled, to the satisfaction of Miss Sophia, who had been nettled by Worcester's attitude and had written of him: "I cannot say of him as I will of God, 'Though he slay me, yet will I trust him.' " Her somewhat tenuous connection with the Board was to be maintained. Worcester, who pitied her as a lorn woman with no relative to turn to, took her with him to the newly rebuilt Brainerd for an outing. When she returned to New Echota, John Ridge sent a servant to fetch her to Running Waters, and there she had been ever since.

Mrs. Ridge (born Sarah Northrup of Cornwall) and Miss Sophia had frankly discussed the possible temperamental difficulties involved in so close an association. Miss Sophia had explained her nervous fits, "how I might at these seasons speak and act *wrong*." Smilingly Mrs. Ridge had assured her that she was prepared to bear with such interludes and asked only that Miss Sophia show a similar forbearance with her husband: he was under great stress; in moments of strain he might speak hastily, but if she were patient, his flash of temper would be quickly over.

Actually the junior Ridges and the difficult mission lady seemed to get on with no friction at all. It did distress Miss Sophia that John, in spite of his training at Brainerd and Cornwall, was "a man without piety," but she thought the world of him, called him her "protector." John in his turn thought highly of her, took time on an anxious—and unauthorized—trip to Washington to buy her a bonnet and shoes, which he presented on his return along with money from himself and Boudinot and a Tanner's *Universal Atlas* from the latter.

So at Running Waters Miss Sophia prospered and was happy. But not altogether so, for such was the troubled state of the Nation that even little children were upset. Now and then a father removed a child from class lest he be contaminated by proximity to one of Ridge's political color. Other children, apprehensive that their own parents would follow suit, sometimes found it hard to keep their minds on geometry, arithmetic, Biblical history, and the solar system, all of which subjects were now included in the accomplished Miss Sophia's curriculum.

Ridge was now openly, in defiance of Council, "engaged with his whole soul to accomplish a treaty." This venture had Miss Sophia's sympathy and approval. Of course the Cherokees must remove: the lowering of moral tone inflicted on them by their present circumstances was deplorable; they must go as quickly as possible to the West, where they would be forever beyond the reach of white man and his temptations, where there would never again be drinking, brawling, thieving, killing. Or so Miss Sophia innocently pictured the West, and so did the other missionaries committed to removal.

However, she had gone through no soul-searching on the question. Mainly she favored removal because the Ridges did; they were her people now; they had taken her in and cherished her when the missionaries contemned her; their political beliefs were her beliefs. She burned with indignation at what Ridge was being made to suffer for his honest conviction. People muttered against him throughout the country; there were threats, and after the fate of Jack Walker none dared dismiss such threats as idle talk.

Sometimes unidentified men, wrapped to the eyes in blankets, haunted the plantation, making no move, just maintaining a sinister vigil at the edge of the woods. The whole household was sometimes thrown into a state of alarm by such episodes. Viciously unfair so to persecute a man whose only crimes were honesty and courage—honesty to speak the truth as he saw it, courage to act accordingly. Sheer moral indignation, if nothing else, would have won Miss Sophia to the side of the Ridges.

4.

During the long cold winter of 1835, when the bewildered, disheartened Cherokees huddled by their drafty
chimney corners, Ridge and Boudinot were in Washington. No one in authority had asked them to go, and they
were no longer limiting their activities to trying to influence the authorized delegation; they were making a
treaty of their own in full consciousness that they were
acting against the will and the law of their people.

So revolutionary a course had not been part of their
original plan. For two and a half years they had limited
themselves to constitutional measures, trying only to persuade their countrymen to accept the inevitable. They
had tried repeatedly, bravely, openly; they had had no
success; their only reward was odium.

Now, since 1834, when Andrew Ross had induced
them to visit Washington with him, their political philosophy had taken a new twist. Because the Cherokees would
not listen to them, they conceived it their duty to act for
the Cherokees. As Boudinot explained later, they considered it the responsibility of an intelligent minority, in
possession of the facts, to take the initiative for an emotional, misinformed, misled majority. By their definition,
true patriotism now required them to act against the will
of the people and in disregard of their threats.

It was a philosophy with some affinity to that of young
John in his boyhood when he protested being held to the
slower pace of his class at Brainerd. Call it sophistry,
call it sense, that was the way Ridge and Boudinot now
reasoned. They went boldly to Washington to make a
treaty that their people had forbidden them to make.
Their usurpation of national authority was not, however,
complete, for under the terms of the Removal Bill no
treaty could be valid until it had been formally ratified
by a national majority. It was their intention to make so

advantageous a treaty that the Cherokees would not dare reject it.

Ross was also in Washington at the head of the official delegation. Jackson received him first, for Jackson, in his own way, was no less intent on legality than Ross himself. He could long ago have disposed of the irksome Cherokee question by sending Federal troops into the country to round up the Indians and send them packing. Unfortunately, however, the Removal Bill contained no provision of such simple efficacy; it called for a treaty ratified by the majority of each nation involved. And since Ross represented, or said he did, the Cherokee majority, Jackson saw him first.

The interview was satisfactory to neither party. Ross had come as usual, to the exasperation of Jackson, with a long list of grievances. As if the Cherokees themselves, whose stubbornness had already outlasted one presidential term and threatened to outlast another, weren't grievance enough! Jackson coldly told Ross that removal was the only subject he would discuss with him; he would kindly get down to business with the delegates and draw up the terms under which removal would be acceptable to his people, or there would be no more conversations.

Reluctantly Ross agreed. But nothing came of his promise; he was only temporizing; when this fact became clear to Jackson, he indignantly turned to young Ridge. He knew that the latter's group had no legal standing, but the hand of Ross must be forced somehow. He arranged for J. F. Schermerhorn, a retired parson, to enter into detailed negotiations with Ridge and Boudinot for a removal treaty.

As Jackson had anticipated, the move brought Ross back. He was ready to set a price for his country—twenty millions. "Filibustering!" snorted Jackson. The land, protested Ross, was worth all of that, but since Jackson didn't think so, let the Senate make an offer. But when the

Senate offered a maximum of five millions, Ross refused it.

Now the negotiations between Schermerhorn and Ridge
were carried through to their conclusion. Thanks to the
chief's obstinacy, Ridge was able to get better terms than
had Andrew Ross the previous year; Ridge exacted four
and a half millions plus such concessions as an annuity
for school funds and extra territory in the West.

When Ridge went back to the Nation in April, he
brought Schermerhorn with him. The latter carried the
treaty and a special message from Jackson urging the
Cherokees to ratify a document that had been drawn up
with every consideration for their welfare.

5.

The Cherokees were not disposed to regard the action
of Ridge and Boudinot as motivated by a form of higher
patriotism. They duly called a Council in May to dispose
of the treaty and also to condemn, unanimously, the
action of the treaty-makers.

At this point and on the advice of Schermerhorn, Ridge
tried really revolutionary action. Inasmuch as there had
been no election since 1828, Council was unconstitutional
in any case. He would go over its head to the people and
summon a council of his own.

The result was fiasco. Even by combining "Council"
with a Green Corn festival he could get only 100 to attend—not even the ghost of the majority required under
the Removal Bill. Young Ridge, son of a distinguished
father and of a whole line of "beloved men," himself a
statesman whose career had opened with great promise,
now made the unpleasant discovery that he had lost
every vestige of political influence. He could command a
handful of followers in his own neighborhood, and that
was all.

Ridge was no man of iron; his resolution was not yet

unshakable; he could still question his conduct. Butler
had noted his craving for popularity; the hostility he had
incurred was a blow and told on him heavily. He was
frightened by the danger to which his family was exposed
from the men who now hung around Running Waters.

And above all he regretted that Jackson had entrusted
the delicate matter of negotiations to such a character as
Schermerhorn.

Chester had now given up his attempt to win over the
Cherokees. He had signaled his surrender by sending the
missionaries a bill that staggered them, especially as
they were now aware that his frequent and expensive
trips to Washington had been impelled less by devotion
to their cause than by private business with Jackson. His
place had been taken by Schermerhorn, and everyone
concerned now perceived that by comparison with Schermerhorn, Chester had been an honest man. He had at least
respected the Cherokees to the extent of trying to win
a true majority to the need of making a treaty; Schermerhorn, it was obvious, would descend to any wile.
The Cherokees improved on his name; it became "Devil's
Horn," and one who had favored removal told Butler:
"We expected to find him a good man, but we find him a
very bad one, even one guilty of profanity."

In his own eyes Schermerhorn was simply a realist.
The Cherokees were intransigent; persuasion would not
move them; other devices must be resorted to. How about
bribery? he asked Jackson. But Jackson said no. Well
then, suggested Schermerhorn, since the National Council
would have none of the treaty, would not ratification by
an intelligent minority satisfy the letter of the law? By
no means, said Jackson; if the Cherokees were mad enough
to refuse what was offered them for their own good, let
them suffer until the consequences of their obstinacy
forced them into line. Thus restrained by his chief, Schermerhorn, acting on a suggestion from Enrolling Agent

Curry to the effect that if the Cherokees were made sufficiently miserable they would have to give up, appealed to Alabama and Tennessee to refuse refuge in their territories to fugitives from Georgia.

The profane parson ended by antagonizing John Ridge. Before summer was over the unhappy young man was avoiding his late collaborator and showing symptoms of a change of heart. At least he consented to a reconciliation with Chief Ross. The latter, aware of the real worth of the Ridges and Boudinot, had never condemned them as harshly as most Cherokees, had restrained Council from impeaching them, and had tried hard to heal the distressing schism that had opened in Cherokee ranks. By the time of October Council, reconciliation had gone so far that Ross appointed young Ridge and Boudinot to a committee to review the whole question of treaty-making.

6.

The proceedings of October Council were watched by an unexpected visitor, another white man, but this time a friendly, disinterested one who was to do the Cherokees no harm and some small good. A wandering journalist, late a child prodigy of the stage, now a famed composer and dramatist, and presently to become a diplomat, John Howard Payne had happened upon the Cherokees quite by accident while he was touring the South in search of material for magazine articles. Chief Ross had invited him to stop over in his cabin at Red Clay. Payne accepted the invitation, and was thereby immediately and sensationally initiated into Cherokee history.

He watched Ross receive the members as they came into Red Clay to attend October Council. "The woods echoed with the trampling of many feet; a long and orderly procession emerged from the trees . . . halted at the humble gate of the Principal Chief; he stood ready to receive them. Everything was noiseless. The party,

entering, loosened the blankets which were loosely rolled
and flung over their backs and hung them with their tin
cups and other paraphernalia . . . on the fence. They
formed diagonally in two lines, and each in silence drew
near [the chief] to give his hand. . . .

"All wore turbans except four or five with hats; many
of them wore tunics with sashes and nearly all some
drapery, so that they had the oriental air of the old
Scriptural pictures of patriarchal processions." Most
had come sixty miles on foot to attend Council; only old
women and a few men rode horseback.

Concerning Council proceedings, Payne was less specific. The details were lost on one who had not the
language, whose interest was chiefly in local color,
and who in spite of his ready sympathy looked on the
more intricate complications of Cherokee affairs with
detachment. It was not for him to appreciate the sensation caused by the appointment of the erring Ridges
and Boudinot to a committee. He could hardly realize
how great a sensation the committee was in itself, since its
function was to discuss with the Federal authorities what
the Cherokees had until now refused to discuss at all—a
treaty—and it was appointed now only because Jackson
would consent to deal with the Cherokees on no other
basis.

He could, however, appreciate a step the Council took
to counteract the influence of Schermerhorn: an appeal
addressed to the governors of Georgia, Alabama, Tennessee, and North Carolina that they induce their legislatures
to abstain from passing laws to "further harm a people
already so deeply galled that a renewal of irritating
means at a moment so critical might entirely defeat the
object of those who have nothing but the peace and
happiness of their own countrymen and friendship with
yours. . . .

"We are the earlier possessors of the soil we retain,

but where events which we have had no share whatsoever in producing surround us with all the anxieties and privations of war although in a state of perfect peace. . . . We have been misunderstood. We have been slandered. . . ."

All these matters Payne observed with the detachment appropriate to his calling. But detachment was something that no one who came close to a Cherokee in that period could keep; on November 7, immediately after the close of Council, Payne lost his. Abruptly, without warning, for no imaginable reason, a bewildered literary man found himself ridden off to jail by the Georgia Guard. And not alone, for with him, unsurprised and self-possessed as ever, rode another captive, Chief Ross.

7.

Ross was unsurprised, not because he had any reason for expecting arrest at that moment, but because he had anticipated that the Guard would do something of the sort sooner or later. He had instructed his associates that in the event of such an emergency the Cherokees were on no account to rescue him; leave that to the lawyers.

In spite of this precaution the Cherokees clamored for action. The prisoners were taken no farther away than Spring Place, hardly a ten-mile ride from Red Clay. The Guard was not overpowering; only twenty-four had come with fixed bayonets to seize Ross and his astonished guest. It would be entirely practicable to muster a party to ride to the rescue, shoot up the Guard, and make off with the captives. And what a joy to do so! After the endless years of humiliating, frustrated sick waiting, what a release!

But Ross, even helpless in prison, had too powerful a hold on his people for them to act against his express will. Long ago he had schooled them to non-violence, to waiting on the law. They must wait now in spite of this supreme indignity. To act as their instincts directed would be to bring the whole armed might of Georgia crashing down upon them.

Spring Place, Georgia, has marked the spot where it thinks the prisoners were confined: the earthern basement of the fine Vann mansion, which still commands its knoll overlooking Fort Mountain. However, the Vann basement has several barred windows, and Payne, who made prompt literary capital of his misadventure, stresses the fact that the prison had no windows at all, but only a door kept open all day so the natives of the community that had ousted Brother Clauder could come and stare at the prisoners. This establishment the latter shared with the Guards and a son of Going Snake, speaker of the house, who was chained to a table.

For a time the prisoners were kept incommunicado and in ignorance of the charges against them. As far as Payne was concerned, no charges had yet been evolved. The none-too-literate Guard was spending this time going through a manuscript on which Payne had been working at Ross's. They were rewarded by the discovery of some uncomplimentary remarks about their organization, which he had characterized as so many *banditti*.

A homespun *agent provocateur*, one Dr. Farmer, talked with Payne in French and later told the Guard that in that tongue he had confessed to the additional guilt of being an abolitionist and a Frenchman. The Guard, which had taken a dark view of a copy of Sequoia's alphabet found in Payne's effects, was now enlightened. So that was what French looked like.

Ross was less interested in the nature of the charges than in a technicality of the arrest. It had taken place at Red Clay by authority of the state of Georgia. But Red Clay was over the Tennessee line. How did it happen, inquired Ross, that Georgia sovereignty now extended so far?

The reply of Sergeant Young of the Guard was evasive.

The prisoners had an inspiration. Payne smuggled a letter out to the governor of Tennessee.

Visitors were admitted at last. To Ross came a brother, a son, and John Ridge. The brother was not allowed to see him; the son was interrupted when he began to talk Cherokee; but Ridge, being in favor with Governor Lumpkin, was allowed more liberty. He reported that the stories about Payne had been enlarged upon and applied to them both. They were supposed to be abolitionists who were plotting to unite the Negroes and the Indians in an insurrection against the whites. At least, that was the story around town.

Actually Georgia seems to have had it in mind to hold Ross as a white man living among Indians. Payne believed that Schermerhorn had engineered the whole affair. He recalled a remark of the latter, "John Ross is unruly now, but he'll soon be tame enough." Schermerhorn later denied any such complicity, but it was significant to Payne that when Ross wrote an appeal to Governor Lumpkin he was not allowed to send it until he added a postcript advocating a treaty.

On November 15 John Ross was given his papers and allowed to leave, apparently as the result of a second visit from Ridge. But Payne, poor Payne, who had never defied Georgia, never memorialized Congress, who wasn't even a missionary, was left behind.

On one occasion he heard Colonel Absolom Bishop humming "Home Sweet Home."

"I wrote that," said Payne wistfully.

On another occasion, when some Guards, more sympathetic than others, were fraternizing with him, admiring his possessions, particularly a buffalo hide and watch for which they hoped to make a swap, he told them that he wrote for a living.

"Go on!" said the Georgia Guard.

Payne remained four long days more, reading *Gil Blas*

and *The Belgian Traveler*, which Sergeant Young had found for him, wishing he had friends as influential locally as those of John Ross, from whom he had had one message. Then finally, on November 20, he was released.

But not without ceremony. First he was ordered to mount his horse and ride with Colonel Bishop to view an assembly of the Georgia Guard.

"Those are the men," said the Colonel, "whom you called *banditti*."

"Then I should apologize to the *banditti*," said Payne, but at the moment not aloud.

Then he had to listen to a lecture.

"You've come into this country to pry, since you arriv, into things you've no business with. You're a damned incendiary, sir. You've come into this country to rise up the Cherokees against the whites. You've wrote agin these worthy men. You've wrote agin the general government of the United States. Above all, Sir, you've wrote agin me. Now, Sir, I order you to cut out of Georgia. If you ever dare again to show your face within the territories of Georgia, I'll make you curse the moment with your last breath. Clear out of the state forever, and go to John Ross, God damn you."

Payne did as he had been told. He cleared out of Georgia as fast as he could make it. He rode straight for Tennesssee and made himself heard there. On December 2, 1835, the *Knoxville Register* printed in large detail his account of his arrest.

There were loud and immediate repercussions. Enrolling Agent Curry spoke out and called Payne a liar. Schermerhorn disclaimed any connection with the arrest, but called Payne a busybody who deserved what he had got.

Over Tennessee went a wave of anger against Georgia. In the eastern end of the state volunteers organized an armed force to patrol the borders and "keep the rambunctious Georgians on their own side."

In Georgia, the *Georgia Journal* of Milledgeville had cutting things to say about the behavior of Governor Lumpkin's "strong arm gang." A committee of the legislature scored the Guard and passed a resolution disapproving the unconstitutional violation of Tennessee soil. Governor Lumpkin admitted the unfortunate technicality, but called Payne one of that type of Northern fanatics "whose avocation is to repent for the sins of everybody except themselves."

And Colonel Bishop, late so eloquent at Spring Place, resigned his commission.

8.

Whatever the faults of J. F. Schermerhorn, onetime parson, now emissary extraordinary for Jackson, infirmity of purpose was not one of them. He had come to the Cherokee Nation determined to conclude a removal treaty; in December 1835, after months of setbacks, he was if anything more undiscouraged and determined than ever.

Any man of less toughness of moral fiber would have been disheartened by this time. The Cherokees had rejected the treaty on which he and Ridge had collaborated. In his work in the Nation he had lost more ground than he had gained; even Ridge had wavered to the extent of coming to an agreement with John Ross. A letter that Schermerhorn had sent October Council, exposing Ross as an illegal usurper, had not even been read, at least not all the way through; Council had angrily interrupted as soon as they grasped its import.

Even Jackson had placed obstacles in his path. Every suggestion that Schermerhorn had made for dealing realistically with the situation had been vetoed by Washington. No funds for "greasing the wheels" of stubborn chiefs. No ignoring the majority voice of National Council to make arrangements with a more common-sensible, intelligent minority. Everything, said Jackson, must be "honest and open." Well, Jackson had to talk that way for the sake of the record. Wasn't it possible, however, that the President, in delegating authority to Schermerhorn, was trusting him to use his own discretion on the spot without embarrassing Washington with the pettier details? In the long run would Jackson look too closely into the means by which Schermerhorn effected a treaty, so long as that document was signed, sealed, and safely delivered to Washington?

By the end of 1835, Schermerhorn had convinced himself that Jackson would not. He had been empowered to conclude a treaty, and now he would conclude it.

The old treaty, drawn up with Ridge and Boudinot, he threw aside. It had been rejected by Council; well and good, no more of that. But negotiations for a new treaty would be opened in New Echota on December 23; Schermerhorn broadcast announcements to this effect, urging everyone to attend. As an additional inducement he promised a gift: blankets would be distributed to all comers.

Ross and his followers disregarded this invitation. The chief later put it on record that he and his committee were about to leave for Washington when they were approached by a representative of Jackson and asked to negotiate on the premises. Ross refused; he and his committee said that it was too late to cancel their plans and continued on their way. Schermerhorn's meeting, they knew, was bound to be another such fiasco as the one Ridge had called in the summer. Their departure at just this juncture was none the less a crucial strategic error.

The Ridges and Boudinot stayed behind. In spite of young Ridge's friendly services in getting Ross freed, he had again fallen out with the chief. The reconciliation had been based on an understanding that the committee to which Ridge and Boudinot had been appointed would work on a *bona fide* treaty. That Ross had no such inten-

tions, that the committee was merely a gesture of appease-
ment to government insistence, became clear to them when
the chief rewrote a document they had signed, substi-
tuting for the word "treaty" the phrase "adjustment of
difficulties."

The Ridges and Boudinot considered that they had
been hoodwinked; Ross had been using them under false
pretenses for his own purposes. They had agreed in good
faith to make a treaty. Well, come what might, they
would remain in New Echota with Schermerhorn and do
so.

December 23 came; it was a fine day, and Cherokees
plodded into New Echota. Counting women and children,
three hundred of them came; but of legal voters there
were, according to Butrick, only seventy-nine, and many
of these were of the type that took a livelier interest in
the promised blankets than in the treaty. Considering
that October Councils often drew thousands, it was hardly
a representative gathering. In fact, the Cherokees were
boycotting Schermerhorn's Council. The boycott, however, like Ross's absenteeism, was a mistake; they could
hardly vote down the proposals of the minority faction
without presenting themselves to do so; indeed, Schermerhorn now announced that all Cherokees failing to appear
would be counted as voting in the affirmative.

Their absence did, however, present an embarrassing
problem. It would not be politic to present Washington
with a treaty signed by seventy-nine voters out of so
numerous a nation. It was decided to disguise this weakness by appointing a committee of twenty, not only to
carry on negotiations, but also to ratify the results. For
the unique feature of this treaty was that it need never
be presented to Council; it would be ratified by a "majority of the nation," in conformity with the terms of
the Removal Bill, right there in New Echota.

The committee met at the home of Boudinot. Occasionally they paused for refreshment—sometimes liquid refreshment, a circumstance that came to the ears of Daniel Butrick, who later spoke his mind on the subject to the distressed Harriet Boudinot. Towards midnight of December 29 their work was complete; the treaty lay before them ready for their signatures.

The Ridge was asked to set his mark before all the others. It was a tribute to his quality; the signers honored The Ridge as the noblest Cherokee of them all.

But was it an honor? It was The Ridge himself who had invoked the blood law on Cherokees who sold their land against the will of the Nation—who did exactly what he was doing now. Was it an honor that his name should have any place at all on such a document?

The Ridge was a simple Cherokee without book learning. If he had doubts, he did not, like Samuel Worcester, set them on paper. No one can know whether at the last moment the question flashed through his mind if his son and nephew were really right in setting themselves against the Cherokee folk spirit, if it was true that a farsighted minority had the duty of acting for an irrational majority.

But having set his mark to paper, so tradition says, he did make one significant comment.

"I have signed my death warrant," said The Ridge.

CHAPTER XVII

The Times of Trouble

Ross was certainly unwise and possibly disingenuous in disregarding insistence that he remain in the Nation to negotiate with Schermerhorn, but not all the disingenuousness was on his side. The War Department received him kindly; he was given an audience by the President, and in general recognized as the legitimate representative of his people.

But these promising conversations were rudely terminated by an announcement that they had become superfluous—that a treaty had already been concluded with the Cherokee Nation, the final details of which would be arranged with a committee en route to Washington with the Reverend Mr. Schermerhorn.

The latter had triumphantly written the Secretary of War: "I have the extreme pleasure to announce to you that yesterday I concluded a treaty. Ross, after this treaty, is prostrate. The power of the Nation is taken from him as well as the money, and the treaty will give general satisfaction."

Schermerhorn's statement was not wholly accurate. Ross was stunned indeed, but by no means prostrate. And, far from giving general satisfaction, the treaty was being passionately protested. Even now, as the Ridge delegation reached Washington, Second Chief Lowry was assembling a meeting to protest the treaty and put it on record that the New Echota group had acted without any authority whatsoever. It was bitterly cold in January; smallpox and dysentery had broken out in the Nation; only four hundred were able to attend Lowry's meeting, but these were at least voters, and each was diligent in circularizing the Nation to get signatures for the series of protests that the Cherokees sent to Washington.

Schermerhorn, however, had correctly read the mind of Jackson. The President was not disposed to question the validity of a treaty drawn up in the capital of the Cherokee Nation by Cherokees, ratified by Cherokees, and now presented by Cherokees in Washington. He sent it to the Senate for approval, and was merely annoyed by the protests that came his way.

Particularly irritating to Jackson was the fact that agents and military men now sent to maintain order and prepare the Cherokees for removal showed a disposition to turn pro-Cherokee. Especially officious was a protest from Major W. M. Davis, appointed to enroll emigrants to the Arkansas, and not to collect a poll of Cherokee sentiment.

"Sir," Davis addressed the Secretary of War, "that paper called a treaty is no treaty at all, because not sanctioned by the great body of Cherokees and made without their participation or assent. I solemnly declare to you that upon its reference to the Cherokee people it would be instantly rejected by nine-tenths of them and I believe by nineteen-twentieths of them. . . . The delegates taken to Washington by Schermerhorn had no more authority to make a treaty than any other dozen Cherokees accidentally picked up for the purpose. I now warn you and the president that if the paper of Schermerhorn's called a treaty is sent to the Senate and ratified you will bring trouble on the government and eventually destroy this Nation. The Cherokees are a peaceable, harmless people, but you may drive them to desperation, and this treaty cannot be carried into effect except by the strong arm of force."

John Mason, a confidential agent sent in late summer to collect evidence that Ross was inciting the Cherokees to hostility, turned not only pro-Cherokee but pro-Ross.

"The opposition to the treaty is unanimous and irreconcilable," he reported. "They say it cannot bind them because they did not make it. . . . The influence of this chief is unbounded and unquestioned. . . . It is evident that Ross and his party are in fact the Cherokee Nation. . . . Yet though unwavering in his opposition to the treaty, Ross's influence has constantly been to preserve the peace of the country. . . . He alone stands between the whites and bloodshed. The opposition to the treaty on the part of the Indians is unanimous and sincere, and it is not a mere political game played by Ross for the maintenance of his ascendancy in the tribe."

Most annoying of all from Jackson's point of view was the fact that General Wool, sent into the country to avert violence by disarming the Cherokees, took it on himself to forward for them a protest signed by nearly 16,000.

This protest was remarkable in several ways. Boudinot claimed it was written by Payne, who, himself a member of a much abused minority group, was never to lose his sympathy with the Cherokees. Whoever wrote it, it was eloquent. It summarized the grievances of the Cherokees and denounced the treaty. "We are denationalized. . . . We are deprived of membership in the human family! We have neither land nor home nor resting place that can be called our own. . . . We . . . appeal with confidence to the justice, the magnanimity, the compassion of your honorable bodies against the enforcement on us of a compact in the formation of which we have no agency. . . .

"In truth our cause is your own. It is the cause of liberty and justice. It is based on your own principles which we have learned from yourselves; for we have gloried to count your Washington and Jefferson as our great teachers.

"We are not ignorant of our condition; we are not insensible to our sufferings. We feel them! . . . And anticipation crowds our breasts with sorrows yet to come. . . . On your sentence our fate is suspended. . . . Spare our people! Spare the wreck of our prosperity!"

More remarkable even than the wording was the number of signatures. The Georgia census of 1835 had listed only 16,542 Cherokees, including children and any number of people old or young who couldn't write in any alphabet. The inference in Washington was that so many names could have been collected only by duplication and forgery. Worcester, commenting on the event later, said that some of the names were of babes at the breast; he considered this circumstance the one wholly dishonorable act ever committed to his knowledge by John Ross.

Ross, however, could hardly have collected the signatures in person. Rather one visualizes an artless delegate saying to a mother: "And the baby on your back, have you signed for him? For him it is even more important than for us who have lived our lives. He too must sign."

Such reasoning had a childlike logic, but was not calculated to impress skeptical legal minds in Washington.

And this was the document that General Wool tacitly sanctioned by forwarding it to Jackson with the comment that he could not persuade even the poorest of Cherokees to accept government rations lest such action be construed as acceptance of the treaty.

Coldly Jackson replied that memorials from the Cherokees served no purpose and would not be entertained by his government.

Washington itself, however, was not silenced. In the House, David Crockett, returned by constituents who decided they could trust a man who spoke for his conscience, denounced the treaty, and Representative (later Governor) Henry Alexander Wise of Virginia pointed out that no treaty could be binding unless it had the assent of both parties, a circumstance manifestly lacking in this case. Frelinghuysen and Daniel Webster protested it, and Henry Clay, still a presidential possibility—or at least the Cherokees hoped so—considered the whole treatment of the Cherokees a violation of the Treaty of Ghent, and expressed his concern not only for the Indians but also for the "deep wound" that such breaking of faith might inflict on the American character.

Advocates of the treaty made no attempt to hold that it represented the will of the Cherokee majority. Their argument at its crudest was Governor Lumpkin's charge that nineteen twentieths of the Cherokees were too ignorant or depraved to know what was good for them anyway. Boudinot, justifying himself, put this view more delicately when he wrote in a series of letters published in Athens, Georgia: "If one hundred persons are ignorant of their true situation and are so completely blinded as not to see the destruction that awaits them, we can see strong reason to justify the actions of a minority of fifty persons to do what the majority *would* do if they understood their condition to save a *nation* from political thralldom and moral degradation."

On May 23 the Senate ratified the treaty of New Echota by a margin of one vote. The Cherokees must evacuate by May 1838 or suffer forcible removal.

2.

In June 1836 an extraordinary event took place. In precisely those parts of the Nation where the whites had most completely dispossessed the Indians and outnumbered them six to one, the whites fell prey to panic.

"Massacre!" they cried, and crowded their women and

children into makeshift stockades, where they cowered listening for the sound of a distant drum. There were no drums. There were Indians, but only the same harmless neighbors they had always been, going about their farm chores as usual. They were sad-eyed people these days, hardly diverted from their despondency even by the odd antics of white folks.

"They act," commented Missionary Chamberlin of the whites in Willstown, Alabama, "as if they had committed some heighnous [*sic*] crime and were expecting every moment that the hand of justice would overtake them. . . . They have got it into their heads that the Creeks and Cherokees are about to unite and cut the white people all off."

The rumor, which Ross charged that the Georgians had inspired to get Federal troops sent into the country, was widespread. Governor Gilmer, returning from Creek country, where there really were disorders to give plausibility to the myth of the Cherokee uprising, swung around on a wide circle to avoid being scalped by a people who might have their reasons for desiring to scalp him.

Governor Dunlap of Tennessee thought the situation serious enough to warrant a personal investigation. He returned from a tour of inspection to make some uncomplimentary remarks about "the lawless rabble of Georgia" (the recent invasion of Tennessee soil had not yet been forgotten) and the observation that it was the Cherokees who needed protection from the whites, not the reverse. "I could never," he added, as a further dig at Georgia, "dishonor the Tennessee arms in a servile service by aiding to carry into execution at the point of a bayonet a treaty made by a lean minority."

General Wool, sent into the country in July, was for a while persuaded that the Cherokees were violent; he ordered them to fight or get out. The alternative fell strangely on the ears of a peaceful farm folk who for three generations had forsworn the warpath except for the unfortunate once when they had contributed to the rise of General Andrew Jackson. The tradition of resisting white men by force was something of which only the oldest men had any experience. They would not get out, and they knew better than to fight. The people in Valley Towns docilely surrendered their shotguns on demand and then came around asking when they could have them back. They needed them to keep varmints off their farms; and by varmints they referred neither to Georgians nor to General Wool's military.

Wool, in fact, speedily became pro-Cherokee, though not anti-removal. "If I could," he wrote indignantly, "and I would not do them a greater kindness, I would remove every Indian tomorrow beyond the reach of white men, who, like vultures, are watching ready to pounce on their prey and strip them of everything they have or expect to have from the government of the United States."

He did not confine his sympathies to words. When he saw Indians plundered by whites, with no recourse to justice in white courts, where no Indians could testify against white intruders, he began dispossessing the latter, particularly in Alabama, and reinstating the Cherokees. For this, the governor and legislature of Alabama charged him with usurping the power of the civil tribunals and demanded an investigation; but Wool, who had only been acting under the terms of the treaty, was vindicated by a military tribunal in Knoxville.

3.

The treaty of New Echota offered no speedy solution to the Cherokee problem. The stiff-necked people still had two years left them in which to make up their minds to remove peaceably before they were driven out by force. All but members of the treaty faction elected to wait. Much could happen in two years. Henry Clay might be elected; Chief Ross might get the treaty voided. Something might come of a trip he made to the Arkansas late in 1836 to enlist the support of Chief Jolly and other leaders of the Cherokee Nation West who had hitherto worked for removal.

In January 1837 The Ridge left for the West with a party of some five hundred treaty adherents. The trip gave the lie to those who thought that migration was necessarily mortal: there were no deaths en route. Boudinot also went West to continue his work with Worcester, who was waiting for him there.

John Ridge was the last of his clan to leave. He remained long enough to experience considerable disillusionment at the manner in which his treaty was executed. Georgians were not restrained from ousting Cherokees prematurely, in disregard of its provisions, and sometimes the "fortunate drawers" sued the Cherokees for back rent of their own property. Such action Ridge protested as bitterly as Ross himself; but the treaty itself he did not repent. To the American Board he wrote that the Cherokee sensible enough to decide for himself to emigrate underwent a "quiet revolution. . . . He loves those who are in favor of removal and dislikes those who encouraged him to stay under delusive hopes."

Deluded or not, the mass of the Cherokees continued to hope, or at least to endure. So far as they could arrange it they went on with business as usual.

Butler was now setting up his mission at Red Clay. Thirty Cherokees took time out from their own preoccupations in January 1836 to perform the neighborly service of splitting oak taken from the virgin forest and of giving him a house-raising.

People still crowded in to attend the classes in Sequoia's alphabet offered by the ex-ball-player Jesse. He had now 440 pupils in twenty-five places over a circuit of 137 miles and an assistant, one Run About. But these comings and goings and the abracadabra in crowded cabins were viewed as suspect by white folks. One of these, a man who hated Presbyterians because he had once been excommunicated by them, presently brought the Presbyterian Jesse to grief. He detained Jesse to demand $100 for the slaying of a sheep that Jesse had supposed was his own, and made him drunk—so drunk that Butler found it his unhappy duty to suspend the heartbroken Jesse from his services as teacher.

Children still went gladly to Miss Sophia's school, but it is noteworthy that the letters some of them wrote to Boston under her inspiration were now less concerned with celestial geography and Patagonia than with local and current events. Rachel rambled on about a grandfather, Big Cabin, who had been very wicked, but had been converted, and was now in Heaven, she hoped. She mentioned people turned out of their homes, told of two aged Cherokees who died near New Echota for want of food. Also she mentioned the ratification of the treaty; now that this had happened, commented young Rachel hopefully, there would soon be food for everyone.

This term at Running Waters was Miss Sophia's last in the East. She was ill, subject to strange dreams, and for once found her pupils and "their ceaseless inquiries" hard to bear. By midsummer she was on her way to her home in Rindge, New Hampshire. She went by way of Georgia, and in her turn found that there were Georgians she could like, Georgians, moreover, who were most sympathetically eager to hear of her work among the Cherokees. She was to see the latter again; the arrangement was that when the Ridges were ready to remove they would send for her and build her a school in the West.

Butrick by this time had thrown aside some of his scruples about taking an interest in political affairs. "Did not St. Paul as well as other inspired writers," he wrote in his diary, "censure traitors and rebels?" Such was his view of the Ridges and Boudinot, and in common with many Cherokees he suspected, unjustly it seems, that Boudinot had acted on the advice of Worcester.

The emotional little missionary now put aside a document on which he had been working for years, designed to prove that Indians in general and Cherokees in particular were really Jews, descendants of a lost tribe of Israel, while he compiled a long essay on the controversy between the Cherokees and Georgia. He must not participate, but he could and would bear witness.

He was also at this time writing a whole series of urgent letters to caution the Board against accepting the $25,543 which the government appraisers offered them for the mission properties. That the missions should be compensated by a deduction from the total due the Cherokees for the sale of their lands had been Schermerhorn's idea. In Butrick's eyes (and also Butler's) acceptance of this money would be an injustice to the Cherokees in that the mission land had been a free loan from the Nation, and the schoolhouses and dwellings in large part constructed by Cherokee labor. To exact from them payment for what had been a gift would be like asking the Indians to buy the mission twice over. Worse, it would be tacit recognition of a treaty repugnant to the Cherokees. If the missions were to maintain their prestige, said Butrick, they must not be convicted of profiting from Cherokee misery.

4.

The misery of the Cherokees had increased as the Georgians flooded into the country and found one means or another of getting Cherokee property into their hands. Sometimes dispossession took place at a season when the corn was already in the ground and it was too late to plant elsewhere even if the means could be found.

For many the misery was by no means wholly mental; there was hunger, even, as Rachel had reported, to the point of starvation.

Yet, whether it was folly or courage, the Cherokees clung to their hills and sullenly rejected offers of government rations. They would not live by the bread of treachery; better to live on what rations the hills could provide, the game, the roots, herbs whose properties their ancestors had understood and they could learn again.

"Jewish inflexibility," Butrick called it. Governor Lumpkin, appointed with Carroll of Tennessee to supervise appraisal of property, attributed this inflexibility to the influence of John Ross, "a very reserved, obscure, and wary politician." Exactly how Ross exerted this influence Lumpkin could not discover. There never seemed to be any overt act; all he knew was that whenever Ross returned from one of his expeditions afield, every impetus toward removal immediately collapsed; even Cherokees already committed to emigration became suddenly evasive. Some other time, they said; they would wait first to see what Chief could do.

On the borders they were haunted by spectral evidence of what came of such obstinacy as theirs. The Creek Nation had surrendered long ago, yet there were still Creeks about; homeless, starving, half naked, they roved in bands in the Alabama end of the Nation looking for food, hunted by whites who had orders to relieve them of their one remaining means of livelihood, their guns.

Could the Cherokees expect a better fate than these Creeks? Yes, for the Creeks at least had confirmed a treaty for removal. These that were left were a mere intransigent minority. With the Cherokees the reverse was true. It was a minority that had treated, with no more authority to speak for the Nation than had the Shah of Persia, and the treaty could not by any stretch of justice be considered binding on their fellows.

"We shall never submit to it!" Butler's parishioners told him.

Butler commented sorrowfully: "Not, as I suppose, that they intend to fight, but flee. Where is a serious question."

The Cherokees were as stubborn as so many rocks placed to obstruct the course of one of their streams. Rock-like also was the impassivity with which by racial tradition they endured, or tried to endure, their sufferings. Yet Cherokee hearts were no more stony than those of other men; it was only their hard determination that kept them now from giving way to a violence of grief.

In letters of observers, whether of missionaries or ordinary homesteaders, written at this time, there is a recurrent, involuntary refrain, "Oh the poor Cherokees!"

Probably the tender-hearted Butrick came the nearest of any white observer to understanding what they were going through. In 1836 he was indignantly calling the attention of the Board to an article that rationalized white men's treatment of Indians by the theory that God had preordained the race to perish and to this end had mercifully deprived them of any capacity for real feeling.

"Americans do not feel towards the Indians as they do towards other heathen nations," wrote Butrick, "therefore reports of their wretchedness do not excite sympathy as they ought, but paralyze every exertion; thereby that old and cruel theory Indians are to be destroyed."

The watchful eye of Butrick detected the feeling of the Cherokees in a hundred small signs. The very calm with which they had endured major injustices from white men whom they had trusted, whose ideals they had embraced, whose civilization they had hopefully imitated, had now brought them to a point of sensitivity where the smallest act of neglect was too much to be borne—a white friend forgetting to speak in passing; a white keeper of an ordinary inn at which they were accustomed to stop, now ignoring them while he attended to white customers. To such neglects the Cherokees offered no protest; they merely turned silently away; but in their eyes, looking out of faces kept rigidly impassive, Butrick read their desolation.

"The Cherokees," he wrote, "are now prepared to feel most tenderly any token of kindness and also every token of neglect and every look of contempt. That treatment, or that little neglect on the part of their friends which ten years ago they could bear cheerfully now breaks their hearts and sinks them into despondency."

To endure the unendurable in silence has a kind of nobility about it. Yet the noisy grief of the whites that Lieutenant Harris had found contemptible in contrast to the unspoken grief of the Indians may have had superior psychological justification. Under the silence of the Cherokees during the long ordeal in the East something corrosive was at work. When the intolerable end came, many of them had exhausted their endurance. For some, for thousands, this meant death; for others it meant an end to self-control.

Certain missionaries were already aware of this corrosion. Chamberlin, who had recently advocated removal and had received a warm invitation from The Ridge to set up a mission near his new home, had been explicitly told by Council that he would not be wanted if removal actually took place. And Worcester, safe in the West, where the good life was supposed to begin, and where presumably everyone favored removal, since everyone there had removed, was experiencing a very disagreeable surprise. Boudinot was unpopular, and this unpopularity was reflected on Worcester, his employer.

Worcester at first made light of the prejudice. It would pass. "The feeling of the Cherokees is founded on interest or supposed interest, not on principle," he wrote. "It is not that he has done morally wrong that they are excited against him."

But Worcester underestimated the depth of the feeling against Boudinot. Even Western Cherokees who had been in favor of removal had been repelled by the means by which The Ridge's party had concluded the treaty; indeed, Worcester himself, though he did not condemn, seems to have been shocked. The Western Cherokees, perhaps as a result of their recent visit from John Ross, felt so strongly on the subject that Worcester was made to realize that he himself might not be allowed to remain if he persisted in his association with Boudinot. Presently the National Council of the Cherokee Nation West sent him a direct request to get rid of his translator. Worcester appealed to Chief Jolly, who reluctantly gave him a permit to continue work; but the permit was only temporary, was subject to the approval of Council, and the second chief would not put his name to it.

There was something ominous in all this, happening as it did in the West, where all discords were to be harmonized. Worcester, returning to his new home at Park Hill with his permit, found himself shaken. Never in his worst experiences with the Georgia Guard had he received so severe a shock or been so profoundly dismayed.

CHAPTER XVIII

The Trail of Tears

On their way West overland early in 1837 The Ridge's party had stopped in Nashville to shoe their horses. Hard by lived an old friend of the Creek campaign from whom The Ridge had until recently been estranged. The Ridge and some friends dropped in at the Hermitage, and a gaunt, snowy-thatched veteran, General Jackson, now retired from public office, was delighted to receive the migrant Cherokees.

The Cherokees had at last realized one hope: they had as a nation outlasted Jackson as president.

Their enemy, however, had not been replaced by Clay. It was Van Buren who now sat in the White House, and though Van Buren was not such a one as Jackson, being diminutive and dandified (and moreover from the friendly North) where the other had been rangy and rugged, he was nevertheless Jackson's man, committed to carry out the obligations he had inherited from Jackson.

Ross's delegation called on him soon after his inauguration. The President was charming to his guests, but his charm was exerted only in the interest of persuading them to yield to the inevitable. And when Lumpkin afterward warned him that Chief Ross would make capital of such audiences to encourage the Cherokees to further resistance, there were no more audiences.

The Cherokees presented still another protest to the Senate. "For adhering to the principles on which your great empire is founded and on which it has advanced to its present elevation and glory, are we to be despoiled of all we hold dear on earth? Are we to be hunted through the mountains like wild beasts, and our women and children, our aged, our sick, to be dragged from their homes like culprits and packed on board loathsome boats for transportation to a sickly clime?"

Ross had also gone North to appeal to sympathizers to make themselves heard while there was yet time to save his people. His own memorial, *A Letter to a Gentleman in Philadelphia*, was printed and circulated. It was an impressive document. It contained not only facts and figures, but also philosophy and a warning. "I knew," he wrote of the aggressions of Georgia, "that the perpetrator of a wrong never forgives his victims, and that there were some who would excite our people to open indications of resentment as a pretext for violence and justification of themselves. . . . We distinctly disavow all thoughts, all desires to gratify any feelings of resentment."

Then came his warning. "That possessions acquired and objects attained by unjust and unrighteous means will sooner or later prove a curse to those who sought them is a truth we have been taught by that holy religion which was brought to us by white men. Years, nay centuries may elapse before the punishment follow the offense, but the volumes of history and the sacred Bible assure us that period will certainly arrive. We would with Christian sympathy labor to avert the wrath of Heaven from the United States by imploring your government to be just."

In this appeal Ross rose to something like greatness; he

was one with Clay in fearing that the act of injustice
would inflict an irreparably "deep wound" upon American character, and one with Jefferson, who had written
in another context: "Indeed I tremble when I remember
that God is just and that his justice cannot sleep forever."
The chief had proved the sincerity of his renunciation of
revenge; but for Ross, according to Worcester, who was
not an admirer, the leaders of the Treaty Party would
not have been allowed to leave the Nation alive.

Ross's petition was thoughtfully read in the North.
Protests from citizens of New York, Pennsylvania, Massachusetts, and New Jersey were sent to the House to
reinforce the Cherokee memorial—and to be tabled with
it. The familiar voices of Crockett, Clay, Everett were
again raised in Congress to denounce the treatment of the
Cherokees, and Frelinghuysen, no longer a senator, for-
warded his own protest. Wise of Virginia reminded the
country of the debt it owed John Ross for what had been
done at Horse Shoe Bend; Webster denounced the treaty
as "a great wrong."

Even Van Buren was moved. He was not, after all,
another Old Hickory. In the spring of 1838 he yielded to
these pressures to the extent of proposing to allow the
Cherokees two more years of grace. But this impulse of
clemency was frustrated by an ugly warning from Georgia, where Gilmer was governor again. Permit such delay,
said Gilmer, and there would be a collision on Cherokee
soil between Federal troops and the Georgia militia; the
consequences would be on Van Buren's head.

Jackson could have met such a threat on its own terms,
had he chosen to incur it; he had forced South Carolina to
back down on exactly such a bluff. But Van Buren, again,
was no Jackson. Presented with this ultimatum he merely
threw up his hands. There was nothing, then, that he
could do for the Cherokees; the treaty must be executed.

2.

The Cherokees, meanwhile, had made no more preparations for removal than if they had never heard of the proposal. The whole arrangement had for them the irrational and preposterous quality of a nightmare. Harried though they were, here still were the familiar contours of their hills about them, and these hills were theirs. They had not been unworthy of such a land. Their soil they had tended lovingly, learning the newest and best methods of making their cornfields and their orchards fruitful. They had cared for their woodlands and chestnut groves, keeping the latter parklike by burning off the underbrush in spring and fall, tending their fires carefully lest the forests suffer. Their own affairs they had managed soberly; they lived in peace and order; they had been good neighbors; in the memory of man no Cherokee had done unprovoked violence to a white man.

White men talked of a treaty; there was no treaty, for they had never made one. "Indeed," one of their memorials had set forth, "the Cherokee Nation need never have been consulted or their signatures obtained. The president might of his own mere notion dictate the terms of a treaty to the Senate and by the ratification of that body it becomes binding upon all who never saw or assented to it."

In vain the friendly Wool pleaded with them that they were largely dispossessed in any case, and that such protection as he had been able to give them must soon be withdrawn.

General Winfield Scott, who came into the country in the spring of 1838 with authority not only to command Federal troops but also to call out as many militiamen from the states involved as he needed to enforce submission, had no better success. Stolidly the Cherokees watched his men construct eleven stockade forts at strategic points in the Nation to serve as concentration camps; they saw the keelboats built and the chartered steamers brought up to the landings. And they were not moved. They would not lift a finger to get their possessions in order for transportation West; they were not going West.

On May 10, Scott addressed a last appeal to them from his headquarters at New Echota. "Will you, by resistance, compel us to resort to arms? Or will you by flight seek to hide yourselves in the mountains and forests and oblige us to hunt you down?"

Some Cherokees, dispossessed anyway, acted on the hint contained in these not wholly discreet words. But those who still had homes remained in them, going about their chores as usual. Why should they take flight? Their consciences were clear; they had nothing to run away from.

But on May 23 the roundup began.

3.

Georgia's great moment had come at last, after thirty-six years. The militia—not the Georgia Guard, which after the unfortunate Payne episode had been denounced and disbanded by the Georgia assembly—was in the country in force, ready for anything, ready to fight Federal troops if Governor Gilmer gave the word, but now most happily ready to collaborate with them in ridding the country of the Cherokee varmints.

They were in robust humor. One heard them roaring out snatches of a song that someone had composed at the time John Marshall was insulting the sovereign state of Georgia with his decisions:

> *The Georgians are coming, oho, oho,*
> *The Georgians are coming, oho, oho,*
> *The Georgians are coming*
> *With roaring and humming*
> *And cruikshanks with rum in, oho, oho.*

Bestriding a Cherokee pony, great Lumpkin,
With phiz beaming bright as a lightning bug's tail,
With nullification grown full as a pumpkin,
He'll puff like a Steamboat and spout like a whale.

They'll grapple old Marshall and choke him to death . . .
The Georgians are coming, oho, oho. . . .

So the Georgians came, and according to Butrick one detachment of high-spirited zealots desired permission from General Scott to make an example of sixteen Cherokees they had seized at New Echota by giving them a public whipping outside the stockades. This desire the General did not gratify. On the contrary he warned them to watch their language in handling the Cherokees and expressly forbade them to fire on the Indians even if they attempted to escape. In the main these orders were observed. But a bewildered deaf-mute who turned right when told to go left was shot and killed. A man who dared strike a soldier for goading his wife with a bayonet was handcuffed and given one hundred lashes.

On the whole, however, there were surprisingly few such incidents. Many Cherokees fled when they could, but with the exception of the half legendary Tsali, of whom more anon, they did not resist. On the march to the camps, the soldiers formed them into platoons with soldiers forward and to the rear and in single file along the flanks. The Georgians, being mostly farm folk, liked to urge the band along with the cries they used in driving hogs as more appropriate to the mentality of the Cherokees than military orders. Those who had bayonets found it good sport to use them to prod a laggard. But there was less of this sort of thing than might have been expected. Joel Chandler Harris, some of whose Uncle Remus stories came straight out of Cherokee country, was stretching a point when he wrote that "there has never been any complaint as to the manner in which the troops performed their duty"; but there was among the troops more decency than not; the indecency lay rather in what they were asked to do.

4.

It is a terrible and wonderful thing, not unlike the Last Judgment, for a day to be appointed when an entire nation shall be set upon the road. Strange fish were caught in the white man's net. There were men and women so old and gnarled that they seemed more like supernatural beings than human flesh. There were newborn babies; indeed, there were unborn babies who elected just this moment to thrust themselves into the world, so that their mothers were left by the road, sometimes to die there. There were the blind; until that moment the missionaries had no idea that there were so many blind in the Nation. There were dying consumptives who had to be carried on litters. There were idiots.

There were the devout; Epenetus was picked up on the road when he was returning from helping Butrick administer the sacrament at Brainerd, and he was not allowed to return there to fetch his young son, but was thrust into a keelboat on the Tennessee and shipped all the way to Arkansas without having a chance to find out what would become of his boy.

Sometimes when the soldiers came battering at the doors, gentlefolk said, "Let us pray first." Then the soldiers stood sheepishly by while a man fitted spectacles over his nose, got out a queer little book printed in Sequoia's characters, and read from it to his family.

One woman senselessly filled her apron with corn, stepped to the door, and threw a last handful to her chicks and stood staring at them blindly until someone took her arm and guided her away.

Children took fright at the appearance of the white

men, and fled into the woods, and their weeping mothers were not permitted to go and find them.

A man came down the hills from a hunt, a buck slung over his shoulders, and walked straight into the Georgia militia. He was luckier than some who had been away and returned to find despoiled and empty cabins, and nothing to tell them what had happened except a howling dog and a stray cow moaning because her milking was overdue.

With the devout came also the wicked. Smoke came, that same Smoke who had terrified Miss Sophia with his drunken fits at Haweis.

Butrick saw his first refugees on May 31, when sundown caught a company of two hundred, two and a half miles from camp, and the lieutenant in command asked permission to stop where they were. They had been plodding through a heavy rain, and they were drenched. Butrick's Elizabeth brought the mothers into her kitchen and helped them strip their shuddering, blue-lipped babies by the fire, warmed milk for them, and helped dry their clothes.

Others were taken into the meetinghouse, where the lieutenant gave his orders. After they heard the drum beat, he told them, none must leave the building again, on pain of being shot, until daybreak.

"But sir, some have dysentery," said his Cherokee interpreter. (Bilingual Cherokees were in great demand as interpreters at $2.50 a day; a son of Sequoia's was acting in that capacity.) The lieutenant revised his order: they might go out only if they asked permission first.

They were not the last Cherokees to take refuge at Brainerd or at Butler's station at Red Clay. Cherokees fled over the line from Georgia seeking sanctuary in Tennessee. One hundred came on a rainy Sunday to hear Butler preach on a text out of Lamentations. And after the sermon Butler found that it was with him as with the disciples in the wilderness; no good shepherd could dismiss this forlorn flock unfed. He distributed a ration of corn and meat from his own stores and arranged for forty to sleep in the meetinghouse; the rest found shelter with Ross and Hicks. "Homeless," commented Butler, "on their own soil."

But Tennessee was an impermanent sanctuary; on June 5, the work in Georgia being virtually complete, 8000 Cherokees in custody, the roundup began there as well. But still some Cherokees roamed from place to place, evading arrest, grateful to the missionaries for giving them refuge for a night.

5.

The troops had not come among the Cherokees unattended. Homesteaders crowded on their heels on the lookout for bargains in such household furnishings and livestock as the Cherokees could not take with them.

In this matter there were many kinds of procedure. Sometimes the Cherokees were interrupted when they tried to gather possessions in a blanket, and were ordered to leave everything as it was: arrangements would be made later. Sometimes sales were made on the spot, and the more unsophisticated Cherokees, bewildered when their cabins suddenly filled up with armed white men, distracted by the weeping of their children and clamor of their dogs, were no match for hard-headed bargain-hunters. Beef creatures, rocking chairs, cherrywood tables, castiron kettles, fiddle saws, homespun blankets, and patchwork quilts went for a twelfth of their value or for nothing at all. One Cherokee recalled that his cabin had been made the scene of an impromptu auction; very distinctly he recalled the price fetched for his blue-edged plates, twenty-five cents apiece. But who got the money? The auctioneer perhaps? Anyway, *he* never saw it.

Some soldiers were agreeable about the delays caused

by such transactions. They saw no reason to interfere when a Cherokee protested that he was being swindled. It wasn't cheating when you cheated a Cherokee, who had no right to be where he was, had got what he had by holding back Georgia from her lawful rights, and had disregarded repeated orders to get ready to move. To help oneself to the unexpectedly desirable possessions found in the cabins was like helping yourself to the berries off the bush; they were there for that purpose, and if you didn't take them someone else would.

Some Cherokees had the presence of mind to refuse to sell on the spot. These locked up, went to camp, and as quickly as they could arrange it came back on parole to see to their belongings. But those were as often as not gone when they came back.

6.

The roundup had gone so smoothly that by June 17 Scott was able to dismiss the militia that had assisted his regulars. Already 1675 Cherokees had been launched by water towards the West in two detachments, and on June 17 a third detachment of 1070 was sent after them.

"Towards the West" is the way to put it, for these parties did not arrive in force. The Cherokees had told Butrick they could be taken only if they were "bound to the bottom of a boat." Some of them told the truth. The guards had found embarkation hard to handle; the Cherokees wouldn't give their names, wouldn't accept rations. Driven into boats, they did perforce stay there so long as the boats were afloat, but when they were encamped by the way some of them got drunk and others, observing that the guard had been reduced, left the place and made for home overland. One party of eight hundred numbered only 489 by the time it reached Paducah.

The large group that left overland on June 17 was the most unmanageable of all, because the emigrants had

heard that emigration was about to be suspended until
fall. When their petition to be allowed to turn back was
refused, as many of them as could manage it went anyway. By June 25 a hundred had escaped, and on that date,
when a second petition was refused, three hundred took
to the woods and the rest mutinied. White men were liars,
said one spokesman; the Cherokees would not follow them
further; they would go home and fight for John Ross.

A company of volunteers had to be enlisted to restore
order and beat the woods for the fugitives and marshal
what was left of the party on its way. But the Cherokees,
unable to continue open defiance, could still be crafty.
They watched every relaxation of vigilance; the party
continued to melt away from its captors. Women and children followed their menfolk into freedom, living off the
countryside by an ancient, half forgotten lore, walking on
stubborn feet as many as three hundred miles back to the
hills of home. Only 722 were left of the 1,070 when they
finally reached Little Rock.

There was nothing dangerous about the Cherokees except when some fool let them get blind drunk; but they
were stubborn as death and as hard to handle.

7.

The rumor that removal had been suspended was correct. The season was dry and hot, the rivers were low;
mortality was increasing in the camps at an alarming rate.
Taking cognizance of these facts, General Scott had ordered that all parties not already on their way might
remain in camp until fall.

In setting May 23 for enforced removal, the Senate had
not had any more practical consideration in mind than
that this date would give the Cherokees exactly two years
to reconcile themselves to their fate. Otherwise the date
was as bad a choice as could have been made. All spring
Butrick had been worrying about the perils of a summer

removal. Summer was fever season. The Cherokees, to be sure, had hitherto been a reasonably hardy people. The visitation of smallpox in 1836 had not resulted in a real epidemic in spite of the unhappy circumstances of the Nation at that time. Measles, of which there was again a mild epidemic, was not as disastrous to the Cherokees as it is to most primitive peoples; not, at least, so long as they could have it at home.

But Cherokees removed from the bracing atmosphere of their hills, placed in climates and circumstances to which they were not accustomed, were a different people. The mortality of the exodus of 1834 had proved that; even without the accident of cholera, the death rate had been very high, and yet the emigration had taken place in winter, the season considered the most healthful for travel in these latitudes. What then could be expected from a summer migration, particularly this summer? It had turned out to be unusually oppressive. Day after day the sun blazed out of a cloudless sky, drinking up the wells and springs. When thunderheads came, they hovered ineffectually over the hills, muttering and flashing sometimes, but giving no rain, adding only to the heaviness of the days.

The camps themselves were clumsily contrived. At temporary camps Indians were forced to sleep on bare ground with no overhead shelter. At the larger camps near the river landings, planned to accommodate thousands while waiting for the keelboats, there were tents or sheds, but no provision for sanitation and an inadequate and questionable water supply. No privacy was possible; according to the missionaries the Indians were herded like pigs in a sty. Not the humblest, most ignorant Cherokee living in a windowless one-room cabin with a dirt floor was used to such squalor as prevailed here.

Bitterly Butrick wrote in his journal that the government might more mercifully have put to death at once everyone under a year or over sixty; it had chosen "a most expensive and painful way of putting these poor people to death."

There was a sickness of spirit upon the Cherokees. For the gentle it took the form of heartbreak, for others a deathly hatred of those responsible for this humiliation. Still others profited by the condition of a world turned upside down to enjoy a witches' sabbath. Smoke and his kind found their way to the local whisky supply and made the night hideous with their screaming and shouting. Brawling followed such bouts; someone broke Smoke's jaw, and two weeks later someone shot him dead. That disposed of Smoke, but not of his kind.

With despair Butrick saw Federal soldiers luring Cherokee girls into this saturnalia. They went after the better-bred girls, the ones that had been to mission schools and knew English. (Butrick regretted that any Cherokee had ever been taught a word of the language.) The soldiers induced pretty girls to drink from their bottles, and when there had been a sufficient dose of such medicine the girls forgot their bringing up, their mission training, and all the afflictions that had come upon their parents; and so did some lonesome soldiers.

And out of this saturnalia, out of this humiliation, unprivacy, this heartbreak, came a great sickness that made even the cholera that had overtaken the emigrants of 1834 seem of minor consequence.

Butler now remembered that he was a physician. No orders had come from the Board to resume his practice; he did what he must to save his people. "The Cherokee," he wrote, "seem to be taken off as with a flood."

The sickening began with what Butler called "putrid dysentery." It appeared in a fatal form and became epidemic at once. Butler reported seventeen deaths in one camp in one week, of this cause alone. Measles cropped up again, and whooping cough, and "remitting fever." Babies died by the hundred; children were born into these unhappy camps, but seldom survived to make the pilgrimage. Butler himself in August lost his seven-months-old child.

In October he reported that an estimated 2000 had died in the encampments alone.

8.

During the summer the Cherokees took advantage of the enforced delay to assemble in Council and draw up their own plans for an exodus that not even John Ross had any further hopes of resisting.

Some of the missionaries, Worcester, and even Butler, had supposed that John Ross's reputation would suffer as a result of the tragedy. His leadership had been based on faith that the United States would fulfill its obligations, and that faith had been misplaced. It was Boudinot who had warned them that delay would be ruinous. Boudinot had been right. Had the Cherokees resigned themselves to arrange for removal before the summer heat struck they would have saved lives. Instead they had waited while Ross's delegation made its last appeal to Washington. Besides being ruinous, the delay had been futile: Van Buren had been almost persuaded, but only almost. Ross, returning to the Nation shortly after the roundup started, could no longer hold out any hope that removal could be avoided.

Yet Ross, reported the surprised Butler, had not lost one particle of the confidence his people had placed in him. If he had been wrong, they had been wrong, for his will had been their will. They did not, however, discuss wrongs in connection with Ross and themselves. There had been only one wrong, the treaty of New Echota. That and not "ruinous delay" was responsible for the present tragedy; even Jackson had been powerless to move against them until he had made some sort of phantom treaty to replace the honorable treaty of Hopewell. They had been undone by an act of treachery. All the hatred of the Cherokees was focused like sun through a lens on one object: the group that had perpetrated the treaty of New Echota—the Ridges, Boudinot, and Boudinot's brother, Stand Watie.

Council met in August at the Indian Agency at Rattlesnake Springs. They gave their first attention to the hated treaty, putting it on record that compliance with its demands was not to be interpreted as recognition. The Indians had not been able to keep to their Spartan resolve to accept no government rations; they accepted them, but only as dole.

The constitution and their laws were to be continued in the new country.

Then they gave their attention to the now unavoidable matter of removal. They made a division of what was left of the Nation into fourteen parties of 700 to 1000 each, appointed leaders and a police force. Overland routes were mapped out, the favorite lying through Nashville. The water routes now had a bad odor; too many deaths had occurred on the way; the humiliation of seeing Cherokees driven into the "loathsome boats" was too burning a memory. Even the fact that between Tuscumbria and Decatur the Indians had been transported (to the intense interest of some of them) on a brand-new novelty called steam cars could not induce them to choose that route.

Having made up their minds at last, the Indians drew their plans with methodical efficiency. General Scott could find no flaw in them, helped them assemble the 645 wagons, the 5000 horses, and the oxen needed for the journey. On October 4 the Cherokees began to move out of the country under their own power.

But not all of them. When Butler made his surprised comment on the undiminished prestige of Ross, he had lost sight of one group of irreconcilables who would not have removal on any terms. Many of these were hiding in the hills, living under conditions more primitive than those of their most savage forefathers, for they could neither plant nor build and hardly dared light fires. When Ross at last surrendered to force, other Cherokees detached themselves from his removal parties and joined the fugitives. By some accounts there were as many as a thousand of them. Scott knew about them and sent searching parties after them, but they were as impossible to collect as so many squirrels.

In the eyes of this group, Ross's final capitulation made him no less a traitor than Ridge. It is the descendants of these who today keep alive the confused tradition that Ross was Jackson's man and plotted with him to achieve the abomination of removal.

9.

One by one the parties of the Cherokees set off in the fall of 1838. Their course ran northwest across the Cumberland Plateau to Nashville, through Hopkinsville, Kentucky, to Golconda, where they crossed the Ohio, and then west to cross the Mississippi at the double sandbar near Jonesville. From there on it was a southwest course to the Arkansas country.

Tennessee, Kentucky, Illinois watched them go, often with incuriosity, for they were used to seeing homesteaders on the march. They could not, however, have seen many like these; the cavalcade of wagons, carryalls, horsemen, and plodding pedestrians stretched out for a mile at a time; when they bivouacked at night their camps were like miniature cities. The first of these detachments set out in September, the last in November, so that there seemed to be no end of them.

They met all kinds of reception on their way. The ascent of some parties into the Cumberland Plateau was made hazardous for the heavy wagons by the refusal of a farmer to let them take an improved road leading through his acres. Once in Illinois, a state of which Butrick had a low opinion, some of them cut their wood and pitched their tents in three places before they were allowed to settle for the night.

Many communities took the view that, these being Indians, they were homesteaders with a difference, people who had just profited richly from a land deal with the government. They went after their money, primarily with whisky, and there was disorder in camp, though as time went on the Lighthorse Guard learned to control the worst of it. The price of commodities rose as the pilgrims traveled—apples from six to fifty cents a dozen. Sometimes a white man overtook the leader of a detachment and demanded a price for having buried an Indian who had fallen behind and died on the road.

But not everyone was unkind. Hopkinsville, Kentucky, took up a collection for the relief of one party. Preachers along the way sometimes opened their own meetinghouses to Butrick so that he would not have to assemble his congregation in the open in the bitter November weather. On one of these occasions, when white people crowded into the meetinghouse so fast that there was no room for their invited guests, the Cherokees, Butrick talked not of the children of Israel, but of this lost tribe; he told of their covenant with the government, how the Cherokees had observed it faithfully, how the government had broken it to please Georgia.

Butrick and his Elizabeth slept either in their carryall, whose curtains could not always protect them from a driving snow or rain, or in a tent pitched in the encampment area. In December there were sometimes great winds that tore limbs from the trees and blew brands from the fire all over the tents. But sometimes the missionary folk were given hospitality. They remembered Nashville with particular affection, not alone for its beautiful cedars and the fact that it was the most splendid city Butrick had seen since he left Boston a score of years before, but also because they were invited there to sleep in feather beds, and because after they left, so that they could not refuse, gifts were sent after them—a leghorn bonnet, shoes, a shawl, a "cloke."

Denominationalism was forgotten on the journey. Butrick held the sacrament one Sunday in the home of a Baptist elder; on another occasion he held a joint meeting with a Methodist preacher, a Cherokee. He was grateful when Trott, a Methodist missionary to the Cherokees who had had his own brush with the Georgia Guard, made a special trip to call on him.

Several parties had left the Nation very late. Winter caught them plodding up frozen roads, some of them barefoot, trying to get to the Mississippi before it became impassable. They were too late, and had to wait two weeks to get across.

An observer from Maine saw them at this time. He saw the look of death on the faces of the sick who lay in the wagons; he noted the graves made almost daily by the encampments. It happened that he had just read a message of Van Buren congratulating the nation that Indian removal had at last been peaceably achieved. What he saw filled him with bitterness at these weasel words.

Yet the plodders persevered; by January 4, Elijah Hicks had brought the first of the parties to the place of deposit where they would receive each a year's rations and be dispersed to their new homes. Week by week and month by month the others followed him in. By March 25 the last stragglers had arrived.

10.

Butler had been assigned by Ross to accompany one detachment as physician and chaplain. In spite of his efforts, he had lost forty of his charges, and other parties had fared worse. Old Chief White Path, he who had organized the "rebellion" against the new constitution, had died in Tennessee. Quatie, wife of John Ross, died within sight of her undesired goal, near Little Rock, Arkansas. As early as January 25, 1839, when Butler's party arrived, he estimated the deaths since May at four thousand. Later he revised the figure upward. "From the first of June I feel as if I had been in the midst of death." On his last Sunday with his detachment he had preached a general funeral sermon.

Lucy Ames Butler had been left behind in the Nation, since Butler proposed to return to close the mission. After the departure of Ross with the last detachment she had been alone. The chief, reluctant to leave her unprotected, had offered her a "black man," but Lucy refused. Getting so valuable a property safely to the Arkansas was too great a responsibility.

By March, Butler was back with her at Red Clay. He saw circumstances that saddened him. "It is a shameful fact that some white families have already moved from the country where the Cherokees lived . . . to the West. . . . Before I left the detachment several Cherokees inquired of me with feeling why it was that those white people who had moved among them and robbed them of their country were not satisfied and willing to remain there."

It was on this visit that he heard that Cherokees were still hiding in the mountains. Their condition was miserable; of the thousand that had originally taken refuge there, half were believed to have died during the winter. Hearing this, Butler revised the mortality rates: 4600 deaths since May, more than a quarter of the Nation.

Butler busied himself getting his sacramental furniture, his own belongings, and those of others down to a keelboat at Ross's Landing. When it was ready he and his wife would go aboard and have themselves towed part way on their journey to the new life in the West.

What sort of life? Butrick had written just before his own departure: "With regard to the West all is dark as midnight. . . . O that my head were waters and mine eyes a fountain of tears that I might weep day and night for the slain of the daughters of my people."

CHAPTER XIX

The Law of Blood

Miss Sophia, at the last moment, had nearly decided against accepting the offer of John Ridge, her "protector and benefactor," to build her a school in the West.

The younger Ridge, last of his family to leave the East, had written her from Running Waters in the summer of 1837 to send her $150 for expenses and to urge her to meet him at Creek Path or Nashville by the end of September so that she could help Sarah manage their children on the journey West. There were six of these now, all intelligent, all lively, as none knew better than Miss Sophia. The last of the brood had been born in 1835, the year of the treaty, and was named Andrew Jackson Ridge. John Ridge had come a long way in his thinking since 1831, when he had applied the epithet Chicken Thief to the venerable chief executive.

Miss Sophia appreciated the invitation and was as fond as ever of the Ridges, but still she hesitated. While she delayed she missed the appointment at Creek Path, at Nashville, and a later possible rendezvous at St. Louis. The Ridges, in fact, had to make the journey without the services of Miss Sophia. But in the West the offer of a home and school still stood. When would she join them? And still Miss Sophia tarried; did she really want to cast her lot with the Cherokees again?

[302]

She had had rather a pleasant time of it since she had
left New Echota. After her visit with old friends in New
Hampshire she had stopped in New York, Washington
(where the good Schermerhorn had made her a present of
$50 in Georgia money), and in Philadelphia, and now
she was established in Newark. The travel had been stimulating, though after her association with friendly Georgians she had a low opinion of Yankee manners; she had
been working on a book called *Lights and Shades of Indian Character in Thirteen Years Residence Among the
Cherokees*, which a gentleman in Connecticut had almost
promised to publish, and now she was teaching again.
This time it was an "African school for females." Ever
since her experiences with Sam and Peter, she had had a
soft spot in her heart for colored children. She liked her
work with them, and her relations with her fellow teachers
were immensely satisfying.

Longing for society to her liking had always been a
major frustration for Miss Sophia in the Nation. The
missionaries somehow weren't her kind of people. She had
been unhappy until the Ridges had rescued her. In the
West she would again have the Ridges, but one very dear
friend and collaborator she would not have: Harriet Gold
Boudinot. The latter had died shortly after her departure,
worn out by childbearing and by the intensities engendered by her husband's political activities. The event had
grieved Miss Sophia, who was concerned for Boudinot left
with five children at such a time. The latter, however, remained alone very briefly; he married Delight Sargent,
to the shocked surprise of Worcester, in time to have her
assistance in moving his family West. Miss Sophia knew
Delight, who had also been a mission teacher, but Delight
wasn't Harriet Boudinot.

Nevertheless Miss Sophia had given her word to the
Ridges, and a word must be kept. In the fall of 1837 she
packed up, made several references to Scriptural sacrifice

in her letters to the Board to indicate that her mood was not exactly one of adventurous gaiety, and took a ship for New Orleans and finally a river boat for Fort Smith.

On her ship, the *Little Rock*, Miss Sophia had her first impression of life in the West, and an uneasy impression it was. The boat was infested with gamblers who drank prodigiously and bragged—for all the world like Cherokees bent on proving themselves "much of a man"—of killings. Still worse, and this was not like the Cherokees she knew best, they cursed in a manner "to chill your blood." Lying awake in her cabin Miss Sophia heard strange oaths through the thin partitions. "I had never heard the second and third person of the Trinity used in a profane way but once before." She desired to apply her educational methods to the diction of these gamblers, but her cabin mates dissuaded her. After all, they pointed out, the sinners never cursed before ladies, fell into a respectful hush the moment "a female" appeared. It was not their fault that the acoustics were such that females could follow their lusty male talk even when not officially present.

What most troubled Miss Sophia was the finding of characters like these at the very threshold of the new home of the Cherokees. The whole argument for removal as she understood it was that the Cherokees would thereby be placed forever beyond the reach of white men of such habits. Was it possible that the Cherokees, who were now submitting in agony of spirit to removal, would find the moral conditions of the new land even worse than what they had left behind them in the East?

Such fears were only too well justified. Already there were white intruders in the Nation, and there was whisky and there was violence. Even John Ridge was proposing to sell wine in his new store. His wife and the missionaries were protesting and might yet have their way, but John thought their point of view narrow; his business would be not in spirits, but in light wines, and wine rather than an impossible abstinence was the way to wean Cherokees away from the whisky kegs.

If Miss Sophia took part in this controversy, she loyally forbore writing the Board about it. (She left the tale-bearing to Samuel Worcester.) But looking about her she was almost frightened by what she saw, particularly in the spring of 1839 when the Cherokee Nation East had at last moved in among the Old Settlers.

"The critical situation of the Nation I cannot communicate," she wrote in May from Honey Creek. "It is such a time of excitement and I am always getting into trouble. . . . The atmosphere of the old nation in its most disturbed state, compared to this was like the peaceful lake to the boisterous ocean."

These were unhappy words from one who had believed that conditions in the "old nation" were intolerable, and that salvation lay in the West. But in October, after the incredible worst had happened, she uttered a cry even more despairing. She wrote of the Cherokees: "I felt this morning that if I could escape eternally from them, I would go where I might not hear of their suffering and degradation."

But though Miss Sophia could not help uttering such cries, she was too much a woman of character to behave as she had suggested. She had cast her lot with the Cherokees, and with the Cherokees she would remain until the day of her death.

2.

There were two Cherokee causes for the uproar in the West. The most obvious but least dangerous was the fact that the country now had two governments, each with its own constitution and code of laws: that of the Old Settlers, and that of the newcomers from the East, who had expressly reaffirmed their own constitution just before they took to the road. The second group far outnumbered the first, but the Old Settlers were none the less disinclined to yield priority of position to superiority of numbers; they insisted on due process of law as prescribed by their own constitution.

That problem would have been solved without much difficulty had it not been tangled with a subtler and deadlier circumstance, the implacable hatred that most Eastern Cherokees felt not only for everyone concerned with the Treaty of New Echota, but also for everyone who was suspected of so much as having reconciled himself to it.

This hatred had expressed itself already in the old Nation. In the West it was intensified a hundredfold by what the Cherokees had endured on what they now called the "Trail of Tears." Some remembered the days of fever when they had lain in wagons rocking and lurching along the rough roads; some remembered the sting of frozen ground under bare feet; and all, even Chief Ross himself, remembered a grave dug in alien soil where they had placed a child, a wife, a sister, a father, each dead needlessly and before his time because what they called treachery had driven them from their hills.

Worcester had discovered that the treaty leaders were not liked in the West, even before the Easterners caught up to them. People had made it unpleasant for him because he hired Boudinot. But others were even more unpopular than Boudinot. The Ridge, according to Worcester, bore the real brunt of the odium because he had been "a very distinguished man." Although for practical purposes it mattered little to the Old Settlers what these men had done, there was a very general feeling that it had been wrong, that what Boudinot had defended as a higher, more intelligent form of patriotism was in fact betrayal.

When the Easterners arrived, even the devout did not conceal their hatred of the Treaty Party. Butrick reported that all congregations showed a disinclination to let members of the Party sit with the communicants unless they first made public confession that they had been wrong; indeed, they had taken a resolution to this effect before they left the East. Butrick did not interfere. For one thing the influence of the missionaries was just now at its lowest ebb; though the Cherokees were polite in their presence, among themselves they were saying that the treaty of New Echota had been planned in the penitentiary at Milledgeville when Boudinot had visited Worcester. It was the latter who was held responsible, but even his fellow prisoner Butler was not believed entirely above suspicion, and Butrick recalled that in the encampments there had been Cherokees who would not speak to him.

There was nothing to do about this state of affairs but let it take its course; and Butrick held to his old premise that consciences were private and Cherokees entitled to their opinions. He busied himself with his parochial duties and resolutely kept clear of such dissensions. But by the end of the summer these dissensions had reached so appalling a climax that his parochial duties were nearly nonexistent. "They are the same dear people as formerly," he wrote in August, but in the confusion a congregation was almost impossible to collect, and the missionaries could "do little else than enter into their chambers and weep."

3.

In April there had been a called Council of the Cherokee Nation West. The reason had been local: the need of appointing a new chief, John Brown, to carry out the duties of the recently deceased Chief Jolly until elections could be held in October. But, this business completed, Council had yielded to the plea of John Ross that the government of the Eastern Nation be accorded a formal reception and that the question of how to unite the two governments be considered. The discussion, however, led to nothing but a flare-up of resentment on the part of the Easterners.

To one observer this flare-up was irrational and inexplicable. This observer was the missionary C. Washburn, who had been working at Dwight among the Old Settlers and had small practical knowledge of the politics of the East. He was now making his first acquaintance of Ross, and was forming a most unflattering impression of a man hitherto known for his tact and his patience. There may have been some justice in Washburn's estimate; it is possible that Ross's character, like that of his fellow citizens, had suffered deterioration as a result of the brutal experience of encampment and emigration and the complete frustration of Cherokee hopes.

The dissension had arisen over the fact that the Old Settlers had insisted that confusion could be avoided only if the Eastern Nation came under the Western laws until general elections could be held in October to elect a government and draw up a constitution agreeable to both parties. Ross objected, saying that the Cherokee Nation East must retain its body politic in order to press its claims against the government. Chief Brown agreed to their doing so for that purpose, but Ross, who favored union then, was still dissatisfied; why, Mr. Washburn could not imagine.

"Had he acceded he would have been unanimously chosen principal chief next fall and at the elections his friends would have been chosen to fill nearly all offices in the government, but he rejected all overtures for union and seemed determined to set up his own government and laws. By what motives . . . impossible to say. It does not seem that it was ambition that governed him. . . . He would have been the highest chief and the most popular man in the nation, and by the course he has taken he has lost the confidence of many."

The only clue Washburn could think of to Ross's behavior was that the Federal authorities favored the Old Settlers' proposal and that sheer obstinacy impelled Ross to reject whatever the Americans willed.

There was, however, a deeper motivation that Washburn was not in a position to appreciate. All the missionaries who had made the journey with the Cherokees, and even Worcester, who had preceded them, understood only too well what the real trouble was.

The difficulty was not expressed in the rather captious objections that Ross made to details of the Western constitution. It lay in a conviction on the part of the Easterners that the Old Settlers were acting under pressure from the Ridges and Boudinot. In spite of their unpopularity with the public, in spite of Council's expressed objection to Boudinot's connection with the American Board, the Treaty Party did have considerable political influence among the Westerners. They had preceded the rest of the Nation into the West, had brought their sympathizers with them in force, and had consolidated them in Western communities. Quite recently The Ridge had been invited to address Council.

The Eastern Cherokees also remembered that a delegation of the late Chief Jolly's had once lent John Ridge assistance in conducting his unauthorized negotiations in Washington. And added to everything else was the fact that the Old Settlers refused to commit themselves to a resolution denouncing the treaty as fraudulent.

In insisting on deferring the question of consolidation until the regular October Council, the Old Settlers were merely following correct constitutional procedure. Once the Eastern Cherokees could have appreciated this position; no one in the old days had been more of a stickler for legal form than they. But all these legalities, these Supreme Court cases, had been futile; to maintain their existence at all they had been forced to disregard their own constitution; and in the end they had been undone by the letter of the law, by what was called law—the treaty of New Echota.

They had come to the Old Settlers' Council not to impose their own laws on the West, but to offer a union, immediate and honest. Their offer had been evaded, put off; in the postponement they read something sinister: it was a move on the part of the Ridges to gain in the West a political ascendancy they had not enjoyed in the East.

Butler wrote later that could the union have been effected in the spring, when the newcomers wanted it, lives would have been spared.

4.

According to Washburn, the Old Settlers finally withdrew in disgust from their own Council and left the Easterners to their resolutions and their arguments.

What was remarkable about this rump Council was that the most important subject under consideration was kept from the ears of its presiding officer. There was, after all, one subject on which Ross could not be trusted: the formal execution of a law to which not only he but John Ridge had set his signature. Fulfillment of this law was now long overdue; plans for it were being drawn up in Council, but not openly. The matter was whispered in odd corners; details were arranged in conferences called out of hours. And according to Worcester, himself no admirer of Ross, extraordinary precautions were taken to keep these discussions from the ears of the chief.

Council adjourned at last on Friday, June 21, apparently in a high state of inconclusion. Actually a crucial plan had been matured and action set for Saturday, June 22.

Boudinot at this time was working with Worcester on a translation of St. John. Their two families were living together at Park Hill until such time as Boudinot's own house, under construction about a mile away, could be completed. On this Saturday morning Boudinot set out to have a look at it; he was alone.

It was a hired man who heard a distant cry for help and called for Worcester.

The morning was fine; dew sparkled on the grass, but fear was in the air. It was as if Worcester had always known that this moment would come. He and Delight Boudinot ran in the direction of the cry. Among tall grasses they found Boudinot lying all bloody, stabbed in the back and gashed about the head with a hatchet. He was still alive; he opened his eyes when they called his name; but the eyes set in a stare and glazed in death before he could speak.

"I have done what I could," Boudinot had written. "I have served my country—I hope with fidelity."

Boudinot lay alone in the sparkling grasses, but he was not alone. At dawn, when the household of John Ridge was still asleep, a company of riders had come up to the house.

John stirred drowsily, opened his eyes, and met the hard stare of men who had once been his friends. They dragged him from his bed and from his house.

The woman who had been Sarah Northrup of Cornwall followed them. When she got to the veranda, at first she could see only that the mysterious horsemen were riding away again. Then, shading her eyes from the sun, she saw what they had come for. John Ridge, the handsome Indian youth, the young prince of Cherokees who had taken her away from the safety of Cornwall to strange lands and stranger adventures, lay dead on the ground, twenty wounds in his body.

Her son, young John Rollin Ridge, came to his mother and looked too. Until now in his twelve-year-old eyes the whole removal program had been a zestful voyage of discovery among new flora and fauna. But what he saw that

summer morning he never forgot or forgave. The civilized
Cherokees had revived their savage law of blood revenge;
young John would take up the challenge of the feud.

Miss Sophia came running from another cabin and took
charge. The asperities of a brisk Yankee schoolma'am
were a comfort then. Mrs. Ridge collapsed in her arms and
let Miss Sophia persuade her for the children's safety to
take her away from that place to Fayetteville.

The horsemen who killed John Ridge had not yet completed their mission. They were now riding after Boudinot's brother, Stand Watie, but he had been warned and
eluded them. The Ridge, however, either had no warning
or was too proud to escape. When they reached him at ten
in the morning, he faced them unsurprised. "I have signed
my death warrant," he had said. And so it was.

5.

In the eyes of the survivors of the Treaty Party, in the
eyes of the Federal authorities at Fort Gibson, what had
taken place on June 22 was murder. The survivors fled
to the fort for protection; the authorities demanded of
John Ross that the killers be surrendered.

But although after the event Ross seems to have been
entrusted with full details, he succeeded in evading the
Federal demand. To the American Board, aghast at the
violent death of one of its employees and at the state of
disorder that now prevailed in the most civilized of Indian nations, Butrick vigorously defended the chief's
refusal. To confuse the tragedy with common murder was
unjust to the Cherokees, he insisted; it had simply been
execution of a law to which the victims themselves had
assented.

The Board, as so often before, was startled at the extent of Butrick's identification with the Cherokee point
of view. Actually, however, it is not on record that any
missionary had protested the Cherokee law of 1819 and

1828 to provide the death penalty for traitors. In any society treachery is usually punishable by death, and the missionaries well understood the grim necessities of the Cherokee struggle.

The aspect of the law that the missionaries might have protested for the good of the Cherokees was that execution did not follow trial by jury, but was left to any patriot who cared to take the responsibility. From this point of view it was no more than a partial restoration of the ancient law of blood feud which the Moravians had induced the Cherokees to renounce in 1810, a regression to an earlier and more savage code. No public trial preceded the execution of Boudinot and the Ridges; the all-important question of their guilt was left open for endless generations to wrangle over. The chief result was to thrust the tormented Cherokees back to the days of blood feud.

It was Delight Boudinot who first anticipated this result. Something of a heroine, the young wife, left now with five children, none of her bearing, wasted no time giving way to grief until she had taken practical measures to avert further calamities. She sent messages. One went to her brother-in-law, Stand Watie, warning him to escape and pleading with him to seek no revenge. Another went to Ross, whom neither she nor any other missionary suspected of complicity, telling him that she feared for his life.

Her warning saved Stand Watie, but it took him seven years to bring himself to give in to her appeal. His immediate answer was to recruit fifteen men and prowl the country in search of the assassins. However, the Ross party was incomparably stronger than his; Ross himself was well guarded. Watie, too, fled to Fort Gibson. For the moment no vengeance was possible; nevertheless a bloody tradition had been revived that was long to haunt the tumultuous country in the West.

Even the missionaries were not left unmolested. But-rick, who in spite of his sorrow had found much to delight him in the new country—seashells strewn unaccountably across the prairie, "ancient low red houses with roofs over-grown with moss"—was forced to run for his life. Avengers appointed by the stern old wife of The Ridge were after him; for it must be admitted that the apostle who had consistently denounced every semblance of missionary meddling had very strong opinions about the Treaty-makers, and these opinions were well known.

In the midst of the wild uproar caused by the triple killing a new Council of the Eastern Nation met in July. By now the Old Settlers were disposed to give them a wide berth; Chief Brown expressly warned his people to keep away from Council. Some attended, however, among them Sequoia, who is credited with playing an important part in the eventual reconciliation of East and West.

It was an assembly of uneasy conscience, given to taking fright at rumors that armed Treaty men were about to fall upon it. As a matter of fact, Treaty men were present, and were given the choice of being classed as out-laws or being reinstated in tribal membership if they would publicly confess the error of their ways. Seven of them actually made such confession.

The recent tragedy received oblique attention in a law, considered gratuitous by Worcester, granting general par-don for all crimes committed since emigration. In the eyes of most Cherokees there had been no crimes to pardon; but as Federal authorities took a different view, it was neces-sary to strengthen the hand of John Ross, lest he be forced to deliver authorized executioners to what white men called justice.

6.

Life went on, even in the violent West. In time the Old Settlers and the newcomers patched up a *modus vivendi*. John Ross became chief of them all, and remained chief for more than two decades. Common folk turned to their planting and building.

For a time they were listless about it. Gone was the splendid drive that had made them the most remarkable Indian nation in the country. The attitude of many was epitomized for Butler in an old man with whom he talked one January day.

"For whom do I build here?" the old man asked. "I had three sons. One died in General Scott's camp. One died on the trail. The third died here. For whom do I build my house?"

Butler tried to talk of the consolations of religion, but he found it difficult to bring the proper conviction into his voice. The old man shook his head and walked away trembling, for he had an ague.

Miss Sophia had no use for such despondents. She was busy now with a new school at Fayetteville, managing its finances through a bank that threatened to close down faster than she could get to it, but she found time for a call on the Nation in January 1840.

What she saw put her out of patience. There sat the Cherokees huddled up in their blankets at the doors of their slovenly huts, talking of their dead, asking for sympathy. They got something else from Miss Sophia: they got a piece of her mind.

"We have all wept enough!" said Miss Sophia. "Go to work and build houses and cultivate your land. Talk no more about little huts with wood chimneys but let your houses be such as will make suitable homes, such as shall tell to all around, 'We are helping ourselves.'"

CHAPTER **XX**

A Remnant Shall Return

The feuds precipitated by the deaths of the Treaty Party leaders amounted to something very like civil war. The stabilizing effect of an act of union between the Old Settlers and the newcomers, which took place in June 1840, when the former ratified the constitution drawn up in 1839 by Ross's followers, was nullified by Boudinot's vengeful brother Stand Watie, who in 1842 set off a new train of violence by killing James Foreman, one of the alleged assassins of The Ridge.

It was not until 1846 that a truce was called between factions. President Polk had suggested to Ross that, since the Cherokees seemed unable to agree, it might be best to subdivide their territory and their government into two or three independent groups. Dismayed by the suggestion, Ross brought himself and his followers to make sufficient concessions to the Treaty Party to effect a reconciliation in the Treaty of 1846.

Life was still not quiet. The notorious "Starr boys," descendants and associates of that James Starr who had first caused division in Cherokee ranks by negotiating independently with Jackson in 1833, roved the country, murdering and terrorizing, until in 1848 they were vanquished by a group of Cherokee vigilantes in a pitched battle.

But more peaceful pursuits were becoming possible again. Missions were being established, and the Cherokees were opening schools of their own. In 1844 they again had a paper, published partly in Sequoia's alphabet: *The Cherokee Advocate*, edited by a Princeton graduate, young W. P. Ross, who, though a nephew of the Chief, proved himself an impartial editor and no mere mouthpiece. The paper continued until 1854, when it was suspended for lack of funds; taxation was still one function of government that the Cherokees had not mastered.

Worcester at Park Hill continued his labors as translator in spite of the tragic death of his collaborator. Boudinot was replaced by Stephen Foreman, and that Foreman consented to the arrangement was proof that animosity against Worcester was diminishing, for Foreman was a strong Ross man. Worcester also had to find a new printer, for the long-suffering Wheeler, who back in the Cherokee Nation East had suffered arrest with Worcester, fled for his life after the assassination, and though his friends and his wife assured him that no man pursued him, he could not be induced to return. Worcester, very dubiously, made shift with a former Cherokee apprentice named Candy, and presently found to his surprise that the arrangement was not impossible.

His work went forward vigorously. The *Cherokee Almanac*, started in 1836, continued until 1861, two years after Worcester's death. The translation of the Bible was completed and published, a Cherokee primer devised, and material also made available in Sequoia's alphabet for the Creeks and Choctaws. Worcester's mission at Park Hill flourished and became the largest in Indian Territory.

But Worcester's gentle wife Ann did not live to see all this enterprise. She died in childbirth in May 1840, and Worcester, left with several children (the baby had survived), married a mission teacher, Erminia Nash, in 1841.

Miss Sophia Sawyer continued her school at Fayetteville, and though she was no longer connected with the American Board, she continued to favor Boston with her lively observations of life in the West and with poems and letters from her children. She led a rough life sometimes. Accused once of working like a man, she tartly retorted that God had entrusted her with a man's responsibilities. She had great adventures with the unstable currencies of the West; she would borrow money from one source to purchase silver dollars from another, turn these into double the amount in Arkansas currency, and apply the total to her school's indebtedness. Her last letters, dated 1848, are full of references to ill health, and though this was no new thing for Miss Sophia, it is impossible to imagine her living in silence, so probably she died soon after.

Her most distinguished pupil, John Rollin Ridge, joined the California gold rush about that time, and presently, thanks surely in part to his training with the eloquent Miss Sophia, attained fame as writer and editor. But he never forgave the assassins of his father, and was involved in one killing and in some of the later convolutions of the feud.

Butrick lived first at Mount Zion, where his parishioners were beset by the prowlings of the "Starr boys," and then at Dwight, where he died in 1851 after well over forty years spent continuously in the service of the Cherokees. His last years were uneventful, though he was beginning to show symptoms of an active interest in the abolitionist movement. He seemed to be on good terms with his fellow missionaries, above all with the Methodists. In 1847 he indulged himself in a visit to the Choctaws.

Butler's end was less happy. For a year or more after

removal he had been employed by the Cherokees as their national physician. "We have buttoned you and Mr. Butrick to us," Assistant Chief Lowry told him, "and when we thus button a person on to us we will hang on to him and never desert him." Later, in 1843, when Butler decided to settle again in a mission station of his own, Major Lowry himself, then seventy-six, and members of Council turned out to roll logs and raise his house and school at Fairfield.

In 1851 Butler left Fairfield for the Cherokee Female Seminary, whose directors, one of them Chief Ross, had unanimously voted him religious instructor. In 1852 his connection with the Board was severed, apparently as a measure of economy; the event was a bitter blow to Butler and saddened his last days. In 1855 he removed to Van Buren, Arkansas, where he and his wife lived by taking in boarders, and Butler himself helped with the household tasks. "How meekly and quietly that good man performed those daily duties," said Lucy Ames Butler, reporting his death to the Board in March 1857.

2.

The Cherokees had meanwhile hardly accustomed themselves to comparative tranquillity and the beginning of prosperity brought about by the Treaty of 1846 when a greater civil war crashed down on them. Jackson, in taking with his right hand from South Carolina what he gave with his left to Georgia, had not after all disposed of the question of states' rights. In 1861 South Carolina was nullifying again, and worse, and Georgia with her, and Alabama, and North Carolina, though Tennessee, just as she had been on the Cherokee issue, was divided.

Idealists such as Worcester had not been able to defend the Cherokees to the end because of the fear of bringing on such a conflict as this. The conflict came anyway. Now it was not red men who provided the issue, but men of yet another color. The war was fought for Miss Sophia's Sam and Peter, for the "black man" whom Ross had wanted to lend Lucy Ames Butler, for the descendants of old Shoe Boots by his wife Lucy. And what in 1831 might have been a local insubordination, easily quelled, was in 1861 one of the bloodiest wars in history; it ripped the entire country apart, including the luckless Cherokee Nation West.

There were among the Cherokees, as elsewhere, two schools of thought on the slavery issue. Cherokee slaveholders were mostly mixed bloods, the so-called "white Indians," and many of these were of the Treaty Party. The full blood Stand Watie led them; he organized them into Knights of the Golden Circle in defense of states' rights, and after the outbreak of hostilities he raised a Cherokee regiment and achieved the rank of Confederate Brigadier General.

But the full bloods seldom had slaves, and inclined to the philosophy that all men, whatever their color, should go free. These had been organizing a society known as "The Pin," directed in part to the preservation of ancient Cherokee tradition, but also to encouraging the abolitionist movement. These were largely anti-Treaty men, and they had at least the tacit sympathy of a slaveholder whose blood was more Scottish than Cherokee, old Chief Ross.

When the conflict broke out, Ross bent every effort to preserving Cherokee neutrality. Although the Choctaws and Chickasaws, the close neighbors of the Cherokees, joined the Confederacy at once, Ross refused propositions from both Texas and Arkansas to make an alliance. But the Nation, placed on the main line between Texas and "bleeding Kansas," was in a bad position for neutrality; the country was flooded with Confederate agents, and Federal forces were at first far away. In August 1861,

Ross gave in and recommended an alliance with the Confederacy, which in October was consummated.

It was the most equivocal act of his life, the one probably most responsible for the ambiguity of his reputation. In the main he seems merely to have given in to superior force. He has been recorded as comparing the Cherokee Nation in that crisis to a man who, standing helpless on low ground while the water rises around him, sees a log drift by. The log might not save him, but "by seizing hold of it he has a chance for his life." The despairing parable is perhaps the most eloquent statement ever made by Ross.

But perhaps also he could not resist the temptation placed in his way by the fact that for the first time in history the Cherokees were enabled to bargain on superior terms with a white man's government. His price for the alliance was the most remarkable treaty that white men had ever made with his people; one significant provision bound the whites to deal only with authorized representatives of the Indians, never with a minority.

But the treaty was of little avail. In 1862 the Nation was overrun by Federal forces and Ross was captured. The old chief, however, made a great and favorable impression on his captor, General Blunt, who wrote Lincoln that the Cherokees "had resisted the Confederate agents as long as possible, and only the lack of communication with the Federal government had kept Ross from being loyal." At his suggestion, Ross went to Washington, and the chief who in youth had known Jefferson and had spent most of his prime negotiating with Jackson now came face to face with Abraham Lincoln. Lincoln, too, was impressed, and promised Ross before a witness that the Confederate alliance would never "rise up in judgment against the Cherokees." But Ross never saw his people again. He died in Philadelphia in 1866.

Ross had hoped the Union forces could remain in occupation of his country, but this was not possible. The unfortunate Cherokees were torn apart by the stresses of the Civil War, and there was suffering as great as on the Trail of Tears. But survivors of the removal could derive a wry satisfaction from the knowledge that Georgia was suffering even more. At least their descendants have relished this circumstance. Not long after the screening of *Gone with the Wind* a historical-minded Cherokee from the Smokies was invited to Athens to talk to businessmen of Sequoia and other curiosities of Cherokee history. He took the occasion to tell them about the removal.

"When Sherman marched to the sea you Georgians got a taste of what your ancestors gave the Cherokees in 1838," he told them, "and I'm bound to say it served your state right."

And the businessmen applauded and came up cordially to shake his hand, for while it is true that the sins of the fathers are visited on the children even to the third generation, by the time the fourth and fifth come along they are usually ready to be broad-minded about the whole matter. Indeed, some Georgia antiquarians of the present era do not hesitate to apply the term "criminal" to their state's behavior.

Just as the leaders of the Cherokee Nation East had foreseen, it was no more possible to keep white men out of the Indian territory in the West than it had been to keep the Georgians out of the East. Although after the Civil War the Cherokees were able to resume their constitutional government and develop peacefully, by 1893 they were being approached by the Dawes Commission sent to the Five Civilized Nations to persuade them to extinguish tribal title to the Indian lands. True to their tradition, the Cherokees were the last to give in to this proposal. It was April 1906 before the Comprehensive

Act was passed which finally dissolved their tribal government. There would, to be sure, still be Council on occasion
in their western capital, Tahlequah, and there would still
be a chief of sorts, but a Council and chief of sharply
circumscribed power. Now indeed their government was
what John Quincy Adams had once called "of purely
municipal character." The old Cherokee Nation was dead.

When the Indian Territory sought statehood the Cherokees asked to give it their most venerated name, Sequoia.
Even this wish was denied them. The new state became
Oklahoma. But it was to be a strongly Indian state,
where one tenth of the population not only confesses to
some degree of Indian blood, but brags about it, and
where fine Amerind profiles are visible even on the most
elite of occasions. Out of the tragic past of the Cherokees
(his blood much diluted to be sure) came a man of sunny
laughter, beloved by all Americans, Will Rogers.

Thus the Cherokee Nation West, which still has headquarters in the pleasant hickory-shaded town of Tahlequah and still debates with some emotion the tragedies
of the past, though it no longer tries to do anything
about them.

But if you really want to see the Cherokees you look
not west, but east. For in North Carolina the Cherokees
still possess their hills almost as if Andrew Jackson had
never been born and the removal never heard of. And
thereby hangs a tale.

3.

As has already been reported, in the removals of June
1838 not all Cherokees gave up, even when driven by
guns and bayonets into the white man's boats. They only
bided their time to elude their captors at the first opportunity and go home again.

This stubbornness persisted even after they reached
the West. When the Western nation was plunged by

feud into a kind of civil war, some peace-loving Cherokees in despair talked of moving still farther West. Others
quietly packed up what they could and went back where
they came from.

How many did this there is no way of estimating. Because they acted furtively, no statistics were kept of this
removal in reverse, of how large were the parties that set
out, of how many died on the way. One only knows from
the traditions of the Eastern Cherokees that it took place,
and that on the eastward journey as on the westward one
babies were born on the way, and given names of hope,
like Going Home. Their descendants bear such names to
this day.

The trip was not too difficult. The government had
kindly provided them with a year's supply of rations,
presumably for use in the Arkansas; when they tired of
that diet, they could set up camp for a few days while the
men hunted 'possum, wild turkey, and deer or fished the
streams, just as in the happy days before red men discovered that white men also infested an otherwise pleasant planet. The road was easy to find; they had been over
it once, and in any case they need only move toward the
point from which the sun rose.

Once the Mississippi was well behind them they could
measure their progress towards home by the lift of the
country underfoot. The flatlands began to roll and un-
dulate; the roads wound upwards into the Cumberland
Plateau. And one day, watching the Eastern horizon, they
saw what had seemed an unusually solid bank of slate-
blue clouds resolve itself into remembered contours. For
there beyond Sevierville were the Great Smokies, the
hills of home, the rugged western wall of the Cherokee
Nation.

The trails into the mountains were steep and rough,
tumbled with black talus fallen down from the ridges.
But they climbed them joyously, for this was home and

its air was sweet. Finally they came to the top of Tennessee, and from Newfound Gap looked down into the forested valleys of North Carolina where the Valley Towns had been. What would they find there now?

Those who came earliest could have expected only what Butler heard of when he returned early in 1839: a precarious hideaway in the mountains. Since they could hope to hide only in the wildest, least productive part of the hills, the living was lean; many of the fugitives starved to death. Those who had returned first from the West could have hoped for little more than this—starvation, but in their own hills, and in freedom.

But those who came a little later to make a cautious reconnoitering of the valley met with a surprise. There were Cherokees there, in the open. They had cabins, and they were planting their corn as they always had, as if there were no doubt of their right to reap it.

Indeed, the planters had no doubt. It was not Georgia, but Carolina land they were cultivating, and North Carolina would not drive them out, because a white man, one William H. Thomas, held the deeds and saw to it that the taxes were paid on time.

By a hard bargain these Cherokees had repossessed their land. What their fathers had received, presumably of the Great Spirit, they were now buying from North Carolina, and what they bought was not yet even technically theirs, since North Carolina, though it had never made any particular noise over the Cherokee question, would not at the moment allow an Indian to hold property in his own name. The Cherokees, who had lost everything through the faithlessness of white men, had now staked their whole existence on the good faith of one. They had given the money accruing to them from the treaty of New Echota to the young trader Thomas, and he was buying back their lands and registering them in his own name.

The bargain was hard. The Cherokees had paid twice over for what had always been theirs: twice, for, besides money, they had paid in blood. Tsali had had to die before they could get permission to remain in the East.

And now those who had come from the West heard for the first time of Tsali.

4.

Tsali was a simple nobody who made history by the merest accident. He was an old man who lived with his wife and his sons in an out-of-the-way cabin somewhere around Valley Towns. When Scott's soldiers came for them, his family put up no more resistance than any other. Dumbly obedient, they shuffled off down the road with the soldiers.

Tsali's wife had been ill. She walked with difficulty and could not keep up the pace demanded by the soldiers. It amused one of these to spur her on by prodding her with his bayonet. And, seeing this, something snapped inside of Tsali.

"We don't have to stand for this," he said. "At the next turn in the road there's a good cover. When I say Ho, each of you grab a gun and get away. Don't shoot or there'll be trouble. Pick your man now and work into a good position."

This piece of insubordination was spoken in Cherokee, in an idle conversational tone, as if Tsali were commenting on the weather. His strategy was not communicated to the soldiers. The latter, used now to the harmlessness of the Cherokees, were taken by surprise when Tsali said Ho and the sons fell upon them with the same energy with which they were used to falling on opponents at a ball play. The soldiers' guns were wrested from them, and the whole family, even the trembling woman, vanished from the trail as completely as if they had never been in the country.

But there had been an accident. One gun in being wrested had gone off. A soldier had been killed.

General Scott knew that removal was not complete, that the hills were haunted by fugitives from the camps, the caravans, and even in time from the Arkansas country. Tracking them down was difficult; there were vast spaces in the mountaintops, and the Indians, who knew these better than the soldiers, faded away more skillfully than deer on their approach. Starvation couldn't bring them out, for these Cherokees preferred death to captivity.

In time Scott, who had no private stake in removal anyway, and was not unsympathetic with the Indians, saw no reason why a people so deadly determined should not have what they wanted. He told Thomas that he was willing to use his influence to get permission for these Indians to live openly in the country they had refused to leave, but on one condition. Tsali and his sons must be delivered to the authorities for punishment.

Thomas, who had lived with the Cherokees twenty years and was looked on by them as a kind of adopted son, knew the hideouts of most of the fugitives. That was probably why the Cherokees were later able to trust him as they did. In this emergency he who knew everything told nothing. But he did consent to act as a go-between for General Scott.

He went to the cave where Tsali had been hiding and laid the proposition before him. Tsali listened and pondered. He was an old man; his wife and one child had already died in the hills. He himself and perhaps the others would probably die soon anyway; why not, as Thomas suggested, die to some practical purpose?

Tsali and his sons came down the mountain and surrendered and were shot; all but the youngest, Washington, who was allowed to go free and still has descendants in North Carolina.

A young man named Lanman, who visited the country

ten years after the event and wrote of what he saw and heard in lush prose, says that Tsali was shot by a squad commanded by a fellow fugitive, Euchella, and that Tsali, before dying, made a long and moving speech.

"Oh Euchella," said Tsali, "if the Cherokee people now beyond the Mississippi carried my heart in their bosoms, they would never have left this beautiful land, this our mountain land. My little son must never go beyond the Father of Waters, but die in the land of his birth. It is sweet to die in one's own country and to be buried by the margin of one's native stream."

That is the story of Tsali in its classic version. There are others. In the vicinity of Cherokee and Birdtown, North Carolina, nearly every family with any considerable degree of Indian blood in its veins has its own version, each guaranteed authentic because it came direct from the lips of a great-grandmother who was present and saw the whole thing. One of these grandmothers saw Tsali help tomahawk some sleeping guards at Fort Loudon in order to assist two Indian maidens to escape the camp. Some saw him acting not so much the part of a self-sacrificing martyr as of a realist who gave himself up only because he had been told that otherwise his fellow fugitives would turn him over to General Scott in order to make the deal already referred to.

No one, however, quarrels over these divergent views of what happened. Everyone is entitled to his own grandmother's opinion. It isn't at all in Cherokee as it is in Tahlequah, where many people feel very strongly indeed about which construction you happen to put on the conduct of Ross and the Ridges. Indeed, there are Cherokees of Cherokee so thoroughly acclimated to the world of Jack Benny, Big Chief Wahoo, and current events as relayed by the Knoxville radio station that they learn of Tsali and of the whole history of their people for the first time when they drop in at the school at the Agency to watch their youngsters act out a pageant some energetic teacher has composed on the subject of removal.

In Tahlequah it is improbable that such a pageant could be presented without provoking discord unless it were written very dreamily indeed, with no characters more concrete than Spirit of the Mountains, First Cherokee, Second Cherokee. To invoke a historical personality, except perhaps Sequoia's, in a Tahlequah pageant would offend somebody. But the North Carolina Cherokees, thanks perhaps to this shadowy Tsali, thanks surely to William H. Thomas, who did not betray them and saw presently that they held their land in their own tribal name, have made their peace with history. For them the glory and the misery of the old Cherokee Nation is an old wives' tale or something that their children learn about in school. It is all very interesting; they are glad to know about it. But they do not let it distract them from the pursuits of the present.

Bibliography

I

THE CHIEF PRIMARY SOURCES

This history owes nearly everything to three major primary sources, each so important as to require discussion in detail. They are the files of *The Cherokee Phoenix;* the papers of the American Board of Foreign Missions and their derivative, *The Missionary Herald;* and the Payne Manuscripts.

(A) *The Cherokee Phoenix*

The *Phoenix*, the national publication of the Cherokees, first appeared 21 February 1828 and thereafter weekly (with a few very brief lapses) until 31 May 1834. Plans made to resume publication were thwarted in the summer of 1835 when the Georgia Guard seized press and type. It was, according to Ross, still in Georgian hands in May 1837. The *Phoenix's* first and most gifted editor was Elias Boudinot; however, Elijah Hicks, who succeeded him in the summer of 1832, had a rather pleasant colloquial style in spite of some tendency to grammatical lapses.

The most nearly complete files of the *Phoenix* appear to be those in the American Antiquarian Society in Worcester, Massachusetts. The second best collection is in the British Museum in London, housed, luckily, in the unbombed wing of the Newspaper Annex. This collection, most of it originally the property of the Missionary William Chamberlin, I have also had the pleasure of examining. The Oklahoma Historical Society at Oklahoma City also has a good collection, and I have studied individual copies at the University of Oklahoma in Norman, and in the Ayer Collection of the Newberry Library, Chicago.

The *Phoenix* is the repository of the early laws of the Cherokees, contains detailed accounts of Council meetings and of Ross's speeches, of relations with the Federal government and with Georgia, and gives details of the early stages of the apparently immortal Ross-Ridge feud. It is a monument to the intelligence and the energy of the Cherokees.

(B). *The Papers of the American Board of Commissioners for Foreign Missions, Houghton Library, Harvard University, Cambridge, Massachusetts.*

(For the sake of brevity these will be referred to as "Mission Papers," or by the code MP; Roman numerals will refer to the volumes, and Arabic numerals to the numbers assigned the individual documents.)

II. Cherokee Mission: Joint Communications Previous to September 1824.
III. Individual Missionaries.
IV. Cherokees, September 1824–September 1831, Part 1.
V. Cherokees, September 1824–September 1831, Part 2.
VII. Cherokees 1831–1837, Part 1.
VIII. Cherokees 1831–1837, Part 2.
X. Cherokee Mission 1838–1844.
XI. Cherokee Mission after 1844.
Papers Relating to the Controversy of Georgia over the Indians, 1833–1840. By Daniel S. Butrick. (In the Notes this will be called Butrick's *Controversy*.)
A Cherokee Missionary on Jews and Indians. Two volumes. By Daniel S. Butrick.
The Journal of Daniel S. Butrick, missionary to the Cherokees, 1819–1846. (To be referred to as Butrick's *Journal*. Since the pages are not numbered, the dates will serve as reference.)
Biographical Notes Relating to Missions to the North American Indians.
The Missionary Herald, 1818–1838.

The Mission Papers are incomparably the most valuable single collection of documents in Cherokee history. So intimately did the missionaries become identified with the Cherokee struggle that there is hardly a page that does not bear witness, consciously or unconsciously, to its progress. The collection also contains letters by such important figures as John Ross, John Ridge, Elias Boudinot, Elisha Chester, J. F. Schermerhorn, and Senator Frelinghuysen, and in Volume II an especially interesting collection of early Cherokee documents.

I have tried to make my notes detailed enough to serve as a

kind of guide through the labyrinth of these papers. Though I
have not attempted to document every statement that I have made,
I have indicated sources of specific detail that might deserve
further study by historians.

One planning to explore the papers for his own purposes will
find the following facts of service. Letters and diaries (aside from
three separate volumes by Butrick) are bound in large volumes
and grouped by authors with a rough chronological arrangement
within groupings. Each of these volumes contains an index by
author, referring to the documents by number.

As authors I particularly recommend Butrick (often spelled
Buttrick in printed missionary material) for the infectious quality
of his enthusiasm and the diversity of his interests; Sophia Sawyer
for her real literary skill and her intimate acquaintance with the
families of John Ridge and Boudinot; Elizur Butler, who, though
apparently not especially fond of literary expression, was always
on hand to report a specific event of consequence, and who seems
to have been as well balanced as he was courageous and humane.
Samuel Worcester, of course, is a historical figure in his own right.
(So is Butler, but he has remained rather in Worcester's shadow.)
A long, forthright report on mission work by Jeremiah Evarts in
MP II :154 ff. is of special interest.

There is one lacuna in these records: so far as I know there are
no documents bearing the date 1820.

(C). *The Payne Manuscripts*

John Howard Payne, who became accidentally involved in
Cherokee history (see Chapter XVI), never lost his interest in
Cherokee affairs and planned to write his own history. The notes
and papers he collected for this purpose (never realized) are contained in nine of the fourteen volumes of Payne Manuscripts in
the Ayer Collection at the Newberry Library, Chicago.

These documents differ from all the others in that Payne looked
on the Cherokees with the eye of an outsider and recorded details
of costume and custom that others, more habituated to Cherokee
ways, never thought to set down. He collected anecdotes, character
studies, and notes on ancient customs.

It would be impossible to get a coherent picture of Cherokee
affairs from this collection alone, but as a supplement to general
knowledge, it is invaluable.

II
OTHER PRIMARY SOURCES
(printed material)

Anonymous editor: *Speeches on Removal*. A record of speeches on the Bill for the Removal of the Indians. 1830.

Cherokee Nation: *A Memorial and Protest of the Cherokee Nation*, 1836.
Presented with Bill R H No. 695, this is chiefly an attack on the treaty of New Echota.

Commager, Henry Steele (editor): *Documents of American History*, 1934.

Boudinot, Elias: *Letter Relating to Cherokee Affairs*. Athens, Georgia, 1837.
Boudinot's own account of his controversy with John Ross, and his defense of the Treaty of New Echota.

Dale, Edward Everett, and Litton, Gaston (editors): *Cherokee Cavaliers*. 1939.
Some valuable letters by Boudinot and John Ridge written between 1832 and 1835.

Evarts, Jeremiah: *Essays on the Present Crisis in the Condition of the American Indian*. 1829.
A collection of the "William Penn" letters that originally appeared in the *National Intelligencer*. Most of these were also reprinted in the *Cherokee Phoenix*.

Gilmer, George: *Sketches of Some of the First Settlers of Upper Georgia*. 1855.
The Georgia governor gives his own side of the Cherokee story, his impressions of Worcester (unfavorable) and The Ridge (favorable).

Kemble, Frances Anne. *Journal*. 1835.
No authority on the Cherokees, the lady did give some lively detail on the Washington and America that the Cherokees also knew.

Lanman, Charles: *Letters from the Alleghany Mountains*. 1849.
Lanman visited the Eastern Cherokees a decade after the removal and recorded some observations of value.

Lumpkin, Wilson: *The Removal of the Cherokee Indians from Georgia*. 1907.
Another Georgia governor's story; he has much to say of John Ross.

Peters, Richard: *The Case of the Cherokee Nation Against the State of Georgia.* 1831.
A repository of memorials and documents relevant to the Removal Bill and the Cherokee Supreme Court case.

Ross, John: *Letter to the General Philadelphia Public.* 1838.
Ross's version of the making of the Treaty of New Echota and his account of subsequent events.

Trollope, Mrs. Frances: *Domestic Manners of the Americans.* 1832.
Caustic observations on the America of the day and of how America's treatment of the Indians looked to an Englishwoman.

III

SECONDARY SOURCES OF CHEROKEE HISTORY

Battey, George Magruder: *History of Rome and Floyd County.* 1922.
Besides incidental material this contains a reprint *in extenso* of Payne's account of his capture as published in the *Knoxville Register* of 2 December 1835.

Brown, John B.: *Old Frontiers.* 1938
Especially rich in Cherokee folkways and Cherokee history through the Revolution. I have also been fortunate enough to see the collection of Cherokee curios assembled by Mr. Brown at his home in Red Bank, Tennessee.

Dunbar, Seymour: *A History of Travel in America.* 1915.
Dunbar presents an especially thoughtful account of the effect of the mistreatment of the Indians on American character, and includes several documents that I have not seen published elsewhere.

Fitzgerald, Mary Newman: *The Cherokees.* 1937.
A pleasant pamphlet by one who has long lived among the modern Cherokees.

Foreman, Grant: *Indian Removal.* 1932.
Foreman is probably the foremost living authority on Indian history. I owe much to this volume.

Harris, Joel Chandler: *Georgia: from the Invasion of De Soto to Recent Times.* 1896.
Here is an optimistic Georgian account of removal expressing the view that everything that was done to the Cherokees was done exclusively for their good.

Mooney, James: "Cherokee River Cult," *Journal of American Folklore*, January–March 1900.
Myths of the Cherokees, Bureau of Ethnology, Annual Report 19, Part 1. 1900.
Though these works and *The Swimmer Manuscript* are primarily concerned with a study of Cherokee folkways, the *Myths* is preceded by one of the most authoritative of Cherokee histories.

Mooney, James, and Olbrechts, Frans: *The Swimmer Manuscript.* Cherokee Sacred Formulas and Medicinal Preparations. Bureau of American Ethnology, Bulletin 99. 1932. A recent anthropological study of Cherokee folkways.

Parker, Thomas Valentine: *The Cherokee Indians*. 1907.
A minute account of Cherokee relations with the Federal government prior to removal.

Royce, Charles C.: *The Cherokee Nation of Indians*. Bureau of Ethnology, Fifth Annual Report. 1887.
The earliest authoritative history of the Cherokees, based primarily on a painstaking analysis of government documents.

Strong, William E.: *The Story of the American Board*. 1910.
This contains detail on early missions to the Indians.

Walker, Robert Sparks: *Torchlights to the Cherokees*. 1932.
A pleasant account of the missions, based largely on the Mission Papers.

Wardell, Morris J.: *A Political History of the Cherokee Nation, 1838–1907*. 1938.
A scholarly account of post-removal history of the Cherokees.

IV

SPECIAL BIOGRAPHICAL DETAIL

Bass, Althea: *The Cherokee Messenger*. 1936.
A study of the life of Samuel A. Worcester.
"Talking Stones," *The Colophon*, Part IX.
An account of the achievement of Sequoia, largely reprinted from the Payne Manuscripts.

Eaton, Rachel Caroline: *John Ross and the Cherokee Indians*. 1921.
A careful study, written, however, without any apparent acquaintance with the Mission Papers or the complete files of the *Cherokee Phoenix*.

Foreman, Grant: *Sequoyah*. 1938.
The definitive account of the great Cherokee genius.

Foster, George E.
Story of the Cherokee Bible.
Sequoyah.
Both books contain valuable material on the invention of the Cherokee syllabary.

Gabriel, Ralph Henry: *Elias Boudinot, Cherokee, and his America.* 1941.
An authority on the life of the first editor of the *Cherokee Phoenix* and sponsor of the Treaty of New Echota.

James, Marquis: *Life of Andrew Jackson.* 1940.
My favorite authority for the Jacksonian background of the Cherokee struggle. I have followed James's account of the Battle of Horse Shoe Bend.

Meserve, John Bartlett: "Chief John Ross," *Chronicles of Oklahoma*, December 1935.
Though this contains little new material, it is one of the best-balanced appraisals of the man who was for thirty-four years chief of the Cherokees.

Notes

Chapter I

In general, Chapter I follows the account of the early history of the Cherokees in James Mooney's *Myths of the Cherokees*. Specific references to the individual sections follow.

2.

The aboriginal neighbors of the Cherokees are described in Mooney's *Myths*, pp. 14ff.

3.

The description of early Cherokee customs is based on the Payne Manuscripts, IV, VI. Polygamy and divorce among the Cherokees are described in the Mission Papers II: 1. The communication from the delegation of women, dated 30 June 1818, is from MP II: 112ff.

4.

For a complete account of the "blood law" see Payne II; cities of peace are described in Mooney's *Myths*, p. 207, the renunciation of the blood law, *op. cit.*, p. 86.

5.

Mooney's *Myths* and Mooney and Olbrechts' *Swimmer Manuscript* are my authority for the analysis of the ancient Cherokee religion. The Black Mountain legend is from Charles Lanman's *Letters from the Alleghany Mountains*, p. 136.

9.

The results of the adoption of agriculture by the Cherokees are appraised by Charles Hicks in MP II: 5; a generalized account of Cherokee progress is found in Charles Royce's *The Cherokee Nation of Indians*, pp. 240ff.

10.

The story of Shoe Boots is from Payne II; references to the administration of his estate are in the *Cherokee Phoenix* of 11 November 1829, 12 June 1830.

The literate and pious slave couple: MP II: 5ff. The census of 1825: Royce, p. 240.

13, 14, 15, 16.

Tecumseh's visit: Mooney, pp. 53ff.; the Creek campaign: Mooney, pp. 91ff. and Marquis James's *Andrew Jackson* I, pp. 181ff.

The incidents involving Shoe Boots are from Payne II; Grant Foreman's *Sequoyah* is the authority for the statement that Sequoia participated in the campaign.

CHAPTER II

1.

John Arch's upbringing is described by Chamberlin in MP IV: 42. For a more extended account of the life of this young convert, see Robert Sparks Walker's *Torchlights to the Cherokees*, pp. 201–213.

It should be noted that the American Board of Foreign Missions, itself Congregationalist, acted as agent of the Presbyterians; thus their early representatives were of both denominations.

2.

The invitation from Hightower: MP II: 33.

3.

The material in the rest of the chapter is a mosaic of at least a hundred letters and journal entries. References of special interest in relation to the early training of the children: The Brainerd Journal, MP II: 129; Jeremiah Evarts's long report of his visit of 1822 recorded in MP II: 154ff.

5.

The report on the indolent Gilbert Wheeler: MP II: 202.

CHAPTER III

3.

The words ascribed to old Pathkiller are from a collection of Indian documents contained in the Brainerd Journal, MP II: 96. His visit to Brainerd in 1823 is described in MP II: 83, 84.

4, 5.

Details about Charles Hicks are found in the Brainerd Journal
MP II: 1 and about John Ross in MP II: 124.

6.

John Ridge's misadventures at Brainerd are recorded in the
Brainerd Journal, MP II: 2; further material on The Ridge is
found in MP II: 140ff. and in Butrick's *Journal* for 1818.

CHAPTER IV

1.

Chamberlin describes the October Council of 1824 in MP IV:
39.

2.

Social notes of a proper wedding were inserted by Waterhunter
in the *Cherokee Phoenix* of 21 May 1829. For material on the
Cherokee dances, see Payne VI.

3.

The lugubrious hymn is from the Brainerd Journal, MP II:
139.

5.

For material on witchcraft and conjure, see the entry of 28
May 1822 in the Brainerd Journal, MP II, and letters by Moody
Hall, MP II: 229, 254. An excellent modern anthropological
analysis of such customs is in Mooney and Olbrechts' *Swimmer
Manuscript.*

6.

The most complete account of the weddings of young Ridge
and Elias Boudinot is found in R. H. Gabriel's *Elias Boudinot.*
For details of the reaction in the Cherokee Nation, see Chamberlin
in MP IV: 43; David Brown in V: 289; Butrick and Worcester
in MP V: 386 and 228 respectively.

7.

Extended accounts of the ancient ball play are found in Payne
IV, VI; Lanman pp. 100ff. Moody Hall's diary of July and

August 1825 describes the national ball play of 1825 (MP V: 338).

CHAPTER V

This account of Sequoia owes much to Grant Foreman's *Sequoyah;* Foreman is my authority for such details as Sequoia's probable ancestry, his army experience, and his life in the West.

Much of Foreman's book and most of the details of the first three sections follow an account written by Second Chief Lowry in October 1835 and recorded in Payne II. The probable date of Sequoia's first experiments, his relations with the Moravians, and the reactions of the white printers of the *Cherokee Phoenix* to his invention are from George E. Foster's *Sequoyah* and his *Story of the Cherokee Bible.*

Mission letters bearing on the early "revival of learning" in the Cherokee Nation: MP IV: 7 (Butrick); IV: 39 (Chamberlin); IV: 166 and 170 (Proctor); V: 230 (Worcester); the *Missionary Herald* for 1827, pp. 212ff.

The *Cherokee Phoenix* of 13 August 1828 and that of 29 July 1829 also contain accounts of Sequoia's life and achievement.

CHAPTER VI

1.

The quotation from President Monroe is from Seymour Dunbar's *History of Travel in America* II, p. 522.

2.

The Cherokee constitution is analyzed in the *Missionary Herald* for 1828, pp. 193ff. "A Cherokee's" attack on the treasurer began in the 28 February 1828 *Phoenix* and continued until Boudinot tired of the subject; the "naked metropolis" quotation is from the 28 March issue.

3.

References to "White Path's Rebellion" (though not under that title) are in the following mission papers: MP V: 236, 237, 238 (Worcester); IV: 185 (Proctor). Proctor's observations on the 1828 elections were reprinted in the *Missionary Herald* of 1828, p. 353. The results and the expense thereof are recorded in the *Phoenix* of 26 November 1828. Another interesting account of

Cherokee officers and of the use of the annuity fund is in the
Phoenix of 1 May 1830.

4.

Montgomery's discussion of the new Cherokee constitution is
described in the *Phoenix* of 24 April 1828.

5.

The Georgian Campbell's defense of the Cherokees is in the
Phoenix of 3 September 1828. The verse quoted at the end of the
chapter is from Joel Chandler Harris's *Georgia*.

CHAPTER VII

1.

The early discovery of gold is described in Althea Bass's
Cherokee Messenger, pp. 108ff.; Rachel Caroline Eaton's *John
Ross*, pp. 51ff.

The 28 February 1830 *Phoenix* mentions 100 Georgians digging
at the sources of the Hightower River; by the 24 March 1830 issue
3000 Georgians are reported in the country in disregard of Montgomery's order to remove; by 22 May these intruders are reported to be extracting $10,000 daily.

Activities of the United States troops: the *Phoenix* of 5 June,
1830; 12 June, 1830. Arrests of the Cherokees at mines: 19 June
1830; 17 July 1830; 4 September 1830; 10 October 1830. Judge
Clayton's opinion: 22 and 29 October 1831.

Worcester wrote a detailed account of the situation in the gold
fields in MP V: 279. Butler in the *Missionary Herald* of 1830, p.
298, describes Cherokee preaching at the mines.

2.

The arrest and the eviction of the intruders is based on Ross's
report in the 17 February 1830 *Phoenix* and Butler's in MP IV:
81, and Montgomery's denunciation of Ross's act in the 8 May
1830 *Phoenix*. The Ridge is described in full war dress by Montgomery.

CHAPTER VIII

1.

The account of the National Council of July 1830 is from the
17 July 1830 *Phoenix* and a letter by Worcester in MP V: 279.

The "law of love" memorial (which may have been written by Boudinot) is printed in the 24 July *Phoenix*. Nancy Reese's comments are in a group of letters in Payne VIII.

Lumpkin's inflammatory citation from Evarts is in his *Removal of the Cherokees* I, p. 57.

The poem sent to the *Phoenix* by some ladies in Hartford is in the 12 March 1831 issue.

2.

Carroll's report on the Cherokees is printed in Royce, pp. 259–60. Frelinghuysen gives further detail of his activities in *Speeches on Removal*, p. 4. All quotations from the speeches defending the Indians are from *Speeches on Removal*. The attitude of the Georgia lawmakers to the memorials from the North is summarized in the *Phoenix* of 3 February 1830 and further editorialized in the 15 May 1830 issue. Mrs. Trollope's indignant commentary on the Removal Bill is in her *Domestic Manners* II, pp. 11ff.

3.

The opinion of the Supreme Court is found in Henry Steele Commager's *Documents of American History*, pp. 255ff.; Justice Johnson's opinion in Richard Peters' *The Case of the Cherokee Nation* II, p. 171. John Ridge described his talk with President Jackson in the 21 May 1831 *Phoenix*.

CHAPTER IX

1.

The text of the missionary resolutions is published in the *Missionary Herald* for 1831, pp. 79ff. In the *Phoenix* of 25 September 1830 there is an account of similar resolutions drawn up by the Methodists.

2.

The Proctor-Butrick inquiry: MP VII: 1.

3.

Georgia's "nerve war" is described by Worcester in MP VII: 132; Beanstalk's misadventure is recorded in the *Phoenix* of 12 February 1831; Ross's attitude to the new Georgia law is contained in extracts from a letter to Boudinot copied by Worcester in MP VII: 131.

4.

The *Missionary Herald* of 1831, pp. 165ff., describes the first wave of arrests; Worcester's own account of his acquittal is MP VII: 135.

5.

Gilmer's correspondence with the missionaries: *Missionary Herald* of 1831, p. 248.

The Baptist incident is described in the 30 April 1831 *Phoenix* and denied by a member of the Georgia Guard in a later issue.

Butler describes his first arrest in MP VII: 77; Worcester confides his anxieties in VII: 140, 139. The second arrests are described in the *Missionary Herald* of 1831, p. 284. Worcester explains the retention of Chester in MP VII: 147.

6.

August arrests: *Missionary Herald* of 1831, pp. 297ff.; the trial, pp. 363ff. The Cherokee gifts to the missionaries are described in the *Missionary Herald* of 1832, p. 44.

CHAPTER X

1.

The description of New Echota at Council time is based on a miscellany of references in the Mission Papers, Payne Manuscripts, and the *Cherokee Phoenix*. Personal observation of Saturday afternoon in Cherokee, North Carolina, has added some touches.

The visit of Colonel Lowry is described in the *Phoenix* of 23 October 1830 and in a letter by Worcester in MP VII: 125. Earlier details of the 1830 Council are in the 16 October 1830 *Phoenix*.

2.

The announcement of the new annuity arrangement is in the *Phoenix* of 18 June 1830; its taking effect, in the 23 July and 19 August 1831 issues. Eaton's *Ross*, p. 53, tells of the Cherokees' borrowing. The agency letter on disbursal of annuity funds is in the 17 September 1831 *Phoenix*.

Early descriptions of the increase of drunkenness: Butrick in MP VII: 11; the *Phoenix* 1 October 1830.

John Ridge's comments on the Creek situation: *Phoenix* 9 July 1831; "Old Ned's" reply: *Phoenix* 12 August 1831. Full details of the general situation are found in Grant Foreman's *Indian Removal*.

4.

The "Pony Club" verse is in the *Phoenix* of 21 October 1832; the hearing on the death of "John—probably white" is reported in the 20 November 1830 *Phoenix*.

5.

Boudinot's brush with the Guard: the *Phoenix* of 12 and 19 August 1831; Colonel Nelson inserted his own ill-spelled version of the affair in the 17 September 1831 *Phoenix*. The assault on Ross: 21 January 1832 *Phoenix*.

6.

A letter from Worcester, MP VII: 156, mentions the Cherokee determination to continue to meet in New Echota; the 15 October 1831 *Phoenix* refers to the Georgia Guard's attempt to arrest Council. Ross's address to the October Council is in the 19 November 1831 *Phoenix*.

CHAPTER XI

1.

The letters to Butler are from Payne VII.

2.

Ann Worcester describes Reese's visit in MP VII: 161; Gilmer's account of the incident is in his *Sketches*, pp. 396ff.

3.

Foreman's *Indian Removal*, pp. 239ff., gives an account of the collaboration of Starr and Walker with the Western delegation. The first reference to the incident in the *Phoenix* is in the 12 May 1832 issue.

4.

Boudinot's letter describing his impressions of Georgia is in the 24 December 1831 *Phoenix*. He explains the purpose of his tour in the 18 February 1832 issue. The account of his appearance with John Ridge in New Haven is reprinted from the New Haven *Religious Intelligencer* in the 24 March 1832 *Phoenix*.

5.

Butrick's private difficulties are mentioned only in his private *Journal*. His accounts of the attitude of the other missionaries and of the charges of Curry are in MP VII: 69.

7.

Miss Sophia Sawyer describes her contact with the Georgia Guard in MP VIII: 173. The *Phoenix* of 17 March 1832 also refers to the incident.

8.

The announcement of the Supreme Court decision is in the 24 March 1832 issue of the *Phoenix*. Other details of Cherokee rejoicing are given in Foreman's *Indian Removal*, pp. 244ff.

CHAPTER XII

1.

Boudinot's reaction to the Supreme Court decision is from Dale and Litton's *Cherokee Cavaliers*, pp. 4ff. The dismal return of the delegates from Washington is described by Lucy Ames Butler in MP VII: 84.

Descriptions of the Georgia land survey: *Phoenix* 21 April and 23 May 1832; Chamberlin in MP VII: 55; Ann Worcester in VII: 173; Butrick in VII: 16. Lucy Ames Butler describes the rumors inspired by Chester in MP VII: 84.

2.

John Ridge's comment on the Supreme Court decision is from Dale and Litton's *Cherokee Cavaliers*, pp. 7ff. The denial of the Newsome article by Ross and Coodey is in the 17 May 1832 *Phoenix*. The repudiation by the Aquohee District: the 14 July 1832 *Phoenix*.

3.

The full text of Ross's proclamation of a day of fasting and prayer is found in Mooney, *Myths*, p. 120. Rather vague references to discouraging advice given to the Cherokee delegation by their

Washington friends, Supreme Court Justice McLean among them, are found in a letter published by John Ridge in the *Phoenix* of 17 August 1833.

4.

The interpretation of The Ridge's character in the crisis is my own surmise, written from my general impression of the known facts rather than from specific detail.

My authority for The Ridge's early anti-removal activity is Eaton's *Ross*, p. 44; her statement is substantiated by MP II: 112, where he is listed as one of the delegates sent to Jefferson in 1808 to refuse the offer of land in the Louisiana Purchase.

I have followed several authorities in saying that The Ridge put his mark to the "blood law," but I can find no proof of that statement. The *Phoenix* of 4 November 1829 refers to a resolution on the subject submitted to Council 26 October 1829 and signed, among others, by John Ridge and William S. Coodey. The full text of this law, passed on 27 October and printed in the 20 July 1830 *Phoenix*, is signed only by Ross, in his capacity as principal chief. However, there can be no doubt where The Ridge stood; his son's signature is as significant as his own. The Ridge's mark is found on several documents printed in the *Phoenix* of 1828, 1829.

One tribute to the quality of The Ridge's oratory is by Worcester in MP VII: 279. An entire speech by The Ridge is printed from the Mission Papers in Walker's *Torchlights to the Cherokees*, pp. 67–9. Gilmer speaks warmly of his personality in his *Sketches* and adds that though The Ridge understood English his command of it was so imperfect that he preferred dealing with white men through an interpreter.

The prophecy is from the 22 July 1832 *Phoenix*.

5.

Chester's letter about the July Council: MP VII: 188. The 6 August 1832 *Phoenix* prints the reply to Cass's proposal, the text of which is in the 8 September 1832 *Phoenix*. Butrick describes the reaction to the suspension of the constitution in MP VII: 1.

6.

Boudinot's resignation, published in the 11 August 1832 *Phoenix*, is further described in his *Letter*, pp. 6–7. Replies to Boudinot are included in the 25 August and 22 September 1832 *Phoenix*.

7.

Miss Sawyer describes her visit to Valley Towns in MP VIII: 174.

Chapter XIII

1.

The account of the October Council is from the 27 October 1832 *Phoenix*. Butler's version of Chester's activities: MP VII: 106.

2.

Butler's cheerfulness: MP VII: 81. The Tennessee resolutions: MP VII: 161. Gilmer's experience with sympathizers of Cherokees in the North is described in his *Sketches*, pp. 402ff.

3.

Dr. Church's visits to Worcester and Worcester's reaction: MP VII: 159, 160. Worcester's first inquiry about the advisability of a pardon: MP VII: 163.

4.

Worcester's unenthusiastic reaction to news of the Supreme Court decision: MP VII: 166. Jackson's reply to the Mission Board: Dunbar II, p. 594.

5.

The appeal to Worcester in April 1832: MP VII: 169; other appeals, including the support from Tuscumbria, Alabama: MP VII: 170. Ann Worcester's dinner with Lumpkin: MP VII: 178.

6.

Worcester's appeal for guidance: MP VII: 180; the vote of the Prudential Committee: MP VII: 189; appeal of Worcester and Butler to Governor Lumpkin: MP VII: 183.

7.

Worcester's discouragement at the decline of Cherokee morals: MP VII: 214. Ross's opinion: MP VII: 87. Adams's experiences: *Missionary Herald* of 1833, p. 242.

8.

The full-time employment of Boudinot by the American Board: MP VII: 178, 180. Prejudice of the Cherokees because of Worcester's association with Boudinot: MP VII: 215. Worcester's plans for schools in Sequoia's alphabet: MP VII: 216. Boudinot's remarks on the improbability of war: MP VII: 213.

CHAPTER XIV

1.

The account of the dispossession of Clauder from Spring Place is from Payne V.

2.

Butler describes the dispossession proceedings against him in MP VII: 88, 93, 96, 98. Worcester's dispossession: MP VII: 69.

The seizure of Ross's property is described in the 19 April 1834 *Phoenix;* other details are given in the Cherokee Nation's *Memorial and Protest* of 1836, p. 5, and Battey's *History of Rome and Floyd County.*

3.

The most complete account of Ross's career is Eaton's *Ross,* to which I am indebted for an account of his ancestry and early life. A brief but discerning appraisal is "Chief John Ross" by John Bartlett Meserve in *Chronicles of Oklahoma,* December, 1935.

4.

Butler's description of Ross in 1830: MP IV: 81; his testimony on Ross's popularity: MP XII: 107. Butrick's tribute: MP VII: 36.

5.

The activities of the 1832–3 delegation in Washington are detailed in the *Phoenix* of 10 August, 21 September 1833. Frelinghuysen describes his relations with this group in MP VII: 193, and Ross gives further details in MP VII: 87. A detailed analysis of the negotiations is furnished by Royce, pp. 272ff. The 21 September 1833 *Phoenix* contains Ross's address to the May Council.

6.

The correspondence on the Henning case: 20 July, 21 September 1833 *Phoenix;* a comment by Worcester on the subject: MP VII: 214; John Ridge's defense: 17 August 1833 *Phoenix.*

7.

Worcester has written an account of the May Council in MP VII: 215. The October Council is described in the 23 November 1833 *Phoenix*, and Judge Adair's decision is further mentioned in the 19 October *Phoenix.*

CHAPTER XV

1, 2.

All of the details on the tragic 1834 migration are from Foreman's *Indian Removal*, pp. 252ff.

3.

John Ridge's reference to this migration: MP VIII: 213; Bolling's letter, Payne VII. Many mission letters describe the methods of persuasion used on the Cherokees; Hicks's editorial on the subject is in the 29 March 1834 *Phoenix;* his arrest is described in the 15 March issue.

4.

The presence of the "kitchen chiefs" in Washington is editorialized in the 5 April 1834 *Phoenix;* John Ridge's letter of 24 July, MP VIII: 213, gives further details from his point of view. The death of Walker is mentioned by J. C. Ellsworth in MP VII: 238.

5.

My authority for Ross's yielding to the pressure of the rival delegations is Thomas Valentine Parker's *The Cherokee Indians*, pp. 30ff. Worcester details Ross's alleged plans in MP VII: 236, 237. The activities of the November 1834 Council are described in Boudinot's *Letter*, pp. 18–20. Ellsworth's comment on Ross is in MP VII: 238.

6.

Worcester admits his unpopularity in MP VII: 237. Butrick's bitter remarks on Worcester's conduct are set forth in his *Journal* and in his *Controversy between Georgia and the Cherokees.*

7.

Miss Sawyer's difficulties were described by Worcester at her request in MP VII: 238. Her account of her school: MP VIII: 184, 182, 186. An account of Jesse's schools: MP VII: 112, 113.

Butrick's account of the eclipse: *Missionary Herald* of 1835, p. 189; his query on polygamy, MP VII: 33. The effect of the translation of the Scriptures is described by Butrick in MP VII: 33.

CHAPTER XVI

1.

The details on Cherokee folklore are derived from *The Swimmer Manuscript* by Mooney and Olbrechts.

2.

References to the "Lapland winter": Butler in MP VII: 105; Ellsworth in MP VII: 243; Miss Sawyer in MP VIII: 185.

3.

The school at Running Waters is described by Miss Sawyer in MP VIII: 185 and by Mary Fields in 186.

The Ridge-Boudinot correspondence on Miss Sawyer's future: MP VIII: 182, 213; VII: 233. Miss Sawyer's description of Ridge's irritability: MP VIII: 187. Miss Sawyer's account of political developments: MP VIII: 185, 186.

4.

Boudinot's theory that an enlightened minority should act for an ignorant majority is set forth in his *Letter*, published in Athens in 1837.

Details of the Washington negotiations of early 1835 are in Royce, pp. 278–82; letters by Boudinot and John Ridge in Dale and Litton's *Cherokee Cavaliers*, 10ff., and by Ross himself in his *Letter*, published in Philadelphia in 1838.

5.

Butler in MP VII: 106 describes Council's unanimous rejection of Ridge's treaty and the fiasco of his called-Council. The bit about the Green Corn Dance is added by Butrick in his *Controversy*.

Comments on the character of Schermerhorn are made by Butler in MP VII: 109; Ridge's temporary break with him is mentioned in MP VII: 108. Other details on this character are from Payne's account of his arrest, Ross's *Letter*, Eaton's *Ross*, p. 67; and Butrick's *Controversy*.

Payne's account of the October Council is from Foreman's *Indian Removal*, pp. 266ff. Butler gives other details in MP VII: 108. The appeal to the Senate is from Ross's *Letter*, pp. 22ff.

7.

Payne's account of his arrest with Ross is reprinted in full from the *Knoxville Register* by Battey in *History of Rome and Floyd County*, pp. 57ff.

8.

For the Treaty of New Echota, see Butrick's *Controversy*, his *Journal*, Ross's *Letter*, and Boudinot's *Letter*.

CHAPTER XVII

1.

Ross describes his reception in Washington in his *Letter*. Schermerhorn's report is from Royce, p. 282. Lowry's meeting of protest is described in Eaton's *Ross*, p. 71.

Major Davis's report is in Royce, pp. 285ff.; Mason's report: Royce, pp. 286ff.

The Cherokee memorial quoted here is presented in Ross's *Letter*, p. 22. Worcester's comment is in MP X: 115.

Boudinot's defense is from his *Letter;* Lumpkin's comment is quoted in Foreman's *Indian Removal*, p. 269.

2.

The panic and the cry, "The Cherokees are up," are described by Ross in his *Letter*, by Chamberlin in MP VII: 67, and Gilmer in his *Sketches*, pp. 504ff. Dunlap is quoted in Royce, p. 286.

Wool's experiences with the Cherokees are described in Dunbar II, p. 605; his sentiments in Foreman's *Indian Removal*, p. 279.

3.

John Ridge's letter: MP VIII: 70. Jesse's downfall is described by Butler in MP VII: 119. Rachel Fields's description of conditions: MP VIII: 190. Butrick's protest of the application of the Treaty of New Echota to mission property: MP VII: 43.

4.

Lumpkin's comments on Ross are in his *Removal*. The plight of the Creeks is described by Chamberlin in MP VII: 67.

Reactions of the Cherokees: Butler's parishioners, MP VII: 120, 123; Evan Jones's viewpoint, Payne IV; Butrick's observations, MP VII: 39, 41; X: 5.

Worcester's trouble in the West: MP X: 115, 112, 122.

CHAPTER XVIII

1.

Van Buren's indecision is described in Eaton's *Ross*, p. 81.

2.

The memorial quoted is from Ross's *Letter*.
Scott's proclamation: Foreman, *Indian Removal*, p. 286.

3.

The Georgia nullification song is from Payne II. Butrick's account of the Georgian request is from his *Journal*, 26 May 1838.

4.

This section is a blend of details drawn from Foreman's *Indian Removal* and Butrick's *Journal*. Butler's description of the sermon from Lamentations: MP X: 67.

5, 6.

All of the facts on the looting of the Cherokees and of the first shipments of the Cherokees are from Foreman.

7.

The conditions in the concentration camps are summarized from Butrick's *Journal*. Butler writes of the illness in the camps in MP X: 69, 70, 72.

8.

The August Council and Ross's continued popularity are reported by Butler in MP X: 70. The organization for removal is described in Foreman, pp. 299ff.

9.

Such of this section as does not directly concern Butrick's journey west (based on his *Journal*) is from Foreman.

10.

Butler's estimates of Cherokee mortality: MP X: 73; his account of the Cherokees hiding in the Smokies: MP X: 75, 76.

CHAPTER XIX

1.

Miss Sawyer's journey and first impressions of the West: MP X: 317, 321.

2.

Accounts of dissension in the West: Butrick's *Journal* during the spring of 1839 and his letter MP X: 9; Butler in MP X: 77.

3.

Washburn's puzzled account of the difficulties between the Old Settlers and the newcomers is in MP X: 85. Butler's account of the event: MP X: 79.

4.

The most detailed account of the assassination is by Worcester in MP X: 136; Miss Sawyer's testimony is in X: 322; in X: 323 young John Rollin Ridge blends an account of his father's death with a description of Arkansas fauna.

5.

Butrick's defense of the assassination: MP X: 11. Delight Boudinot's attempts to avert further bloodshed are described by Worcester in X: 137. Butrick mentions his flight from Mrs. Ridge's friends in his *Controversy*. The uneasy July convention is described by Worcester in X: 137 and in X: 55. According to Mooney's *Myths*, p. 135, Sequoia participated.

6.

Butler's description of Cherokee despondency: MP X: 80; Miss Sawyer's comments: X: 324.

CHAPTER XX

1.

All details concerning the Cherokee feuds are from Morris J. Wardell's *Political History of the Cherokees*, Chapter III. The text of the Treaty of 1846 is in Charles Royce's *Cherokee Nation*, pp. 295ff.

For Worcester's difficulties with translator and printer see MP X: 138, 141, 148, 149. His achievements at Park Hill are recorded in the *Dictionary of American Biography*.

Miss Sophia Sawyer's last letters are placed at the end of MP XI. Butrick describes his visit to the Choctaws and his difficulties with the Starr boys in his *Journal*. The date of his death is given in the American Board's *Biographical Data*.

Butler describes his medical work in MP X: 80, 81; his conversation with Major Lowry in MP X: 83; the building of the Fairfield Mission in MP X: 88. Letters describing his removal to the Female Seminary are MP XI: 183, 198; his wife's report of his death: MP XI: 205.

2.

The description of Ross's activities in the Civil War and of the final dissolution of the Cherokee tribal government is from Wardell.

3.

I have followed the version of the Tsali legend given by Mooney in his *Myths*, p. 131, and by Lanman in his *Letters*, p. 112. Further accounts of Thomas are given by Mooney and Lanman, both of whom knew him personally. The Tsali story may therefore be accepted as authentic; the complete lack of reference to it in the Mission Papers is probably due merely to the fact that none of these missionaries were stationed near the Valley Towns at the time.

INDEX